400 Home Plans

1½ and TWO STORY DESIGNS

HOME PLANNERS, INC.

23761 RESEARCH DRIVE
FARMINGTON HILLS, MICHIGAN 48024
TELEPHONE: (313) 477-1854

Contents

Edited by: Net Gingras
Cover design by: D. M. Naidus

Index to Designs

On the Cover: Cover designs can be found on the following pages: Front cover - Design 12131, pages 28. Back cover - top, Design 12309, page 280; middle, Design 12283, page 97; bottom, Design 11987, page 220.

How to read floor plans and blueprints

Selecting the most suitable house plan for your family is a matter of matching your needs, tastes, and life-style against the many designs we offer. When you study the floor plans in this issue, and the blueprints that you may subsequently order, remember that they are simply a two-dimensional representation of what will eventually be a three-dimensional reality.

Floor plans are easy to read. Rooms are clearly labeled, with dimensions given in feet and inches. Most symbols are logical and self-explanatory: The location of bathroom fixtures, planters, fireplaces, tile floors, cabinets and counters, sinks, appliances, closets, sloped or beamed ceilings will be obvious.

A blueprint, although much more detailed, is also easy to read; all it demands is concentration. The blueprints that we offer come in many large sheets, each one of which contains a different kind of information. One sheet contains foundation and excavation drawings, another has a precise plot plan. An elevations sheet deals with the exterior walls of the house; section drawings show precise dimensions, fittings, doors, windows, and roof structures. Our detailed floor plans give the construction information needed by your contractor. And each set of blueprints contains a lengthy materials list with size and quantities of all necessary components. Using this list, a contractor and suppliers can make a start at calculating costs for you.

When you first study a floor plan or blueprint, imagine that you are walking through the house. By mentally visualizing each room in three dimensions, you can transform the technical data and symbols into something more real.

Start at the front door. It's preferable to have a foyer or entrance hall in which to receive guests. A closet here is desirable; a powder room is a plus.

Look for good traffic circulation as you study the floor plan. You should not have to pass all the way through one main room to reach another. From the entrance area you should have direct access to the three principal areas of a house—the living, work, and sleeping zones. For example, a foyer might provide separate entrances to the living room, kitchen, patio, and a hallway or staircase leading to the bedrooms.

Study the layout of each zone. Most people expect the living room to be protected from cross traffic. The kitchen, on the other hand, should connect with the dining room—and perhaps also the utility room, basement, garage, patio or deck, or a secondary entrance. A homemaker whose workday centers in the kitchen may have special requirements: a window that faces the backyard; a clear view of the family room where children play; a

garage or driveway entrance that allows for a short trip with groceries; laundry facilities close at hand. Check for efficient placement of kitchen cabinets, counters, and appliances. Is there enough room in the kitchen for additional appliances, for eating in? Is there a dining nook?

Perhaps this part of the house contains a family room or a den/bedroom/office. It's advantageous to have a bathroom or powder room in this section.

As you study the plan, you may encounter a staircase, indicated by a group of parallel lines, the number of lines equaling the number of steps. Arrows labeled "up" mean that the staircase leads to a higher level, and those pointing down mean it leads to a lower one. Staircases in a split-level will have both up and down arrows on one staircase because two levels are depicted in one drawing and an extra level in another.

Notice the location of the stairways. Is too much floor space lost to them? Will you find yourself making too many trips?

Study the sleeping quarters. Are the bedrooms situated as you like? You may want the master bedroom near the kids, or you may want it as far away as possible. Is there at least one closet per person in each bedroom or a double one for a couple? Bathrooms should be convenient to each bedroom—if not adjoining, then with hallway access and on the same floor.

Once you are familiar with the relative positions of the rooms, look for such structural details as:

• Sufficient uninterrupted wall space for furniture arrangement.

• Adequate room dimensions.

• Potential heating or cooling problems—i.e., a room over a garage or next to the laundry.

• Window and door placement for good ventilation and natural light.

• Location of doorways—avoid having a basement staircase or a bathroom in view of the dining room.

• Adequate auxiliary space—closets, storage, bathrooms, countertops.

• Separation of activity areas. (Will noise from the recreation room disturb sleeping children or a parent at work?)

As you complete your mental walk through the house, bear in mind your family's long-range needs. A good house plan will allow for some adjustments now and additions in the future.

Each member of your family may find the listing of his, or her, favorite features a most helpful exercise. Why not try it?

How to choose a contractor

A contractor is part craftsman, part businessman, and part magician. As the person who will transform your dreams and drawings into a finished house, he will be responsible for the final cost of the structure, for the quality of the workmanship, and for the solving of all problems that occur quite naturally in the course of construction. Choose him as carefully as you would a business partner, because for the next several months that will be his role in your life.

As soon as you have a building site and house plans, start looking for a contractor, even if you do not plan to break ground for several months. Finding one suitable to build your house can take time, and once you have found him, you will have to be worked into his schedule. Those who are good are in demand and, where the season is short, they are often scheduling work up to a year in advance.

There are two types of residential contractors: the construction company and the carpenter-builder, often called a general contractor. Each of these has its advantages and disadvantages.

The carpenter-builder works directly on the job as the field foreman. Because his background is that of a craftsman, his workmanship is probably good—but his paperwork may be slow or sloppy. His overhead—which you pay for—is less than that of a large construction company. However, if the job drags on for any reason, his interest may flag because your project is overlapping his next job and eroding his profits.

Construction companies handle several projects concurrently. They have an office staff to keep the paperwork moving and an army of subcontractors they know they can count on. Though you can be confident that they will meet deadlines, they may sacrifice workmanship in order to do so. Because they emphasize efficiency, they are less personal to work with than a general contractor. Many will not work with an individual unless he is represented by an architect. The company and the architect speak the same language; it requires far more time to deal directly with a homeowner.

To find a reliable contractor, start by asking friends who have built homes for recommendations. Check with local lumber yards and building supply outlets for names of possible candidates.

Once you have several names in hand, ask the Chamber of Commerce, Better Business Bureau, or local department of consumer affairs for any information they might have on each of them. Keep in mind that these watchdog organizations can give only the

number of complaints filed; they cannot tell you what percent of those claims were valid. Remember, too, that a large-volume operation is logically going to have more complaints against it than will an independent contractor.

Set up an interview with each of the potential candidates. Find out what his specialty is—custom houses, development houses, remodeling, or office buildings. Ask each to take you into—not just to the site of—houses he has built. Ask to see projects that are complete as well as work in progress, emphasizing that you are interested in projects comparable to yours. A $300,000 dentist's office will give you little insight into a contractor's craftsmanship.

Ask each contractor for bank references from both his commercial bank and any other lender he has worked with. If he is in good financial standing, he should have no qualms about giving you this information. Also ask if he offers a warranty on his work. Most will give you a one-year warranty on the structure; some offer as much as a ten-year warranty.

Ask for references, even though no contractor will give you the name of a dissatisfied customer. While previous clients may be pleased with a contractor's work overall, they may, for example, have had to wait three months after they moved in before they had any closet doors. Ask about his follow-through. Did he clean up the building site, or did the owner have to dispose of the refuse? Ask about his business organization. Did the paperwork go smoothly, or was there a delay in hooking up the sewer because he forgot to apply for a permit?

Talk to each of the candidates about fees. Most work on a "cost plus" basis; that is, the basic cost of the project—materials, subcontractors' services, wages of those working directly on the project, but not office help—plus his fee. Some have a fixed fee; others work on a percentage of the basic cost. A fixed fee is usually better for you if you can get one. If a contractor works on a percentage, ask for a cost breakdown of his best estimate and keep very careful track as the work progresses. A crafty contractor can always use a cost overrun to his advantage when working on a percentage.

Do not be overly suspicious of a contractor who won't work on a fixed fee. One who is very good and in great demand may not be willing to do so. He may also refuse to submit a competitive bid.

If the top two or three candidates are willing to submit competitive bids, give each a copy of the plans and your specifications for materials. If they are not each working from the same guidelines, the competitive bids will be of

little value. Give each the same deadline for turning in a bid; two or three weeks is a reasonable period of time. If you are willing to go with the lowest bid, make an appointment with all of them and open the envelopes in front of them.

If one bid is remarkably low, the contractor may have made an honest error in his estimate. Do not try to hold him to it if he wants to withdraw his bid. Forcing him to build at too low a price could be disastrous for both you and him.

Though the above method sounds very fair and orderly, it is not always the best approach, especially if you are inexperienced. You may want to review the bids with your architect, if you have one, or with your lender to discuss which to accept. They may not recommend the lowest. A low bid does not necessarily mean that you will get quality with economy.

If the bids are relatively close, the most important consideration may not be money at all. How easily you can talk with a contractor and whether or not he inspires confidence are very important considerations. Any sign of a personality conflict between you and a contractor should be weighed when making a decision.

Once you have financing, you can sign a contract with the builder. Most have their own contract forms, but it is advisable to have a lawyer draw one up or, at the very least, review the standard contract. This usually costs a small flat fee.

A good contract should include the following:

• Plans and sketches of the work to be done, subject to your approval.

• A list of materials, including quantity, brand names, style or serial numbers. (Do not permit any "or equal" clause that will allow the contractor to make substitutions.)

• The terms—who (you or the lender) pays whom and when.

• A production schedule.

• The contractor's certification of insurance for workmen's compensation, damage, and liability.

• A rider stating that all changes, whether or not they increase the cost, must be submitted and approved in writing.

Of course, this list represents the least a contract should include. Once you have signed it, your plans are on the way to becoming a home.

A frequently asked question is: "Should I become my own general contractor?" Unless you have knowledge of construction, material purchasing, and experience supervising subcontractors, we do not recommend this route.

5

Most people who are in the market for a new home spend months searching for the right house plan and the ideal building site. Ironically, these same people often invest very little time shopping for the money to finance their new home, though the majority will have to live with the terms of their mortgage for as long as they live in the house.

The fact is that all banks are not alike, nor are the loans that they offer—and banks are not the only financial institutions that lend money for housing. The amount of down payment, interest rate, and period of the mortgage are all, to some extent, negotiable.

• Lending practices vary from one city and state to another. If you are a first-time builder or are new to an area, it is wise to hire a real estate (not divorce or general practice) attorney to help you unravel the maze of your specific area's laws, ordinances, and customs.

• Before talking with lenders, write down all your questions. Take notes during the conversation so you can make accurate comparisons.

• Do not be intimidated by financial officers. Keep in mind that *you are not begging for money,* you are buying it. Do not hesitate to reveal what other institutions are offering; they may be challenged to meet or better the terms.

• Use whatever clout you have. If you or your family have been banking with the same firm for years, let them know that they could lose your business if you can get a better deal elsewhere.

• Know your credit rights. The law prohibits lenders from considering only the husband's income when determining eligibility, a practice that previously kept many people out of the housing market. If you are turned down for a loan, you have a right to see a summary of the credit report and change any errors in it.

A GUIDE TO LENDERS

Where can you turn for home financing? Here is a list of sources for you to approach:

Savings and loan associations are the best place to start because they write well over half the mortgages in the United States on dwellings that house from one to four families. They generally offer favorable interest rates, require lower down payments, and allow more time to pay off loans than do other banks.

Savings banks, sometimes called mutual savings banks, are your next best bet. Like savings and loan associations, much of their business is concentrated in home mortgages.

Commercial banks write mortgages as a sideline, and when money is tight many will not write mortgages at all. They do hold about 15 percent of the mortgages in the country, however, and when the market is right, they can be very competitive.

Mortgage banking companies use the money of private investors to write home loans. They do a brisk business in government-backed loans, which other banks are reluctant to handle because of the time and paperwork required.

Some credit unions are now allowed to grant mortgages. A few insurance companies, pension funds, unions, and fraternal organizations also offer mortgage money to their membership, often at terms more favorable than those available in the commercial marketplace.

A GUIDE TO MORTGAGES

The types of mortgages available are far more various than most potential home buyers realize.

Traditional Loans

Conventional home loans have a fixed interest rate and fixed monthly payments. About 80 percent of the mortgage money in the United States is lent in this manner. Made by private lending institutions, these fixed rate loans are available to anyone whom the bank officials consider a good credit risk. The interest rate depends on the prevailing market for money and is slightly negotiable if you are willing to put down a large down payment. Most down payments range from 15 to 33 percent.

You can borrow as much money as the lender believes you can afford to pay off over the negotiated period of time—usually 20 to 30 years.

The FHA does not write loans; it insures them against default in order to encourage lenders to write loans for first-time buyers and people with limited incomes. The terms of these loans make them very attractive. The interest rate is fixed by FHA at 13½ percent, and you may be allowed to take as long as 25 to 30 years to pay it off.

The down payment also is substantially lower with an FHA-backed loan. At present it is set at 3 percent of the first $25,000 and 5 percent of the remainder, up to the $60,000 limit. This means that a loan on a $60,000 house would require a $750 down payment on the first $25,000 plus $1,750 on the remainder, for a total down payment of $2,500. In contrast, the down payment for the same house financed with a conventional loan could run as high as $20,000.

Anyone may apply for an FHA-insured loan, but both the borrower and the house must qualify.

The VA guarantees loans for eligible veterans, and the husbands and wives of those who died while in the service or from a service-related disability. The VA guarantees up to 60 percent of the loan or $27,500, whichever is less. Like the FHA, the VA determines the appraised value of the house, though with a VA loan, you can borrow any amount up to the appraised value.

The Farmers Home Administration offers the only loans made directly by the government. Families with limited incomes in rural areas can qualify if the house is in a community of less than 20,000 people and is outside of a large metropolitan area; if their income is less than $15,600; and if they can prove that they do not qualify for a conventional loan.

For more information, write Farmers Home Administration, Department of Agriculture, Washington, D.C. 20250, or contact your local office.

New loan instruments

If you think that the escalating cost of housing has squeezed you out of the market, take a look at the following new types of mortgages.

The graduated payment mortgage features a monthly obligation that gradually increases over a negotiated period of time—usually five to ten years. Though the payments begin lower, they stabilize at a higher monthly rate than a standard fixed rate mortgage. Little or no equity is built in the first years, a disadvantage if you decide to sell early in the mortgage period.

These loans are aimed at young people who can anticipate income increases that will enable them to meet the escalating payments. The size of the down payment is about the same or slightly higher than for a conventional loan, but you can qualify with a lower income. As of last year, savings and loan associations can write these loans, and the FHA now insures five different types.

The flexible loan insurance program (FLIP) requires that part of the down payment, which is about the same as a conventional loan, be placed in a pledged savings account. During the first five years of the mortgage, funds are drawn from this account to supplement the lower monthly payments.

The deferred interest mortgage, another graduated program, allows you to pay a lower rate of interest during the first few years and a higher rate in the later years of the mortgage. If the house is sold, the borrower must pay back all the interest, often with a prepayment penalty. Both the FLIP and deferred interest loans are very new and not yet widely available.

The variable rate mortgage is most widely available in California, but its popularity is growing. This instrument features a fluctuating interest rate that is linked to an economic indicator—usually the lender's cost of obtaining funds for lending. To protect the consumer against a sudden and disastrous increase, regulations limit the amount that the interest rate can increase over a given period of time.

To make these loans attractive, lenders offer them without prepayment penalties and with "assumption" clauses that allow another buyer to assume your mortgage should you sell.

Flexible payment mortgages allow young people who can anticipate rising incomes to enter the housing market sooner. They pay only the interest during the first few years; then the mortgage is amortized and the payments go up. This is a valuable option only for those people who intend to keep their home for several years because no equity is built in the lower payment period.

The reverse annuity mortgage is targeted for older people who have fixed incomes. This very new loan instrument allows those who qualify to tap into the equity on their houses. The lender pays them each month and collects the loan when the house is sold or the owner dies.

How to shop for mortgage money

New England
Gambrels & Salt Boxes

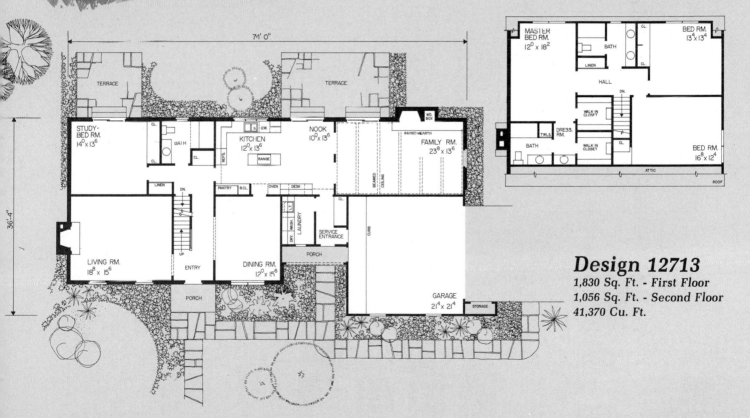

Design 12713
1,830 Sq. Ft. - First Floor
1,056 Sq. Ft. - Second Floor
41,370 Cu. Ft.

● This home with its Gambrel roof and paned windows is sure to be a pleasure for the entire family. Along with the outside, the inside is a delight. The spacious family room creates an inviting atmosphere with sliding glass doors to the terrace,

beamed ceilings and a raised-hearth fireplace that includes a built-in wood box. A spectacular kitchen, too. Presenting an island counter/range as well as a built-in oven, desk and storage pantry. A sunny breakfast nook, too, also with sliding

glass doors leading to the terrace. Note the size of the formal dining room and the fireplace in the living room. A first floor study/bedroom with a private terrace. Upstairs, there is the master suite and two more bedrooms and a bath.

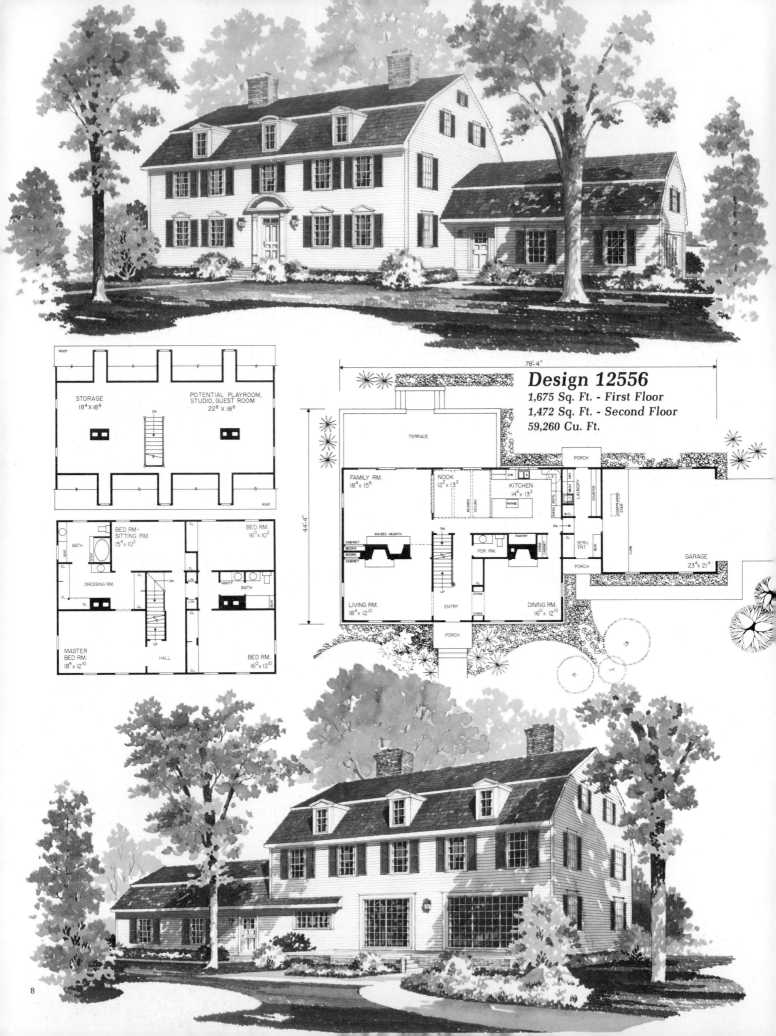

Design 12556

1,675 Sq. Ft. - First Floor
1,472 Sq. Ft. - Second Floor
59,260 Cu. Ft.

78'-4"

44'-4"

STORAGE
18⁴ X 18⁸

POTENTIAL PLAYROOM, STUDIO, GUEST ROOM
22⁸ X 18⁸

DN.

ROOF

ROOF

BED RM. - SITTING RM.
15⁴ x 10²

BED RM.
16⁰ x 10²

BATH

DRESSING RM.

VANITY

BATH

DN.

LIN.

LIN.

CL.

CL.

CL.

CL.

CL.

SEAT

MASTER BED RM.
18⁴ x 12¹⁰

UP

HALL

BED RM.
16⁰ x 12¹⁰

CL.

TERRACE

FAMILY RM.
18⁴ x 15⁶

NOOK
12² x 13²

BEAMED CEILING

KITCHEN
14⁶ x 13²

RANGE

OVENS REFR.

DW

S

WASH

DRY

LAUNDRY

PORCH

COUNTER

CURB

DISAPPEARING STAIR

GARAGE
23⁴ x 21⁴

CABINET

RAISED HEARTH

BOOKS

BOOKS

CABINET

DN.

PDR. RM.

PANTRY

CABINET

B. CL.

DN.

SERV. ENT.

SEAT

CL.

LIVING RM.
18⁴ x 12¹⁰

UP

ENTRY

CHINA

CHINA

DINING RM.
16⁰ x 12¹⁰

PORCH

PORCH

8

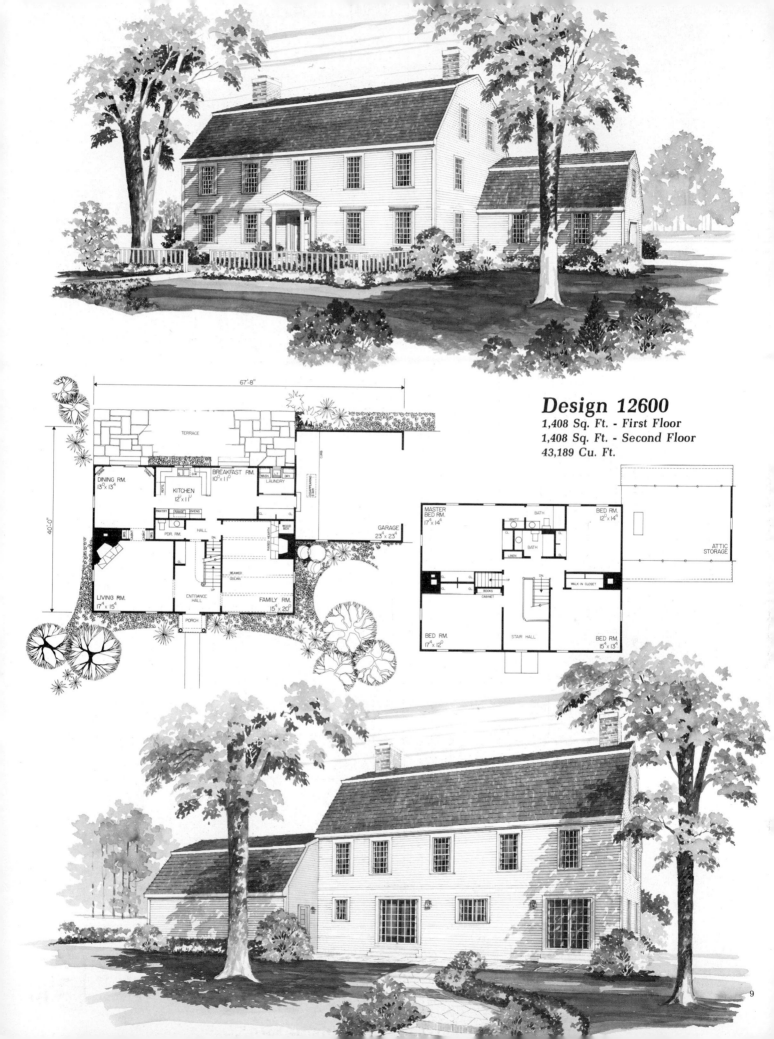

Design 12600

1,408 Sq. Ft. - First Floor
1,408 Sq. Ft. - Second Floor
43,189 Cu. Ft.

67'-8"

40'-0"

TERRACE

DINING RM.
13⁰ x 13⁴

BREAKFAST RM.
10⁰ x 11⁰

KITCHEN
12' x 11'

LAUNDRY

PANTRY RANGE OVENS

PDR. RM.

HALL

WOOD BOX

RAISED HEARTH

GARAGE
23⁴ x 23⁴

LIVING RM.
17⁴ x 15⁵

ENTRANCE HALL

BEAMED CEILING

UP

DN

FAMILY RM.
15⁴ x 20⁰

PORCH

MASTER BED RM.
17⁴ x 14⁴

VANITY

BATH

BATH

LINEN

BED RM.
12⁰ x 14⁴

BOOKS CABINET

DN

WALK IN CLOSET

BED RM.
17⁴ x 12⁰

STAIR HALL

BED RM.
15⁴ x 13⁴

ATTIC STORAGE

9

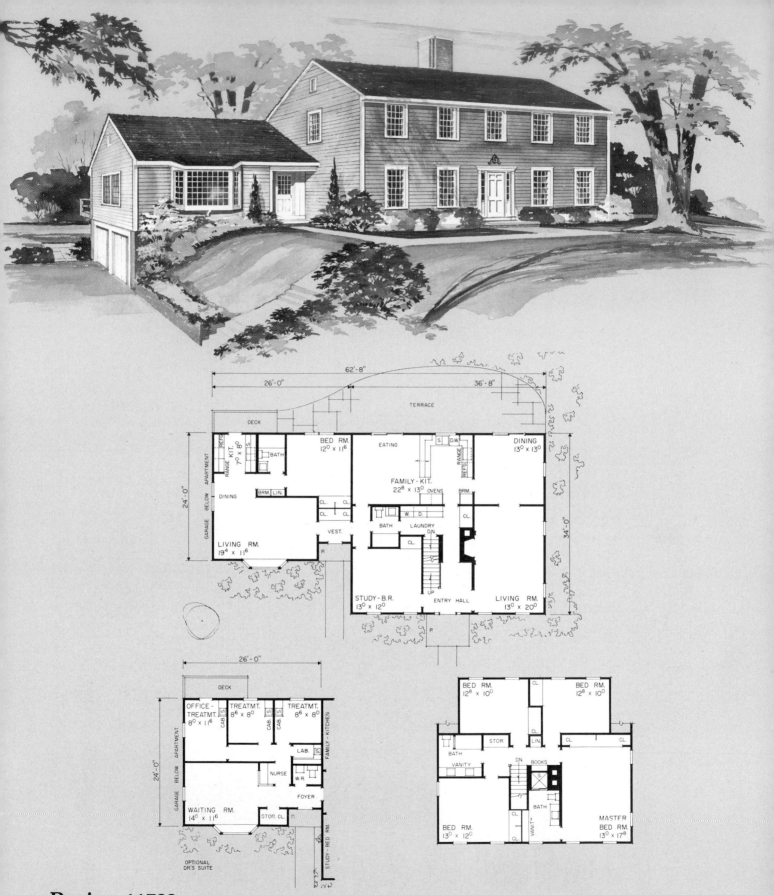

Design 11763 1,246 Sq. Ft. - First Floor; 624 Sq. Ft. - Apartment; 1,054 Sq. Ft. - Second Floor; 42,260 Cu. Ft.

● A charming New England Salt Box designed to satisfy the needs of the large family, plus provide facilities for a live-in relative! Many houses can be a problem in adapting to the living requirements of an in-residence relative. But, not this one. Your family will have all the space it needs, while your relative will enjoy all his or her privacy and independence. This apartment area may also be adapted to function as a doctor's suite.

Design 12399
1,301 Sq. Ft. - First Floor; 839 Sq. Ft. - Second Floor
34,743 Cu. Ft.

• From Early Colonial America comes this Salt Box. Narrow, horizontal siding, muntined windows, a massive centered chimney, carriage lamps and a classic front entrance set the exterior character. Inside, three bedrooms, three baths and two living areas. And much more.

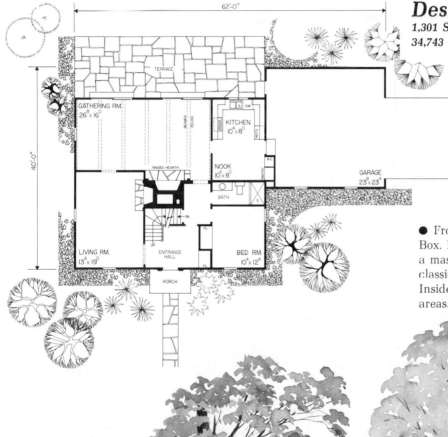

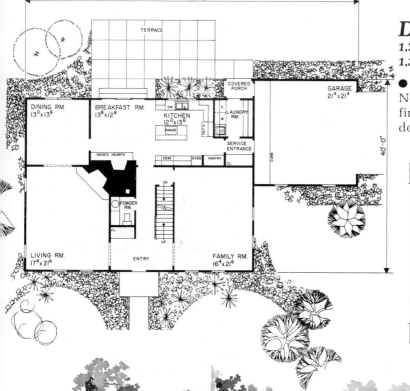

Design 12652
1,728 Sq. Ft. - First Floor
1,308 Sq. Ft. - Second Floor; 47,760 Cu. Ft.

● This two-story Gambrel has features that will delight all. Note the corner fireplace in the living room and the second fireplace in the large breakfast room which has sliding glass doors to the terrace.

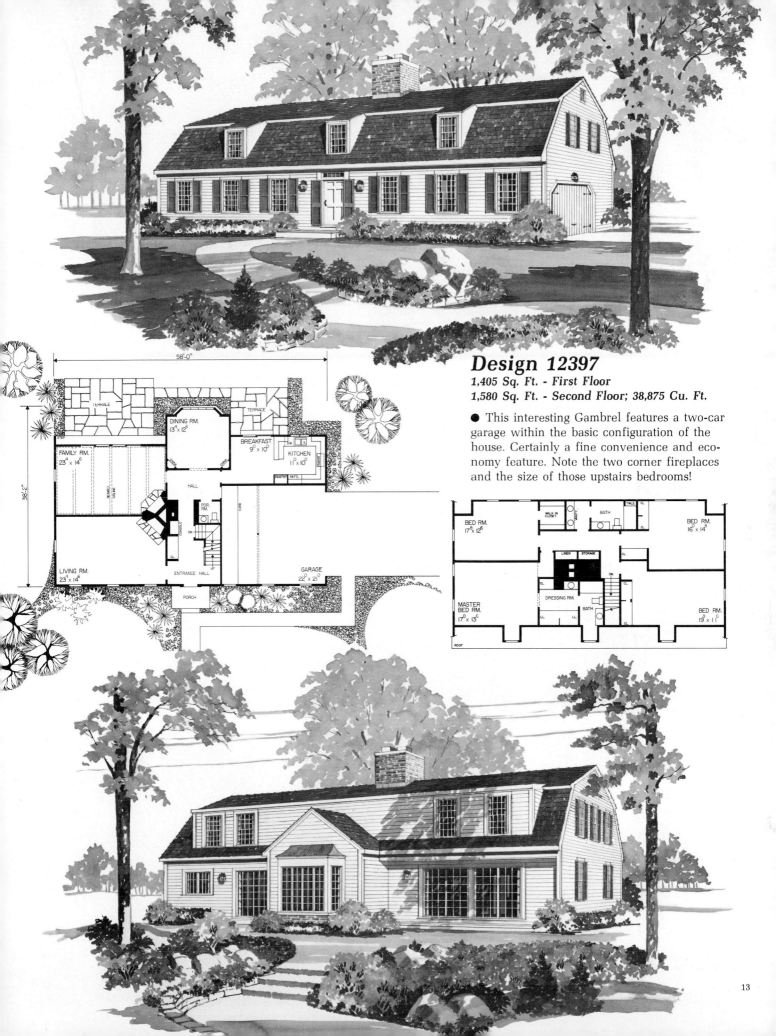

Design 12397

1,405 Sq. Ft. - First Floor
1,580 Sq. Ft. - Second Floor; 38,875 Cu. Ft.

● This interesting Gambrel features a two-car garage within the basic configuration of the house. Certainly a fine convenience and economy feature. Note the two corner fireplaces and the size of those upstairs bedrooms!

58'-0"

38'-2"

TERRACE

DINING RM.
13'⁴ x 12'⁶

TERRACE

FAMILY RM.
23'⁴ x 14'⁶

BREAKFAST
9'⁰ x 10'⁰

KITCHEN
11'⁰ x 10'⁰

PANTRY REFG.

HALL

PDR. RM.

DN

LIVING RM.
23'⁴ x 14'⁶

ENTRANCE HALL

UP

GARAGE
22'⁰ x 21'⁰

PORCH

BED RM.
17'⁸ x 12'⁶

WALK IN CLOSET

BATH

TWLS.

BED RM.
16'⁰ x 14'⁰

LINEN STORAGE

MASTER BED RM.
17'⁰ x 13'⁰

DRESSING RM.

DN

BATH

BED RM.
13'⁹ x 11'⁰

ROOF

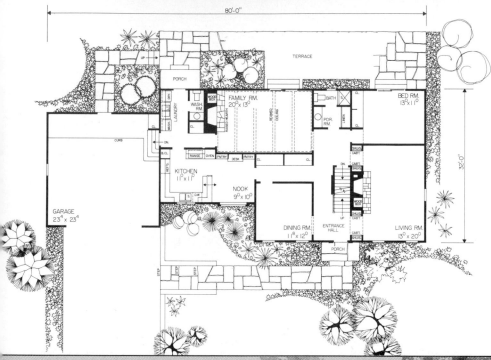

Design 12625
1,640 Sq. Ft. - First Floor
1,072 Sq. Ft. - Second Floor; 39,360 Cu. Ft.

● A 19th Century Farmhouse! So it might seem. But one with contemporary features . . . like the U-shaped kitchen with a built-in desk and appliances as well as a separate dining nook. Or the 20' by 13' family room. There, a beamed ceiling and raised-hearth fireplace add traditional warmth to a modern convention.

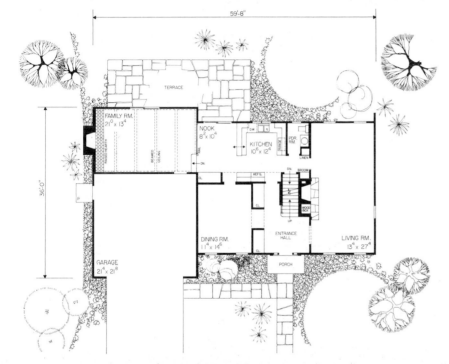

Design 12623
1,368 Sq. Ft. - First Floor
1,046 Sq. Ft. - Second Floor; 35,130 Cu. Ft.

● Take note of this four bedroom Salt Box design. Enter through the large entrance hall to enjoy this home. Imagine a living room 13 x 27 feet. Plus a family room. Both having a fireplace. Also, sliding glass doors in both the family room and nook leading to the rear terrace.

Design 12654
1,152 Sq. Ft. - First Floor
844 Sq. Ft. - Second Floor
31,845 Cu. Ft.

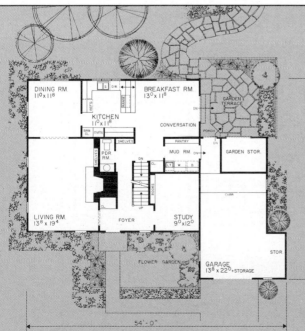

● This is certainly an authentic traditional saltbox. It features a symmetrical design with a center fireplace, a wide, paneled doorway and multi-paned, double-hung windows. Tucked behind the one-car garage is a garden shed which provides work and storage space. The breakfast room features French doors which open onto a flagstone terrace. The U-shaped kitchen has built-in counters which make efficient use of space. The upstairs plan houses three bedrooms.

Design 12616

1,415 Sq. Ft. - First Floor
1,106 Sq. Ft. - Second Floor
36,880 Cu. Ft.

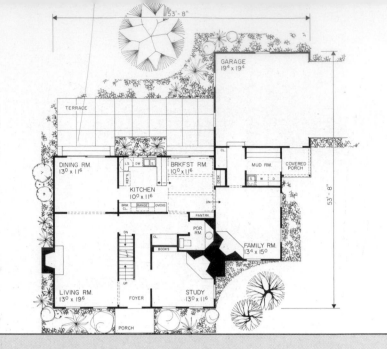

Design 11814

1,471 Sq. Ft. - First Floor
1,052 Sq. Ft. - Second Floor
35,700 Cu. Ft.

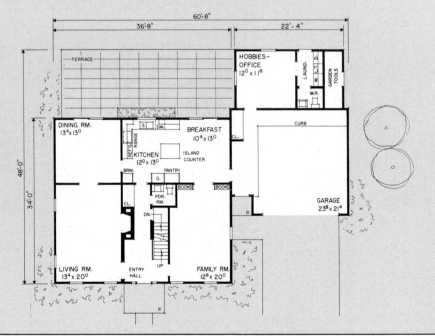

Design 11266

1,374 Sq. Ft. - First Floor
1,094 Sq. Ft. - Second Floor
31,969 Cu. Ft.

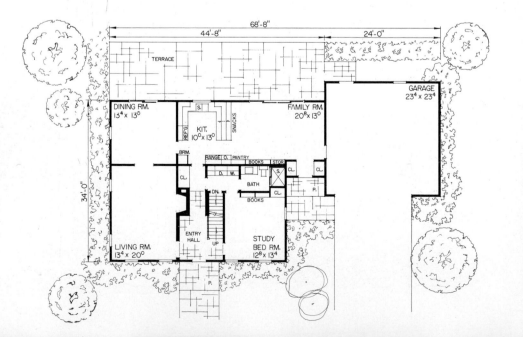

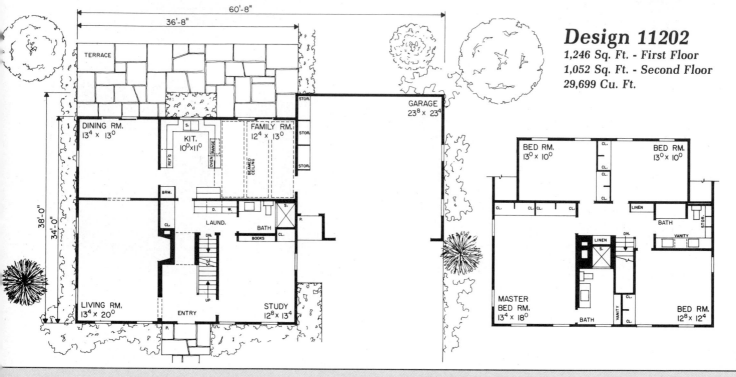

Design 11202

1,246 Sq. Ft. - First Floor
1,052 Sq. Ft. - Second Floor
29,699 Cu. Ft.

First Floor:

- TERRACE
- DINING RM. 13⁴ x 13⁰
- KIT. 10⁰ x 11⁰
- FAMILY RM. 12⁴ x 13⁰ BEAMED CEILING
- GARAGE 23⁸ x 23⁴
- STOR.
- LAUND.
- BATH
- BOOKS
- LIVING RM. 13⁴ x 20⁰
- ENTRY
- STUDY 12⁸ x 13⁴
- 60'-8"
- 36'-8"
- 38'-0"
- 34'-0"

Second Floor:

- BED RM. 13⁰ x 10⁰
- BED RM. 13⁰ x 10⁰
- LINEN
- BATH
- VANITY
- MASTER BED RM. 13⁴ x 18⁰
- BATH
- BED RM. 12⁸ x 12⁴

Design 12632

1,460 Sq. Ft. - First Floor
912 Sq. Ft. - Second Floor
39,205 Cu. Ft.

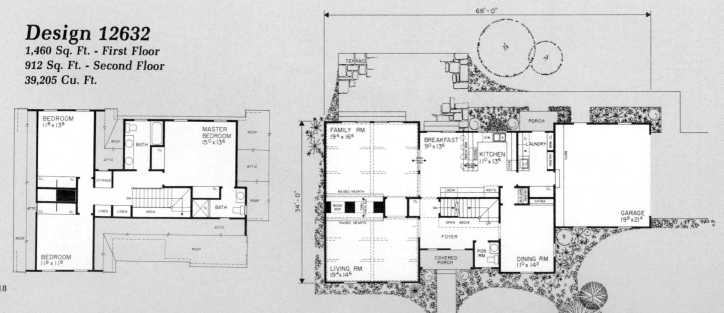

Second Floor:

- BEDROOM 11⁸ x 13⁸
- BATH
- MASTER BEDROOM 15⁰ x 13⁶
- ATTIC
- STORAGE
- LINEN
- OPEN
- BATH
- BEDROOM 11⁸ x 11⁸

First Floor:

- TERRACE
- FAMILY RM. 19⁴ x 16⁶
- BREAKFAST 9⁰ x 13⁶
- KITCHEN 11⁰ x 13⁶
- LAUNDRY
- PORCH
- RAISED HEARTH
- WOOD BOX
- DESK
- BUTLER'S PANTRY
- CHINA
- GARAGE 19⁸ x 21⁴
- LIVING RM. 19⁴ x 14⁶
- FOYER
- COVERED PORCH
- PDR. RM.
- DINING RM. 11⁰ x 14²
- 68'-0"
- 34'-0"

Design 11142 1,525 Sq. Ft. - First Floor
952 Sq. Ft. - Second Floor (1,053 Sq. Ft. - Four Bedroom Option); 32,980 Cu. Ft.

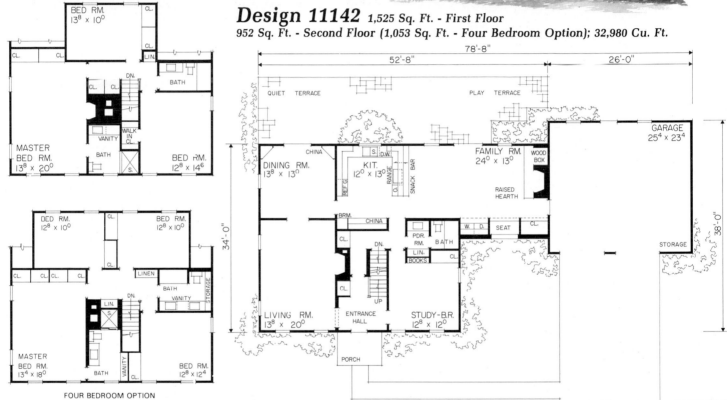

BED RM.
13⁸ x 10⁰

CL.

CL.

CL.

CL.

LIN.

DN.

BATH

MASTER
BED RM.
13⁸ x 20⁰

CL. CL.

VANITY

WALK IN CL.

BATH

S.

BED RM.
12⁸ x 14⁶

BED RM.
12⁸ x 10⁰

CL.

BED RM.
12⁸ x 10⁰

CL. CL. CL. CL.

LINEN

BATH

VANITY

STORAGE

LIN.

DN.

S.

MASTER
BED RM.
13⁴ x 18⁰

BATH

VANITY

BED RM.
12⁸ x 12⁴

FOUR BEDROOM OPTION

78'-8"

52'-8"

26'-0"

QUIET TERRACE

PLAY TERRACE

CHINA

DINING RM.
13⁸ x 13⁰

KIT.
12⁰ x 13⁰

S. D.W.

REFG.

RANGE

O.

SNACK BAR

FAMILY RM.
24⁰ x 13⁰

WOOD BOX

RAISED HEARTH

GARAGE
25⁴ x 23⁴

34'-0"

BRM.

CHINA

CL.

PDR. RM.

BATH

W. D.

SEAT

CL.

DN.

LIN.

BOOKS

CL.

STORAGE

38'-0"

LIVING RM.
13⁸ x 20⁰

ENTRANCE HALL

UP

STUDY-B.R.
12⁸ x 12⁰

PORCH

19

Design 12653

2,016 Sq. Ft. - First Floor
1,656 Sq. Ft. - Second Floor; 60,490 Cu. Ft.

● Livability and special features are absolutely outstanding in this Colonial design. Imagine a living room with beamed ceiling and fireplace that measures more than 20 x 27 feet. And the second fireplace in the luxurious master suite. Make a special note about all the built-ins featured in the dining room.

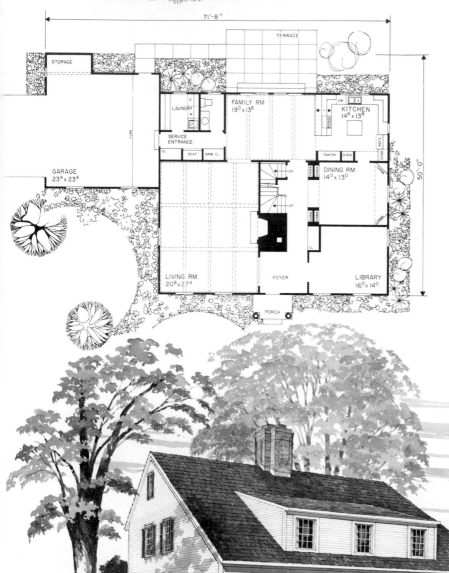

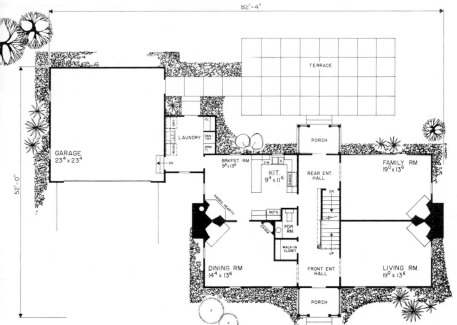

Design 12643

1,446 Sq. Ft. - First Floor
1,281 Sq. Ft. - Second Floor; 41,299 Cu. Ft.

● Four fireplaces! One to serve each of the main rooms on the first floor. Plus an impressive front and rear entrance hall to lead the way through the rest of the interior. Now note the exterior. The main house is identical from the front and back view. This house could hardly be more symmetrical.

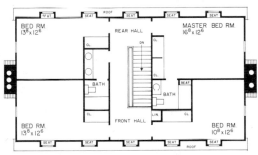

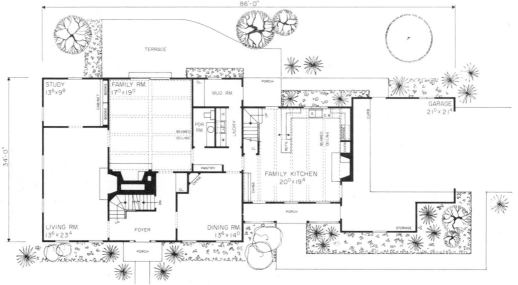

86'-0"

TERRACE

STUDY 13⁶x9⁸

FAMILY RM. 17⁰x19⁰

MUD RM.

PORCH

GARAGE 21⁰x21⁴

BEAMED CEILING

PDR. RM.

LNDRY

BEAMED CEILING

34'-0"

PANTRY

CL.

FAMILY KITCHEN 20⁰x19⁴

CHINA

OVEN

CURB

STORAGE

LIVING RM. 13⁶x23⁴

FOYER

UP DN

DINING RM. 13⁶x14⁰

PORCH

PORCH

Design 11986 896 Sq. Ft. - First Floor
1,148 Sq. Ft. - Second Floor; 28,840 Cu. Ft.

● This design with its distinctive Gambrel roof will spell charm wherever it may be situated - far out in the country, or on a busy thoroughfare. Compact and economical to build, it will be easy on the budget. Note the location of the family room. It is over the garage on the second floor.

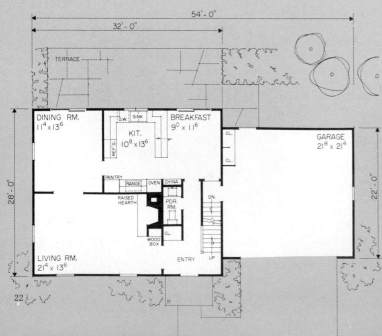

54'-0"

32'-0"

TERRACE

DINING RM. 11⁴x13⁶

KIT. 10⁸x13⁶

BREAKFAST 9⁰x11⁶

GARAGE 21⁸x21⁴

REF'G.

D.W. SINK

CL.

CL.

28'-0"

22'-0"

PANTRY

RANGE OVEN CHINA

RAISED HEARTH

PDR. RM.

DN.

LIVING RM. 21⁴x13⁶

WOOD BOX

CL.

ENTRY

UP

BED RM. 11⁴x13⁶

BATH

PDR. RM.

BED RM. 12⁰x10⁰

BOOKS

BOOKS

CL.

CL.

DN. DN.

LINEN

MASTER BED RM. 17⁸x12⁰

CL.

DRESS. RM.

VANITY

BATH

SHOWER

FAMILY RM. 21⁸x11⁴

22

Design 12320 *1,856 Sq. Ft. - First Floor; 1,171 Sq. Ft. - Second Floor; 46,699 Cu. Ft.*

● A charming Colonial adaptation with a Gambrel roof front exterior and a Salt Box rear. The focal point of family activities will be the spacious family kitchen with its beamed ceiling and fireplace. Blueprints include details for both three and four bedroom options. In addition to the family kitchen, note beamed ceiling family room with fireplace. Don't miss the study with built-in book shelves and cabinets. Gracious living will be enjoyed throughout this design.

Design 11914 *1,470 Sq. Ft. - First Floor; 888 Sq. Ft. - Second Floor; 30,354 Cu. Ft.*

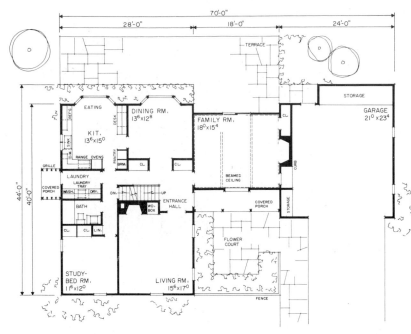

● What an interesting facade for passers-by to enjoy. Here, the delightful configuration of the Gambrel roof is fully visible from the road. The interior has all the features to help assure living convenience at its best. What are your favorite features?

Design 11745 1,440 Sq. Ft. - First Floor; 1,124 Sq. Ft. - Second Floor; 34,148 Cu. Ft.

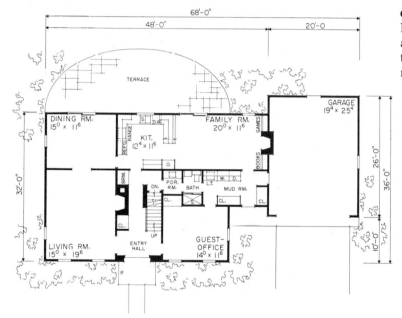

● A picture of charm. For sheer exterior appeal this house would be difficult to top. And inside there is an abundance of livability. Imagine, four bedrooms, three baths, guest room, family room, separate dining room and first floor laundry.

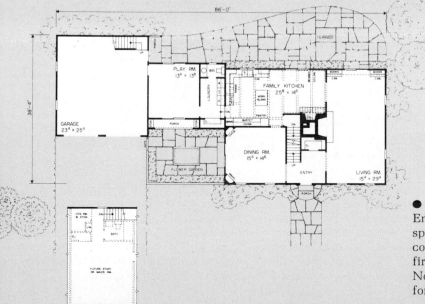

Design 12224

1,567 Sq. Ft. - First Floor
1,070 Sq. Ft. - Second Floor
37,970 Cu. Ft.

● Certainly reminiscent of the charm of rural New England. The focal point of the first floor is easily the spacious family-kitchen. Formerly referred to as the country-kitchen, this area, with its beamed ceiling and fireplace, will have a warm and cozy atmosphere, indeed. Note extra room over garage - an excellent play room for the kids.

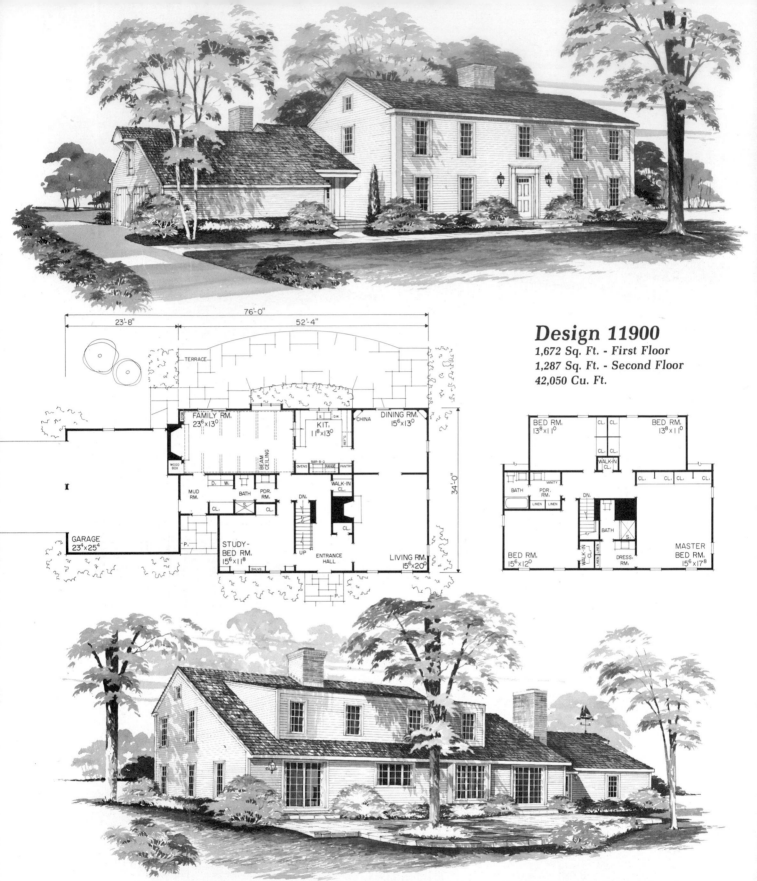

Design 11900

1,672 Sq. Ft. - First Floor
1,287 Sq. Ft. - Second Floor
42,050 Cu. Ft.

● The history of the Colonial Salt Box goes back some 200 years. This unusually authentic adaptation captures all the warmth and charm of the early days both inside as well as outside. To reflect today's living patterns, an up-dating of the floor plan was inevitable. The result is a room arrangement which will serve the active family wonderfully. Formal living and dining take place at one end of the house which is free of cross-room traffic. Informal living activities will center around the family room and expand through sliding glass doors to the terrace. The mud room area is strategically located and includes the laundry and a full bath. An extra study/bedroom supplements four bedrooms upstairs. Count the closets and the other storage areas.

Design 11887

1,518 Sq. Ft. - First Floor
1,144 Sq. Ft. - Second Floor
40,108 Cu. Ft.

● This Gambrel roof Colonial is steeped in history. And well it should be, for its pleasing proportions are a delight to the eye. The various roof planes, the window treatment, and the rambling nature of the entire house revive a picture of rural New England. The covered porch protects the front door which opens into a spacious entrance hall. Traffic then flows in an orderly fashion to the end living room, the separate dining room, the cozy family room, and to the spacious country-kitchen. There is a first floor laundry, plenty of coat closets, and a handy powder room. Two fireplaces enliven the decor of the living areas. Upstairs there is an exceptional master bedroom layout, and abundant storage. Note the walk-in closets.

Design 12364

1,440 Sq. Ft. - First Floor
1,206 Sq. Ft. - Second Floor
38,044 Cu. Ft.

57'-0"

FLAGSTONE TERRACE

FAMILY RM. 14⁴ x 20⁸
NOOK 9⁰ x 13⁶
KITCHEN 12⁰ x 13⁶
DINING RM. 11⁴ x 13⁶

BEAMED CEILING
REF'S PANTRY

MUD RM.
LAUNDRY
DRY WASH
STORAGE
ENTRANCE HALL
LIVING RM. 21⁰ x 15⁶
UP
CURB
COVERED PORCH

56'-0"

GARAGE 23⁴ x 25⁸

ROOF

DRESSING BATH BATH WALK-IN CLOSET
LINEN
BED RM. 15⁴ x 10⁴
SHELF CL
MASTER BED RM. 14⁴ x 12¹⁰
STAIR HALL
DN
BED RM. 11⁶ x 10⁰
BED RM. 11⁶ x 11⁰
CL CL

ROOF

ATTIC STORAGE 17⁴ x 25⁸
DN
ROOF

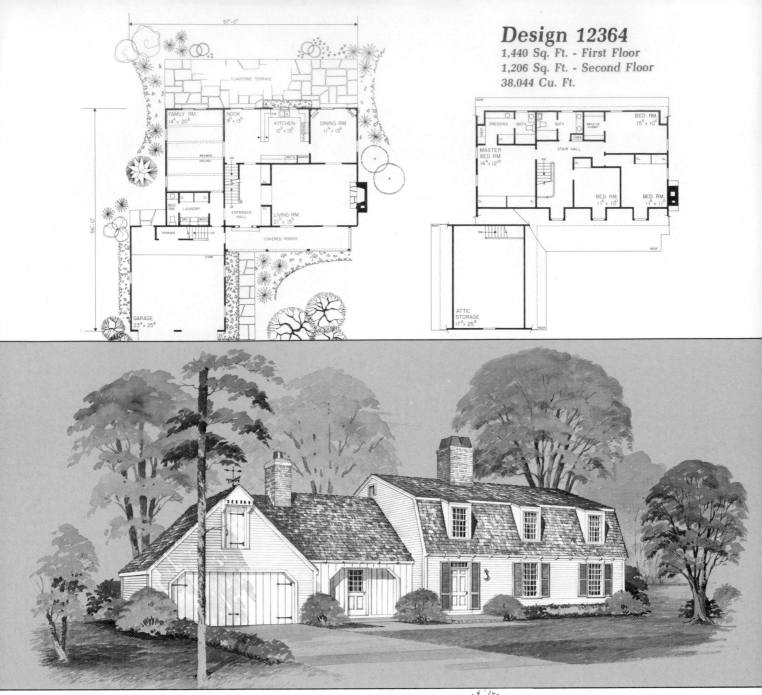

Design 11827

1,442 Sq. Ft. - First Floor
1,098 Sq. Ft. - Second Floor
35,275 Cu. Ft.

72'-10"
35'-7"   12'-5"   24'-0"

TERRACE

DINING RM. 13⁰ x 11⁰
KIT. 12⁰ x 11⁰
BREAKFAST 10⁰ x 9⁰
FAMILY RM. 12⁰ x 19⁴
REF'S
S. D.W.
WOOD BOX

RANGE OVEN PANTRY
LAUND.
D. W.
PDR. RM.
CL.
BEAMED CEILING
RAISED HEARTH
CL. F.
GARAGE 23⁴ x 25⁴

36'-10"
32'-0"

DN
UP

LIVING RM. 13⁰ x 20⁰
ENTRY
STUDY 12⁰ x 12⁰

ROOF

BED RM. 13⁶ x 11⁴
CL. CL. BATH
BATH DRESS. RM.
WALK-IN CL.

DN

BED RM. 13⁶ x 11⁴
LIN.
WALK-IN STOR.
CL.
MASTER BED RM. 12⁶ x 19⁰

ROOF

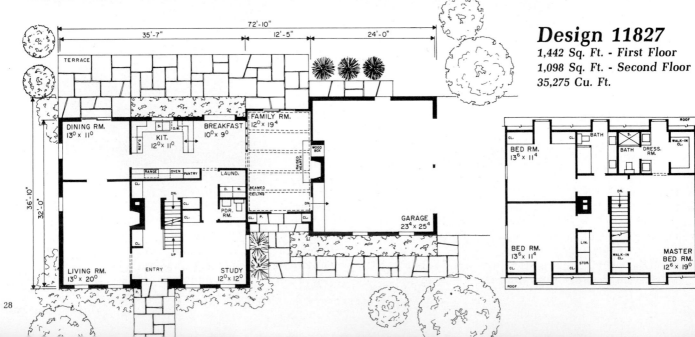

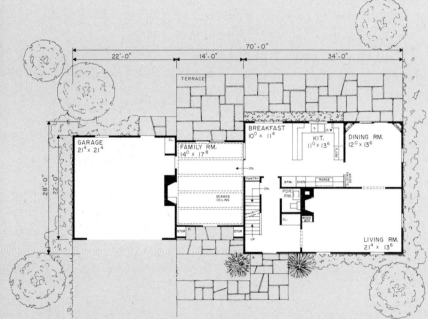

Design 12131

1,214 Sq. Ft. - First Floor
1,097 Sq. Ft. - Second Floor
28,070 Cu. Ft.

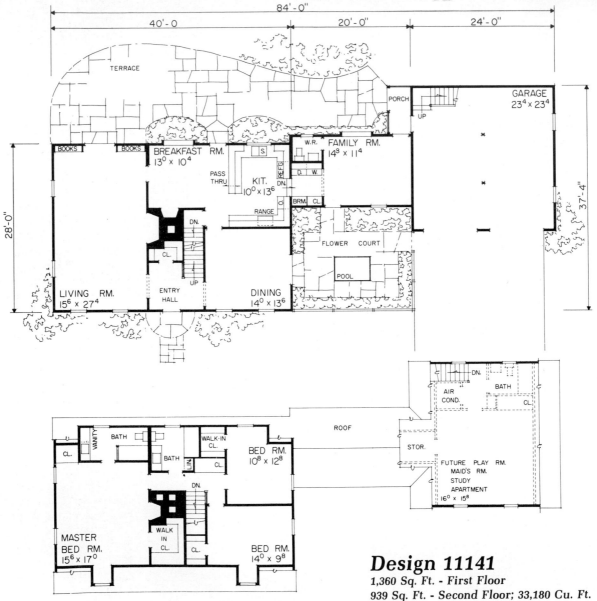

Design 11141
1,360 Sq. Ft. - First Floor
939 Sq. Ft. - Second Floor; 33,180 Cu. Ft.

● A 27 foot end living room, a fireplace in the breakfast room and one in the master bedroom, and a generous area over the garage for possible future development. These are the most unusual features of this uncommonly delightful Gambrel-roofed home. Don't overlook the many other highlights which include the family room, extra wash room, dining room, flower court and basement. A big terrace across the rear is accessible from the living areas.

Design 11712 1,618 Sq. Ft. - First Floor; 1,074 Sq. Ft. - Second Floor; 37,349 Cu. Ft.

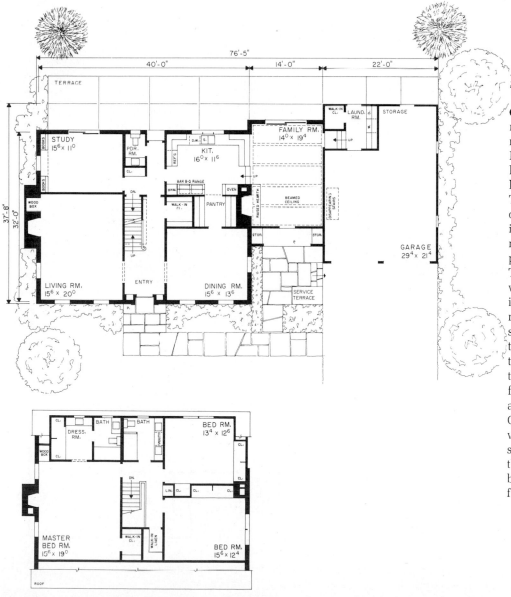

● The Connecticut Gambrel roof design is a fine embodiment of old New England. Here the center entrance hall leads directly through the house to the rear terrace. There will be no annoying cross-room traffic in the living room and the dining room may be completely by-passed whenever desired. Two raised hearth fireplaces will add enjoyment to the living areas. The extra powder room could hardly be more strategically located, while the mud room catches the traffic from the garage and the rear yard. The sunken family room is conveniently accessible from front or rear. Observe such features as the wood box, the built-ins of the study, the walk-in coat closet, the pantry, the kitchen barbecue unit and the bedroom fireplace.

Design 11777

1,136 Sq. Ft. - First Floor
1,004 Sq. Ft. - Second Floor
32,318 Cu. Ft.

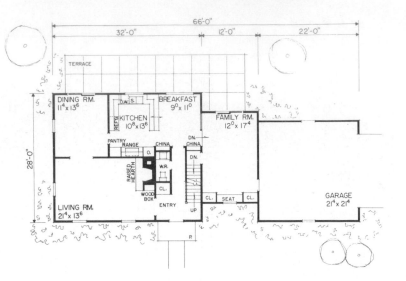

Design 12531

1,353 Sq. Ft. - First Floor
1,208 Sq. Ft. - Second Floor
33,225 Cu. Ft.

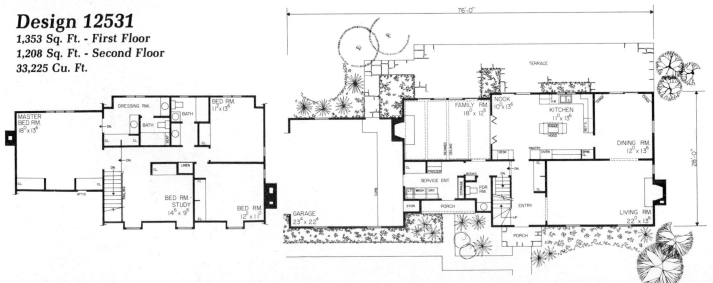

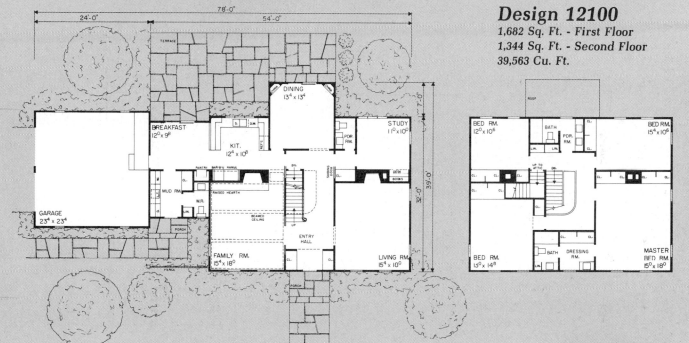

Design 12100

1,682 Sq. Ft. - First Floor
1,344 Sq. Ft. - Second Floor
39,563 Cu. Ft.

First floor labels:
TERRACE
BREAKFAST 12⁰ x 9⁸
DINING 13⁴ x 13⁴
STUDY 11⁰ x 10⁰
KIT. 12⁴ x 10⁸
PDR. RM.
GARAGE 23⁴ x 23⁴
MUD RM.
W.R.
RAISED HEARTH
BEAMED CEILING
FAMILY RM. 15⁴ x 18⁰
ENTRY HALL
LIVING RM. 15⁴ x 10⁰
PORCH

Second floor labels:
ROOF
BED RM. 12⁰ x 10⁶
BATH
PDR. RM.
BED RM. 15⁴ x 10⁶
UP TO ATTIC
BED RM. 13⁰ x 14⁸
BATH
DRESSING RM.
MASTER BED RM. 15⁰ x 18⁰

Dimensions: 24'-0", 78'-0", 54'-0", 7'-0", 32'-0", 39'-0"

Design 12539
1,450 Sq. Ft. - First Floor
1,167 Sq. Ft. - Second Floor; 46,738 Cu. Ft.

● This appealingly proportioned Gambrel exudes an aura of coziness. The beauty of the main part of the house is delightfully symmetrical and is enhanced by the attached garage and laundry room. The center entrance routes traffic directly to all major zones of the house.

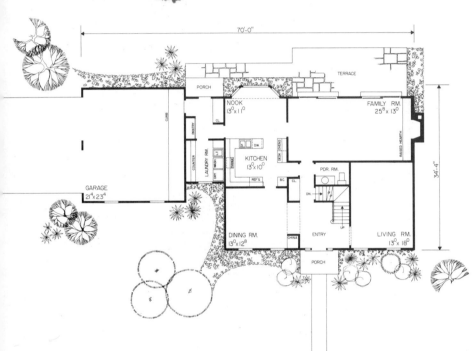

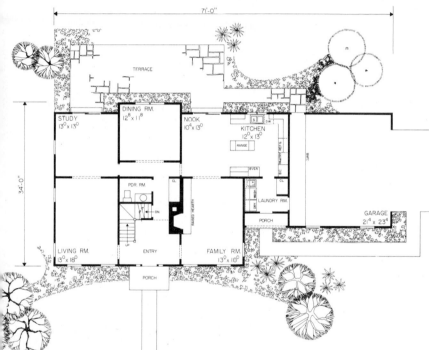

Design 12538
1,503 Sq. Ft. - First Floor
1,095 Sq. Ft. - Second Floor; 44,321 Cu. Ft.

● This Salt Box is charming, indeed. The livability it has to offer to the large and growing family is great. The entry is spacious and is open to the second floor balcony. For living areas, there is the study in addition to the living and family rooms.

Design 12731
1,039 Sq. Ft. - First Floor
973 Sq. Ft. - Second Floor; 29,740 Cu. Ft.

● The multi-paned windows with shutters of this two-story highlight the exterior delightfully. Inside the livability is ideal. Formal and informal areas are sure to serve your family with ease. Note efficient U-shaped kitchen with handy first-floor laundry. Sleeping facilities on second floor.

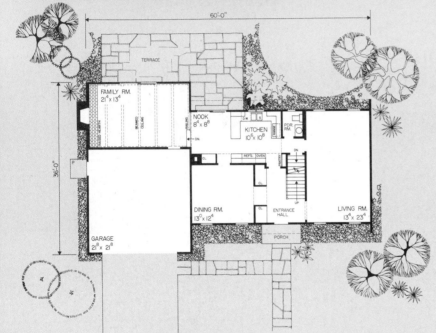

Design 12617
1,223 Sq. Ft. - First Floor
1,018 Sq. Ft. - Second Floor; 30,784 Cu. Ft.

● Another Gambrel roof version just loaded with charm. Notice the delightful symmetry of the window treatment. Inside, the large family will enjoy all the features that assure convenient living. The end-living room will have excellent privacy.

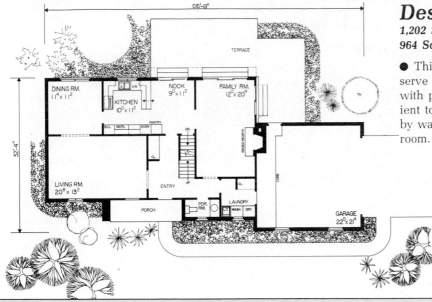

Design 12751

1,202 Sq. Ft. - First Floor
964 Sq. Ft. - Second Floor; 33,830 Cu. Ft.

● This Gambrel roof version of a Colonial is sure to serve your family efficiently. The U-shaped kitchen with pass-thru to breakfast nook will be very convenient to the busy homemaker. The terrace is accessible by way of sliding glass doors in the nook and family room.

Design 12189

1,134 Sq. Ft. - First Floor
1,063 Sq. Ft. - Second Floor; 31,734 Cu. Ft.

● Imagine this Colonial adaptation on your new building site! The recessed entrances add an extra measure of appeal. While each family member will probably have his own favorite set of highlights, all will surely agree that the living patterns will be just great.

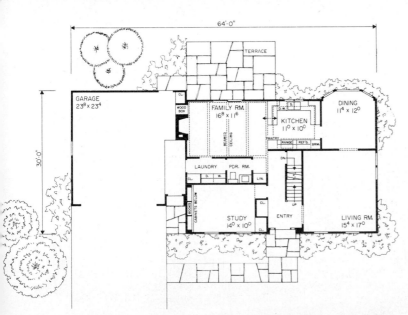

● What a tremendous amount of livability this house has to offer. Of particular note is the spaciousness of the various rooms. Study the room sizes. The traffic circulation is outstanding. The center entrance hall directs the flow most conveniently. The living room and library, each with its own fireplace, will enjoy complete privacy.

Design 12157
1,720 Sq. Ft. - First Floor
1,205 Sq. Ft. - Second Floor
40,963 Cu. Ft.

Tudor & Cotswold
English Adaptations

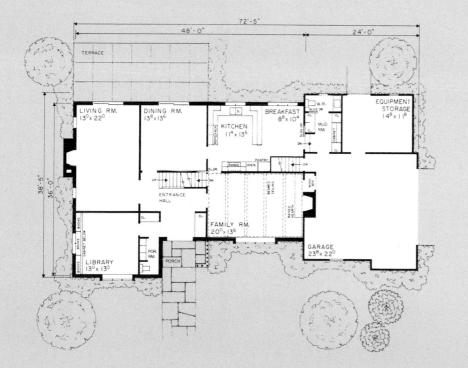

Design 12148
1,656 Sq. Ft. - First Floor
1,565 Sq. Ft. - Second Floor
48,292 Cu. Ft.

● The charm of this Tudor adaptation could hardly be improved upon. Its fine proportion and exquisite use of materials result in a most distinctive home. However, the tremendous exterior appeal tells only half of the story. Inside there is a breathtaking array of highlights which will cater to the whims of the large family. Imagine six large bedrooms, two full baths and plenty of closets on the second floor! The first floor has a formal living zone made up of the big living room, the separate dining room and the sizeable library. A second zone is comprised of the U-shaped kitchen, the breakfast room and the family room — all contributing to fine informal family living patterns. Behind the garage is the mud room, wash room and the practical equipment storage room. Don't miss beamed ceiling, powder room, two fireplaces and two flights of stairs to the basement.

Design 12586

984 Sq. Ft. - First Floor
1,003 Sq. Ft. - Second Floor; 30,080 Cu. Ft.

● A stately Tudor! With four large bedrooms.
And lots of living space . . . formal living and
dining rooms, a family room with a traditional
fireplace, a spacious kitchen with nook.

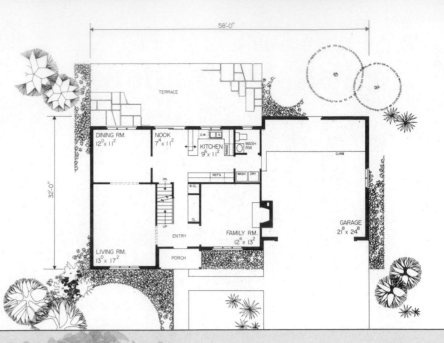

Design 12732

1,071 Sq. Ft. - First Floor
1,022 Sq. Ft. - Second Floor; 34,210 Cu. Ft.

● The two-story front entry hall will be dramatic indeed. Note the efficient kitchen adjacent
to informal family room, formal dining room.
Upstairs, three big bedrooms, two baths.

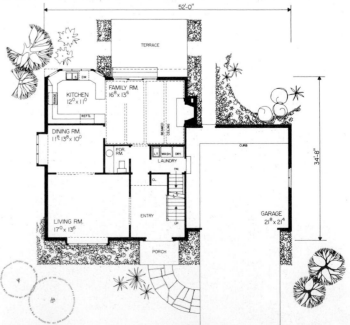

40

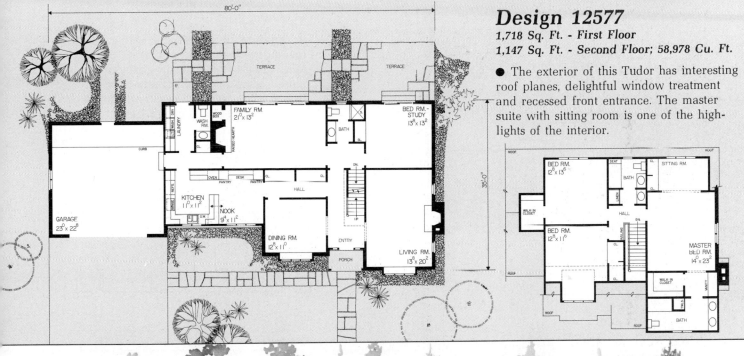

Design 12577

1,718 Sq. Ft. - First Floor
1,147 Sq. Ft. - Second Floor; 58,978 Cu. Ft.

● The exterior of this Tudor has interesting roof planes, delightful window treatment and recessed front entrance. The master suite with sitting room is one of the highlights of the interior.

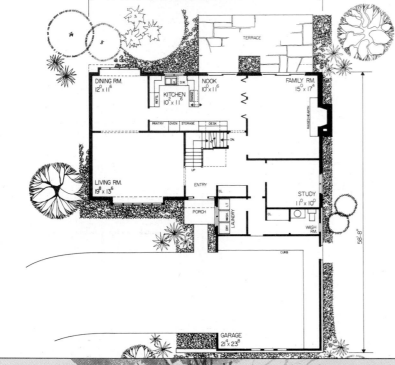

Design 12568

1,512 Sq. Ft. - First Floor
1,480 Sq. Ft. - Second Floor
42,762 Cu. Ft.

● Here's an English version with a hip-roof and an overhanging second story. As with all these designs, the distinctive exterior beam-work is simulated and built-up of readily available and conventional framing members. This is a great plan. Study it carefully.

Design 12618

1,269 Sq. Ft. - First Floor
1,064 Sq. Ft. - Second Floor
33,079 Cu. Ft.

● This four bedroom Tudor design is the object of an outstanding investment for a lifetime of proud ownership and fine, family living facilities. Note that the family room is sunken and it, along with the nook, has sliding glass doors to the terrace.

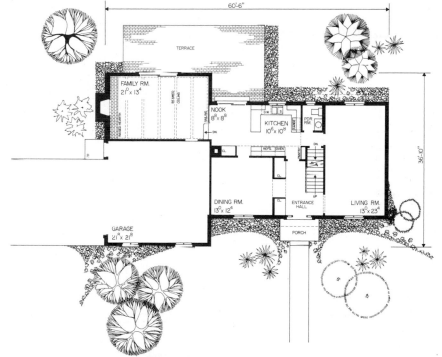

Design 12637

1,308 Sq. Ft. - First Floor
1,063 Sq. Ft. - Second Floor; 34,250 Cu. Ft.

● A generous, centered entrance hall routes traffic efficiently to all areas. And what wonderfully spacious areas they are. Note living, dining, sleeping and bath facilities. Don't miss first floor laundry.

43

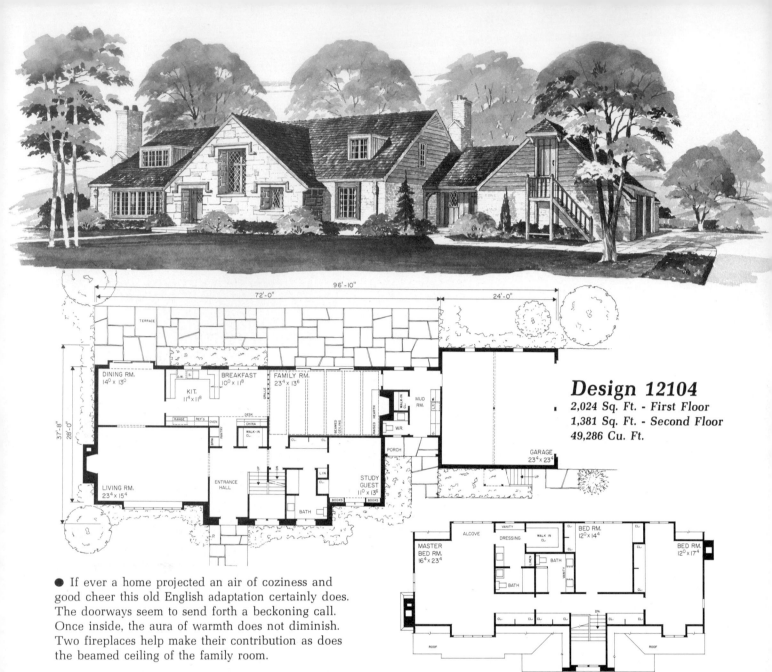

Design 12104

2,024 Sq. Ft. - First Floor
1,381 Sq. Ft. - Second Floor
49,286 Cu. Ft.

● If ever a home projected an air of coziness and good cheer this old English adaptation certainly does. The doorways seem to send forth a beckoning call. Once inside, the aura of warmth does not diminish. Two fireplaces help make their contribution as does the beamed ceiling of the family room.

Design 11991

1,262 Sq. Ft. - First Floor
1,108 Sq. Ft. - Second Floor
31,073 Cu. Ft.

● Put yourself and your family in this English cottage adaptation and you'll all rejoice over your new home for many a year. The pride of owning and living in a home that is distinctive will be a constant source of satisfaction. Count the features that will serve your family well for years.

Design 12175 1,206 Sq. Ft. - First Floor

1,185 Sq. Ft. - Second Floor; 32,655 Cu. Ft.

● An English adaptation with all the amenities for gracious living. Note built-ins.

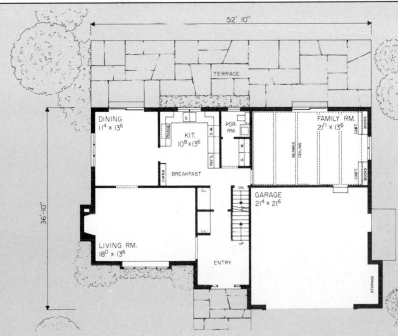

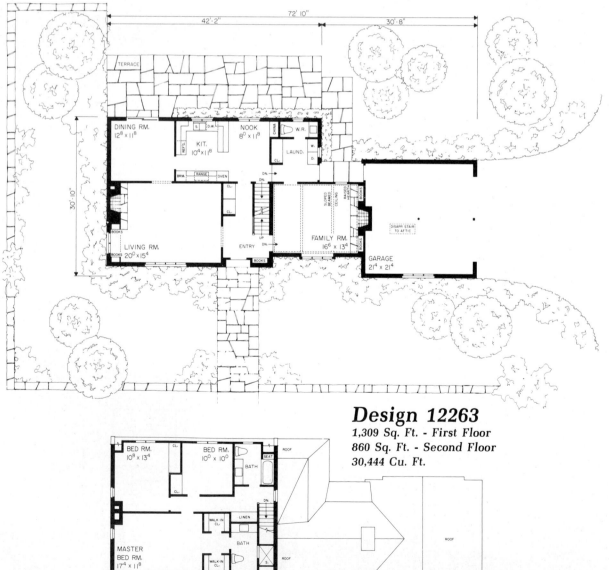

Design 12263

1,309 Sq. Ft. - First Floor
860 Sq. Ft. - Second Floor
30,444 Cu. Ft.

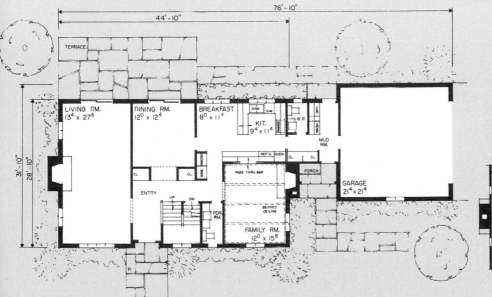

● Here on these two pages are examples of the charm of Cotswold architecture. Their roots go back to 17th Century England. While the old world appeal is retained on the outside, the late 20th Century livability is readily apparent inside. Study these exteriors and floor plans. They have much to offer.

Design 11990 1,412 Sq. Ft. - First Floor; 1,064 Sq. Ft. - Second Floor; 37,282 Cu. Ft.

Design 12126 1,566 Sq. Ft. - First Floor; 930 Sq. Ft. - Second Floor; 38,122 Cu. Ft.

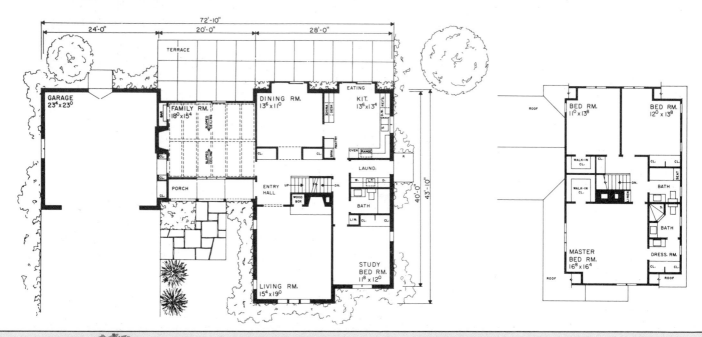

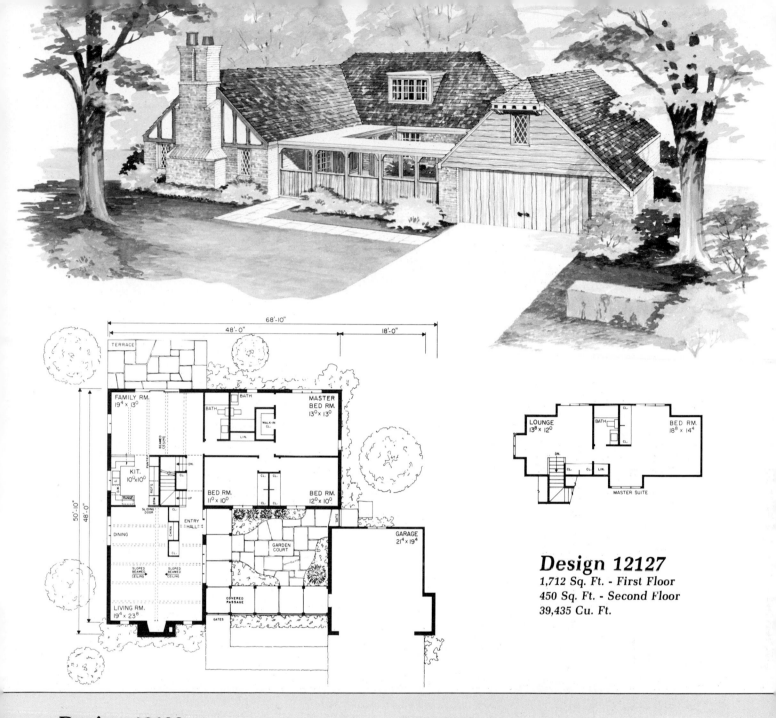

Design 12127
1,712 Sq. Ft. - First Floor
450 Sq. Ft. - Second Floor
39,435 Cu. Ft.

Floor plan labels: TERRACE; FAMILY RM. 19⁴ x 13⁰; BATH; BATH; MASTER BED RM. 13⁰ x 13⁰; WALK-IN CL.; LIN.; KIT. 10⁰ x 10⁰; RANGE; BED RM. 11⁰ x 10⁰; BED RM. 12⁰ x 10⁰; ENTRY HALL; DINING; CHINA; SLIDING DOOR; SLOPED BEAMED CEILING; SLOPED BEAMED CEILING; GARDEN COURT; COVERED PASSAGE; GATES; GARAGE 21⁴ x 19⁴; LIVING RM. 19⁴ x 23⁸; 68'-10"; 48'-0"; 18'-0"; 50'-10"; 48'-0"

Second floor labels: LOUNGE 13⁸ x 12⁰; BATH; CL.; CL.; BED RM. 18⁸ x 14⁴; DN.; CL.; LIN.; MASTER SUITE

Design 12190 1,221 Sq. Ft. - First Floor; 884 Sq. Ft. - Second Floor; 32,042 Cu. Ft.

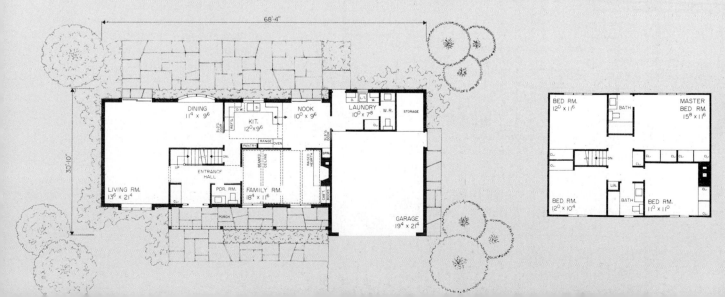

Floor plan labels: DINING 11⁴ x 9⁶; NOOK 10⁰ x 9⁶; LAUNDRY 10⁰ 7⁸; W.R.; STORAGE; KIT. 12⁰ x 9⁶; RANGE OVEN; PANTRY; BEAMED CEILING; RAISED HEARTH; ENTRANCE HALL; UP; DN.; PDR. RM.; FAMILY RM. 18⁴ x 11⁶; LIVING RM. 13⁶ x 21⁴; GARAGE 19⁴ x 21⁴; PORCH; 68'-4"; 30'-10"

Second floor labels: BED RM. 12⁰ x 11⁶; BATH; MASTER BED RM. 15⁸ x 11⁶; DN.; CL.; CL.; CL.; LIN.; BATH; BED RM. 12⁰ x 10⁴; BED RM. 11⁰ x 11⁰

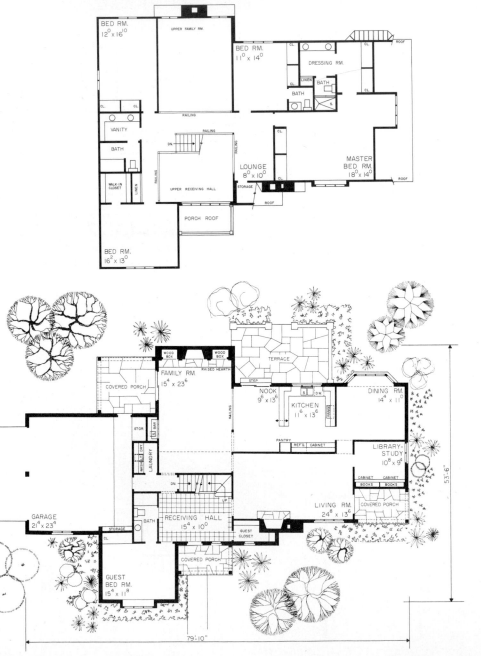

Design 12356

1,969 Sq. Ft. - First Floor
1,702 Sq. Ft. - Second Floor
55,105 Cu. Ft.

● Here is truly an exquisite Tudor adaptation. The exterior, with its interesting roof lines, window treatment, stately chimney and its appealing use of brick and stucco, could hardly be more dramatic. Inside, the drama really begins to unfold as one envisions his family's living patterns. The delightfully large receiving hall has a two story ceiling and controls the flexible traffic patterns. The living and dining rooms, with the library nearby, will cater to the formal living pursuits. The guest room offers another haven for the enjoyment of peace and quiet. Observe the adjacent full bath. Just inside the entrance from the garage is the laundry room. For the family's informal activities there are the interactions of the family room - covered porch - nook - kitchen zone. Notice the raised hearth fireplace, the wood boxes, the sliding glass doors, built-in bar and the kitchen pass-thru. Adding to the charm of the family room is its high ceiling. From the second floor hall one can look down and observe the activities below.

Design 11988

1,650 Sq. Ft. - First Floor
1,507 Sq. Ft. - Second Floor
49,474 Cu. Ft.

● A charming English Tudor adaptation which retains all the appeal of yesteryear, yet features an outstanding and practical contemporary floor plan. With all those rooms to serve a myriad of functions, the active family will lead a glorious existence. Imagine a five bedroom second floor. Or, make it a four bedroom, plus study, upstairs. In addition to the two full baths and fine closet facilities, there is convenient access to the huge storage area over the garage. Downstairs, flanking the impressive, formal front entry hall, there is space galore. The twenty-six foot, end living room will certainly be a favorite feature. The family room is large and will be lots of fun to furnish. The excellent kitchen is strategically located between the formal dining room and the informal breakfast room. The mud room is ideally located to receive traffic from the garage as well as from the rear yard. Don't miss the wash room and the powder room. Note pass-thru from kitchen to family room and abundance of storage available in garage.

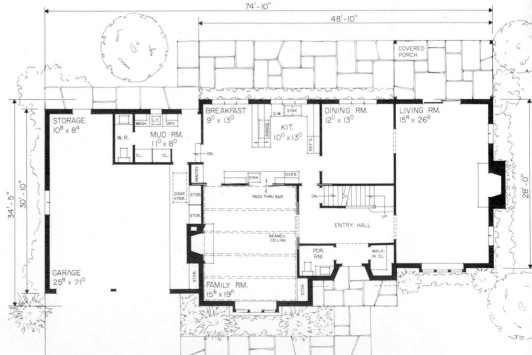

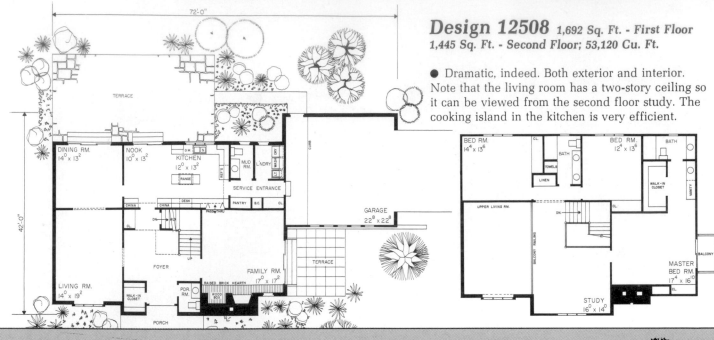

Design 12508 1,692 Sq. Ft. - First Floor
1,445 Sq. Ft. - Second Floor; 53,120 Cu. Ft.

● Dramatic, indeed. Both exterior and interior. Note that the living room has a two-story ceiling so it can be viewed from the second floor study. The cooking island in the kitchen is very efficient.

Design 12128 1,152 Sq. Ft. - First Floor
896 Sq. Ft. - Second Floor; 30,707 Cu. Ft.

● Here is proof that your restricted building budget can return to you wonderfully pleasing design and loads of livability. This is an English Tudor adaptation that will surely become your subdivision's favorite facade. Its mark of individuality is obvious to all.

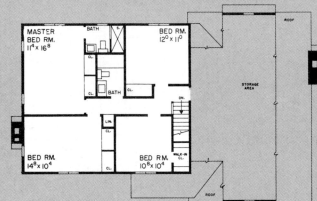

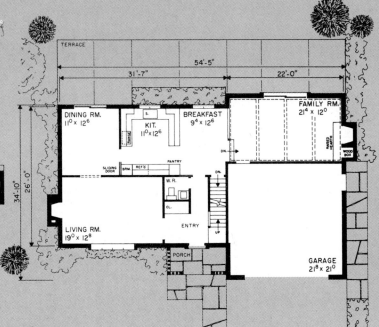

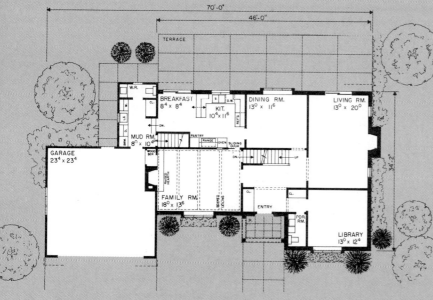

● Imagine, six bedrooms on the second floor. The first floor houses the living areas: family room, living room, dining areas plus a library. Not much more livability could be packed into this spaciously designed home.

Design 12141 1,490 Sq. Ft. - First Floor
1,474 Sq. Ft. - Second Floor; 50,711 Cu. Ft.

First floor plan labels:
TERRACE
W.R.
BREAKFAST 8⁴ x 8⁴
KIT. 10⁴ x 11⁶
DINING RM. 13⁰ x 11⁶
LIVING RM. 13⁰ x 20⁰
MUD RM. 8⁰ x 10⁴
DN.
PANTRY
RANGE
OVEN
SLIDING DOOR
WOOD BOX
GARAGE 23⁴ x 23⁴
FAMILY RM. 18⁰ x 13⁶
BEAMED CEILING
UP
CL.
PDR. RM.
ENTRY
LIBRARY 13⁰ x 12⁴
70'-0"
46'-0"
34'-2"

Second floor plan labels:
BED RM. 10⁴ x 13⁶
BATH
BED RM. 12⁶ x 10⁰
CL.
BED RM. 11⁸ x 13⁶
CL.
LIN.
DN.
LIN.
CL.
BED RM. 12⁰ x 13⁶
WALK-IN CL.
STUDY - BED RM. 12⁰ x 10⁶
DRESS. RM.
SLIDING DOOR
BATH
MASTER BED RM. 18⁴ x 13⁸

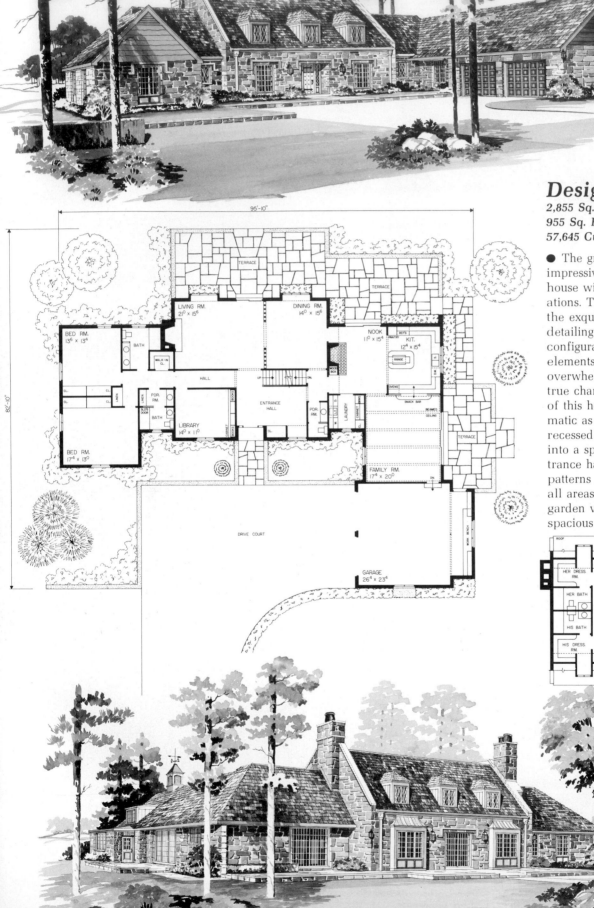

Design 12245
2,855 Sq. Ft. - First Floor
955 Sq. Ft. - Second Floor
57,645 Cu. Ft.

● The graciousness of this impressive English country house will endure for generations. The fine proportions, the exquisite architectural detailing and the interesting configuration are among the elements that create such an overwhelming measure of true character. The interior of this home will be as dramatic as the exterior. The recessed front entrance opens into a spacious, formal entrance hall. From here traffic patterns flow efficiently to all areas of the house. The garden view shows the three spacious outdoor terrace areas.

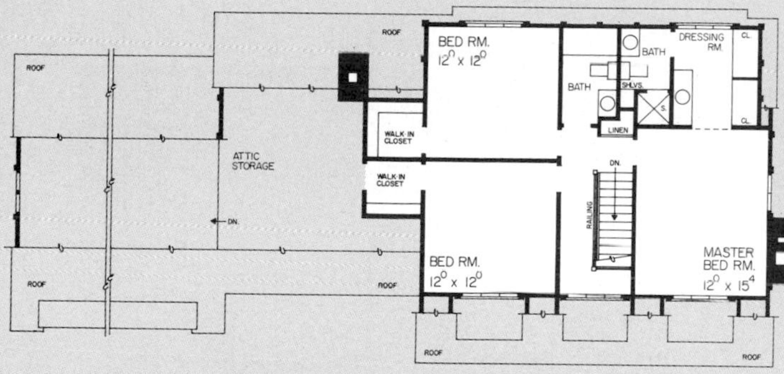

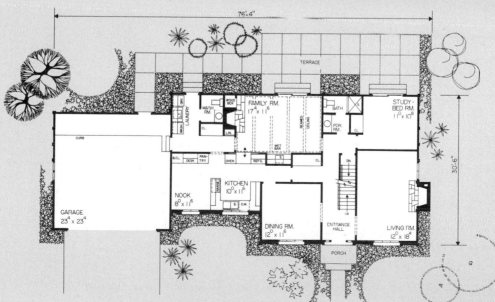

Floor plan labels (upper / second floor):

ROOF · BED RM. 12⁰ x 12⁰ · BATH · BATH · SHLVS · DRESSING RM. · CL · ROOF · ATTIC STORAGE · WALK IN CLOSET · LINEN · WALK IN CLOSET · CL · DN. · DN. · RAILING · BED RM. 12⁰ x 12⁰ · ROOF · MASTER BED RM. 12⁰ x 15⁴ · ROOF · ROOF · ROOF

● This charming, one-and-a-half-story home surely elicits thoughts of an English countryside. It has a beckoning warmth that seems to foretell a friendly welcome. The exterior features are appealing, indeed. The window treatment, the stylish chimneys, the varying roof planes and the brick veneer and stucco exterior, are among the distinguishing characteristics. Inside, the family living potential is outstanding. Notice the extra first floor bedroom with its adjacent full bath. The kitchen overlooks the front yard and is flanked by informal and formal dining areas. Nearby is the laundry and the convenient wash room. The family room, which functions with the rear terrace, will be the favorite gathering spot. Upstairs, a fine master bedroom with private bath and dressing room. A second bath caters to the two large children's bedrooms.

Design 12626 1,420 Sq. Ft. - First Floor; 859 Sq. Ft. - Second Floor; 34,974 Cu. Ft.

Floor plan labels (first floor):

76'-4" · TERRACE · 30'-6" · CURB · LAUNDRY · WOOD BOX · WA.SH. RM. · CL · FAMILY RM. 17⁴ x 11⁶ · BEAMED CEILING · BATH · PDR. RM. · STUDY-BED RM. 11⁰ x 10⁸ · B.CL. · DESK · PAN-TRY · LIN · WET BAR · OVEN · REF. · S · CL · DN. · KITCHEN 10⁰ x 11⁶ · NOOK 8⁰ x 11⁶ · DW · S · UP · GARAGE 23⁴ x 23⁴ · DINING RM. 12⁰ x 11⁶ · ENTRANCE HALL · LIVING RM. 12⁰ x 18⁴ · PORCH

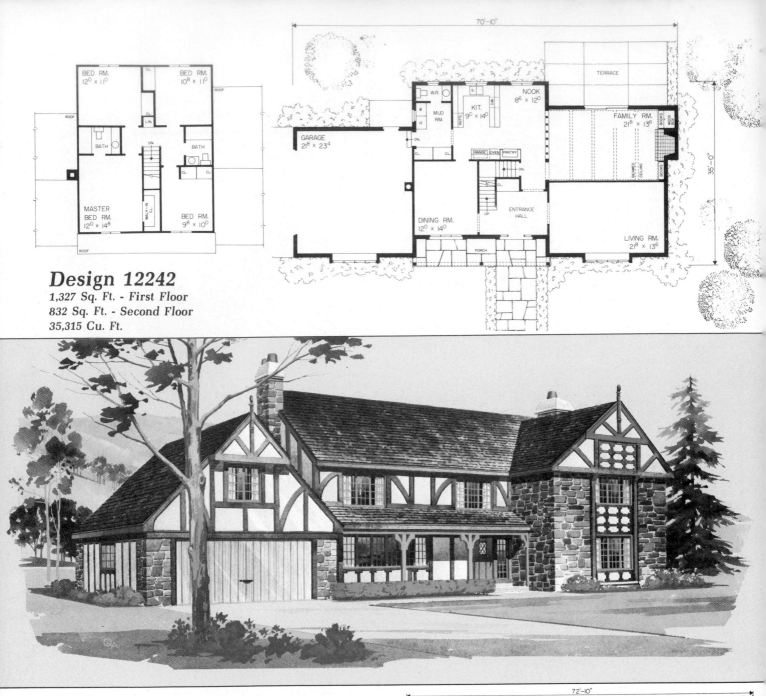

Design 12242

1,327 Sq. Ft. - First Floor
832 Sq. Ft. - Second Floor
35,315 Cu. Ft.

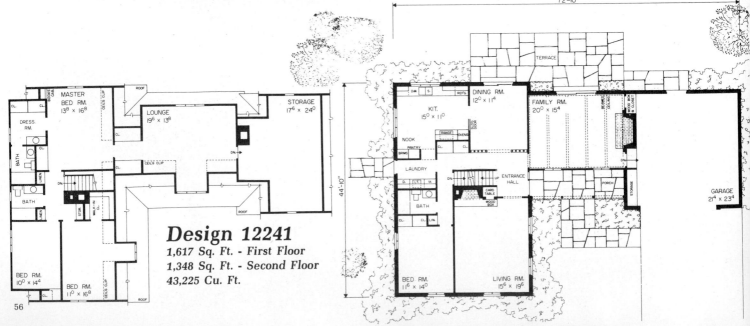

Design 12241

1,617 Sq. Ft. - First Floor
1,348 Sq. Ft. - Second Floor
43,225 Cu. Ft.

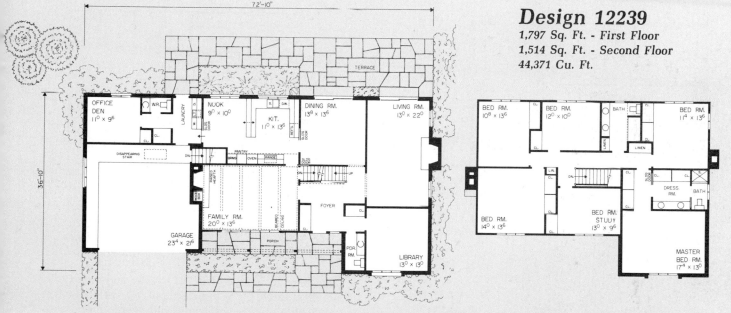

Design 12239

1,797 Sq. Ft. - First Floor
1,514 Sq. Ft. - Second Floor
44,371 Cu. Ft.

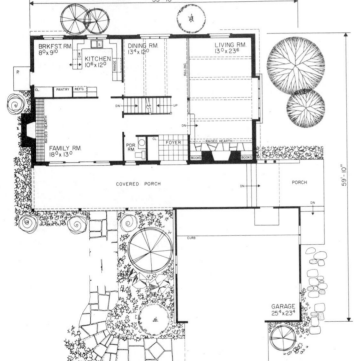

55'-10"

BRKFST. RM.
8⁰ x 9¹⁰

KITCHEN
10⁶ x 12⁰

DINING RM.
13⁴ x 12⁰

LIVING RM.
13⁰ x 23⁶

PANTRY   REF'G.

RAISED HEARTH

FAMILY RM.
18⁰ x 13⁰

PDR. RM.

FOYER

RAISED HEARTH

BOOKS   BOOKS

DN

UP

DN

COVERED PORCH

PORCH

DN

59'-10"

CURB

GARAGE
25⁴ x 23⁴

BEDROOM
12⁰ x 13⁴

CL   CL

BATH   BATH

DRESSING RM.

LINEN   STOR.

MASTER BEDROOM
13⁰ x 24¹⁰

RAILING

DN

DRESS. RM.

BEDROOM
12⁰ x 14⁴

BEDROOM
12¹⁰ x 11⁰

WALK-IN CLOSET

PORCH ROOF

Design 12324 1,256 Sq. Ft. - First Floor
1,351 Sq. Ft. - Second Floor; 37,603 Cu. Ft.

● Dramatic, indeed! Both the interior and the exterior of these three Tudor designs deserve mention. Study each of them closely. The design featured here has a simple rectangular plan which will be relatively economical to build. This design is ideal for a corner lot.

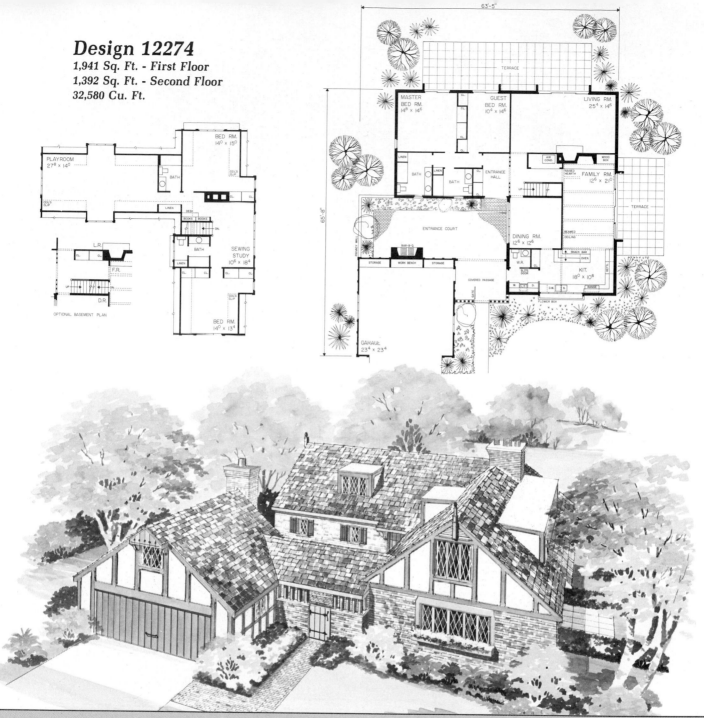

Design 12274

1,941 Sq. Ft. - First Floor
1,392 Sq. Ft. - Second Floor
32,580 Cu. Ft.

PLAYROOM
27⁸ x 14⁰

BED RM.
14⁰ x 15⁰

BATH

L.R.
F.R.
D.R.

BOOKS
DESK
LINEN
BATH
LINEN
SEWING STUDY
10⁶ x 18⁴

BED RM.
14⁰ x 13⁴

OPTIONAL BASEMENT PLAN

63'-5"

TERRACE

MASTER BED RM.
14⁸ x 14⁶

GUEST BED RM.
10⁴ x 14⁶

LIVING RM.
25⁴ x 14⁶

65'-8"

LINEN
BATH
LINEN
BATH
ENTRANCE HALL

AIR COND.
WOOD BOX

RAISED HEARTH
FAMILY RM.
12⁶ x 21⁰

TERRACE

ENTRANCE COURT

BAR-B-Q

DINING RM.
12⁶ x 12⁶

BEAMED CEILING

STORAGE
WORK BENCH
STORAGE

W.R.
SLDG. DOOR

SNACK BAR
OVEN
KIT.
18⁰ x 10⁶
RANGE

COVERED PASSAGE

FLOWER BOX

GARAGE
23⁴ x 23⁴

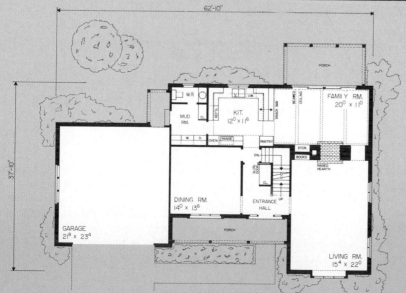

62'-10"

PORCH

37'-10"

GARAGE
21⁸ x 23⁴

W.R.
MUD RM.
KIT.
12⁰ x 11⁶

OVEN
RANGE

BEAMED CEILING
FAMILY RM.
20⁰ x 11⁰

SNACK BAR

W.   D.
PANTRY
STOR.
BOOKS
RAISED HEARTH

DN.
SLDG. DOOR
CL.

DINING RM.
14⁰ x 13⁶

ENTRANCE HALL
UP

PORCH

LIVING RM.
15⁴ x 22⁰

Design 12276

1,273 Sq. Ft. - First Floor
1,323 Sq. Ft. - Second Floor
40,450 Cu. Ft.

BED RM.
11⁸ x 12⁰

BATH

BED RM.
11⁸ x 12⁰

LIN.
LIN.

BATH

MASTER BED RM
15⁰ x 15⁰

WALK-IN
CL.

DN.
CL.

BED RM.
11⁸ x 11⁴

BED RM.
16⁰ x 12⁰

Design 12275 1,421 Sq. Ft. - First Floor; 1,456 Sq. Ft. - Second Floor; 45,330 Cu. Ft.

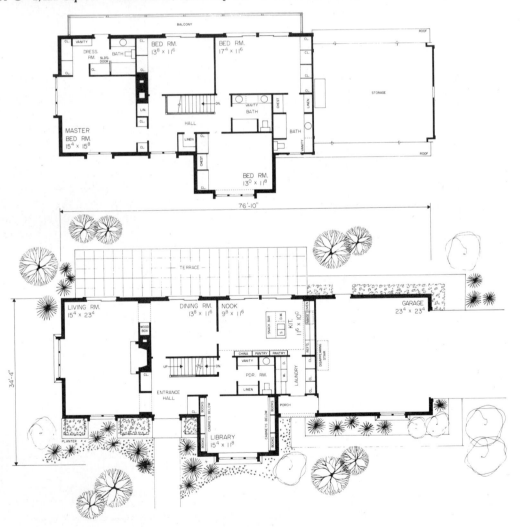

● This stately Tudor version is impressive, indeed. The fine proportion and architectural detailing give it a distinctive character all its own. Upon passing through the double front doors one is quickly aware of the excellent traffic circulation. No-

tice how the entrance hall routes traffic to the various rooms. The end living room will enjoy the utmost in privacy. No unnecessary cross-room traffic here. The dining room is but a step or two from the hallway, the living room and the kitchen/nook

area. The arrangement of the kitchen and its eating area will create a nostalgic country-kitchen atmosphere. The library can be called upon to serve a multitude of functions. Note powder room and laundry. Upstairs, four big bedrooms and three baths.

Design 12541

1,985 Sq. Ft. - First Floor
1,659 Sq. Ft. - Second Floor; 59,012 Cu. Ft.

● Here is English Tudor styling at its stately best. The massive stone work is complemented by stucco and massive beams. The diamond lite windows, the projecting bays, the carriage lamps and the twin chimneys add to the charm of this exterior. The spacious center entrance routes traffic effectively to all areas. Worthy of particular note is the formal living room with its fireplace, the adjacent family room overlooking the terrace, the quiet study with fireplace, two sizeable dining areas and an excellent master suite. Plus two more sizeable bedrooms.

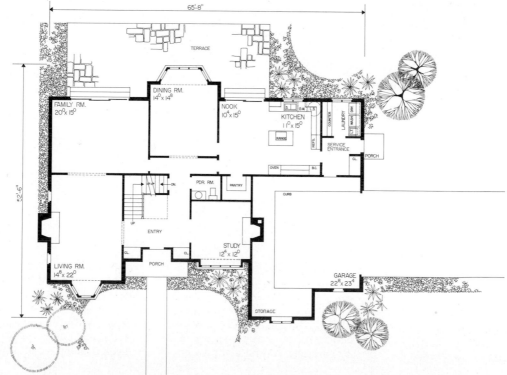

Design 12278 1,804 Sq. Ft. - First Floor; 939 Sq. Ft. - First Floor; 44,274 Cu. Ft.

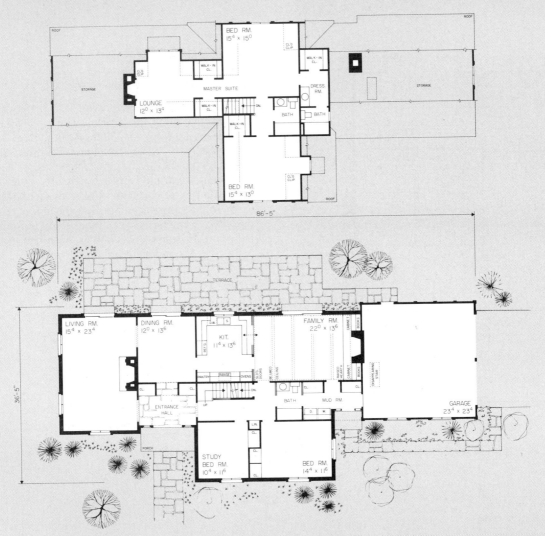

● This cozy Tudor adaptation is surely inviting. Its friendly demeanor seems to say, "welcome". Upon admittance to the formal front entrance hall, even the most casual of visitors will be filled with anticipation at the prospect of touring the house. And little wonder, too. Traffic patterns are efficient. Room relationships are excellent. A great feature is the location of the living, dining, kitchen and family rooms across the back of the house. Each enjoys a view of the rear yard and sliding glass doors provide direct access to the terrace. Another outstanding feature is the flexibility of the sleeping patterns. This may be a five bedroom house, or one with three bedrooms with study and lounge. Don't miss the three fireplaces and three baths.

Design 12373 1,160 Sq. Ft. - First Floor; 1,222 Sq. Ft. - Second Floor; 33,775 Cu. Ft.

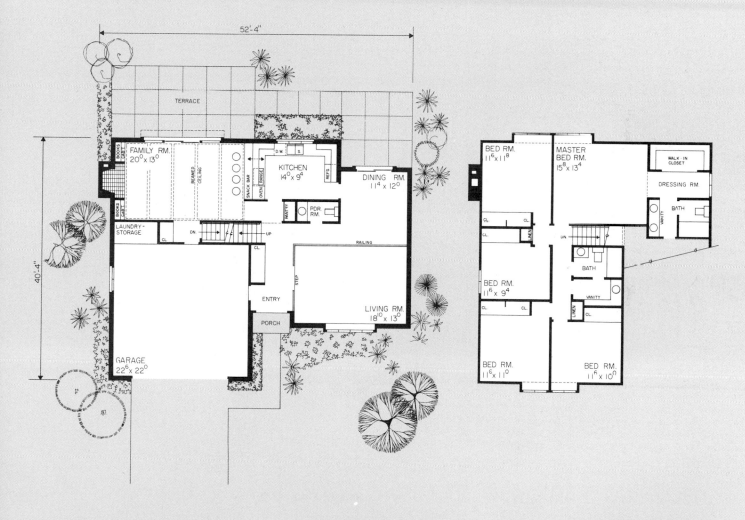

● Finding more livability wrapped in such an attractive facade would be difficult, indeed. This charming Tudor adaptation will return big dividends per construction dollar. It is compact and efficient. And, of course, it will not require a big, expensive piece of property. The location of the two-car garage as an integral part of the structure has its convenience and economic advantages, too. The living room is sunken and is divided from the dining room by a railing which helps maintain the desirable spacious atmosphere. The family room with its beamed ceiling, attractive fireplace wall, built-in storage and snack bar functions well with both the kitchen and the outdoor terrace. Four bedrooms, two baths, plenty of closets and built-in vanities.

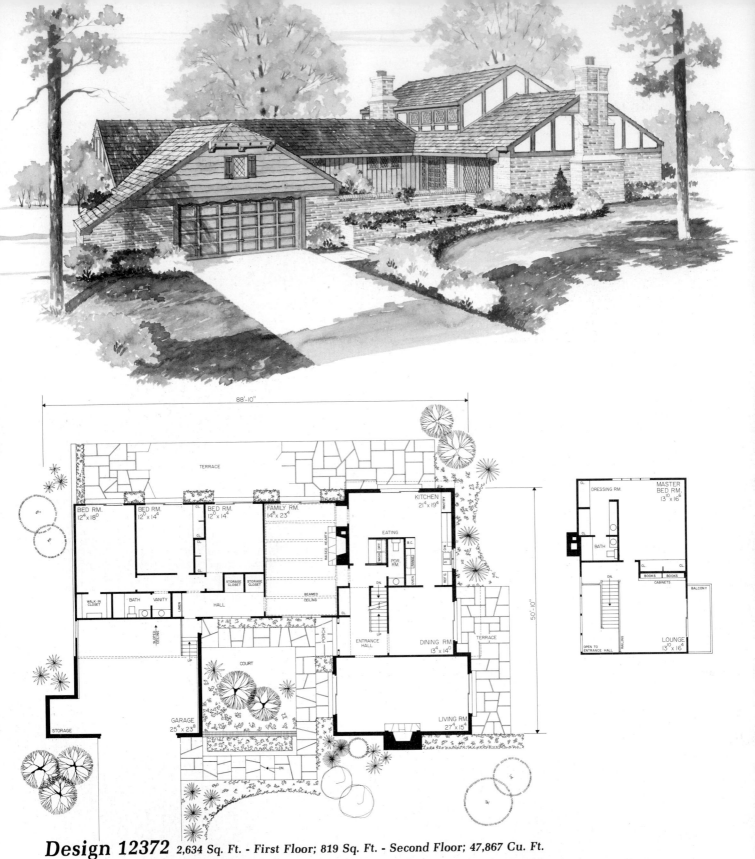

Design 12372 2,634 Sq. Ft. - First Floor; 819 Sq. Ft. - Second Floor; 47,867 Cu. Ft.

● What a wonderfully different and imposing two-story design this is! The Tudor styling and the varying roof planes, along with its U-shape, add to the air of distinction. From the driveway, steps lead past a big raised planter up to the enclosed entrance court. A wide overhanging roof shelters the massive patterned double doors flanked by diamond paned sidelites. The living room is outstanding. It is located a distance from other living areas and is quite spacious. The centered fireplace is the dominant feature, while sliding-glass doors open from each end onto outdoor terraces. The kitchen, too, is spacious and functions well. Two eating areas are nearby. It is worth noting that each of the major first floor rooms have direct access to the outdoor terraces. Note second floor suite which includes a lounge with built-in book cabinets.

Design 12391 *2,496 Sq. Ft. - First Floor; 958 Sq. Ft. - Second Floor; 59,461 Cu. Ft.*

● Here is a stately English adaptation that is impressive, indeed. The two-story octagonal foyer strikes a delightfully authentic design note. The entrance hall with open staircase and two-story ceiling is spacious. Clustered around the efficient kitchen are the formal living areas and those catering to informal activities. The family room with its beamed ceiling and raised hearth fireplace functions, like the formal living/dining zone, with the partially enclosed outdoor terrace. Three bedrooms with two baths comprise the first floor sleeping zone. Each room will enjoy its access to the terrace. Upstairs there are two more bedrooms and a study. Notice the sliding glass doors to the balcony and how the study looks down into the entrance hall. The three-car garage is great. Your own list of favorite features will surely be lengthy.

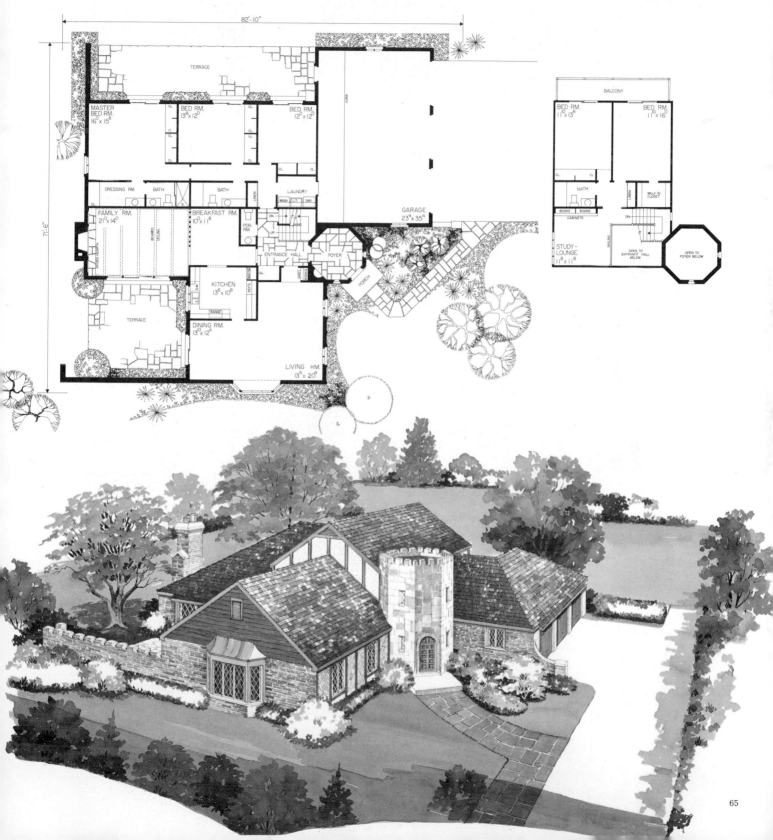

Design 12525

919 Sq. Ft. - First Floor
1,019 Sq. Ft. - Second Floor
29,200 Cu. Ft.

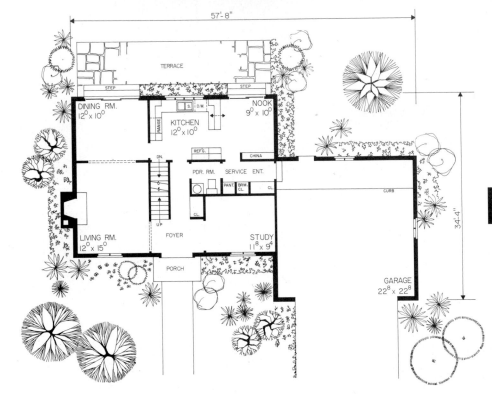

● Here is an economically built home that can be constructed with either of the two illustrated exteriors. Which is your favorite? The two study areas provide plenty of multi-purpose, informal living space.

The Formality Of
French Mansards

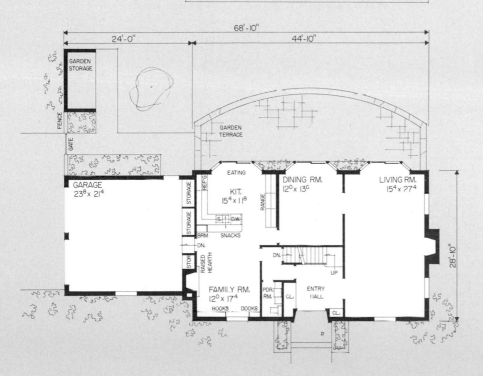

Design 11275

1,314 Sq. Ft. - First Floor
1,080 Sq. Ft. - Second Floor
33,656 Cu. Ft.

● Of French origin, the characteristic feature of this two story design is its Mansard roof. Also, enhancing the formality of its exterior are the beautifully proportioned windows, the recessed front entrance with double doors, the two stately chimneys and the attached two-car garage. The wonderfully efficient floor plan highlights a large end-living room with centered fireplace and a separate dining room. There is also a fine family room-kitchen arrangement with a pass-thru, raised hearth fireplace and strategically located powder room. Upstairs there are three family bedrooms, bath and glamorous master suite. The area over the garage may be utilized for bulk storage or developed as the fifth bedroom. Other bulk storage areas are to be found in the garage and the outdoor unit. Don't miss the sliding doors.

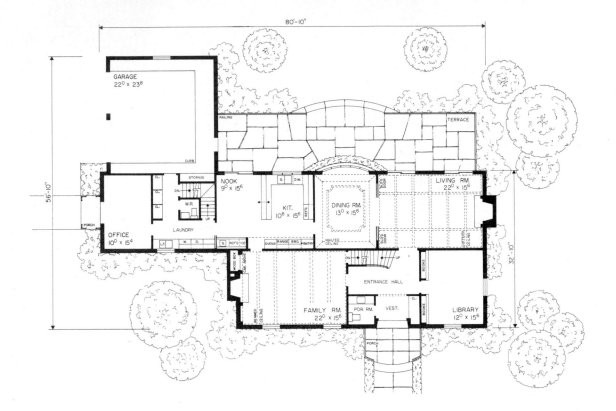

Design 11839 *2,204 Sq. Ft. - First Floor; 1,486 Sq. Ft. - Second Floor; 330 Sq. Ft. - Maid's Area; 55,683 Cu. Ft.*

● Imagine, five bedrooms, a quiet library, a home office (use it as a first floor hobby room if you prefer), a big family room, a first floor laundry, a maid's suite and three full baths plus an extra powder room and wash room! Note the large formal living and dining rooms which look out upon the raised terrace.

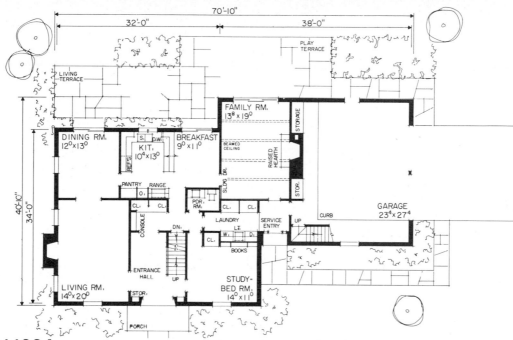

Design 11934 *1,622 Sq. Ft. - First Floor; 2,002 Sq. Ft. - Second Floor; 51,758 Cu. Ft.*

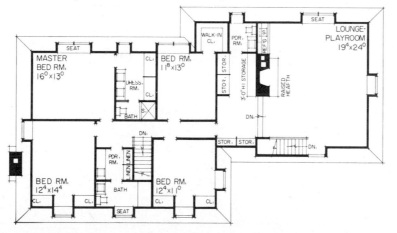

● The two-story French Mansard has become a favorite of many during the past few years. Its attractive proportion and pleasing formality have become familiar to most of us. Be sure to observe the fine architectural detailing such as the dentils at the cornice, the brick quoins at the corners, the recessed and paneled front entrance, the carriage lamps, etc. The interior of this home is even more outstanding. Here is a house that could function as a four, five or even a six bedroom home!

And with plenty of space left over for formal and informal living and dining. For efficient housekeeping, there is the U-shaped kitchen and the separate first floor laundry. Observe the central location of powder room. Note hall storage facilities.

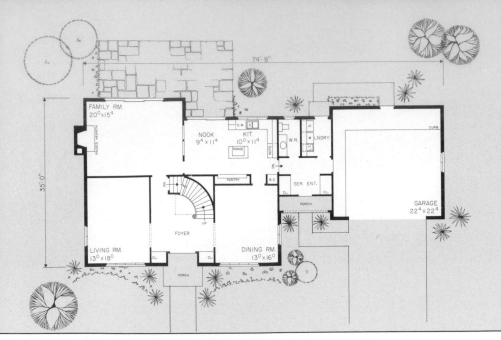

Design 12507

1,529 Sq. Ft. - First Floor
1,206 Sq. Ft. - Second Floor
40,960 Cu. Ft.

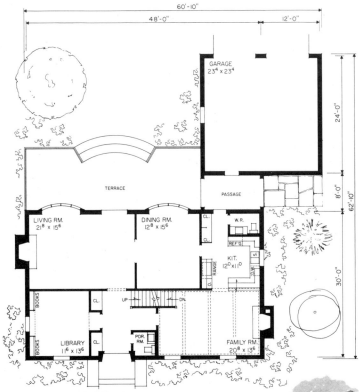

Design 11277

1,504 Sq. Ft. - First Floor
1,243 Sq. Ft. - Second Floor
38,058 Cu. Ft.

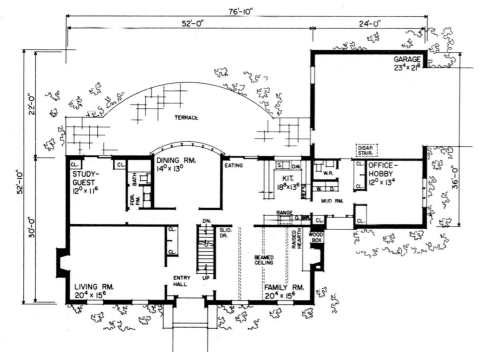

GARAGE 23⁴ x 21⁸

TERRACE

DINING RM. 14⁰ x 13⁰

EATING

OFFICE- HOBBY 12⁰ x 13⁴

STUDY- GUEST 12⁰ x 11⁶

KIT. 18⁸ x 13⁶

W.R.

MUD. RM.

RANGE

CL.

WOOD BOX

DN.

SLID. DR.

BEAMED CEILING

RAISED HEARTH

LIVING RM. 20⁴ x 15⁶

ENTRY HALL

UP

FAMILY RM. 20⁴ x 15⁶

76'-10"
52'-0"
24'-0"
22'-0"
52'-0"
30'-0"
36'-0"

DISAP. STAIR.

CL. DRESS. RM.

BATH

VANITY VANITY

MASTER BED RM. 18⁴ x 14⁸

BATH

VANITY

CL.

BED RM. 16⁰ x 12⁶

DN.

BOOKS

BOOKS

BED RM. 16⁰ x 12⁶

Design 11733
1,944 Sq. Ft. - First Floor
1,308 Sq. Ft. - Second Floor
61,152 Cu. Ft.

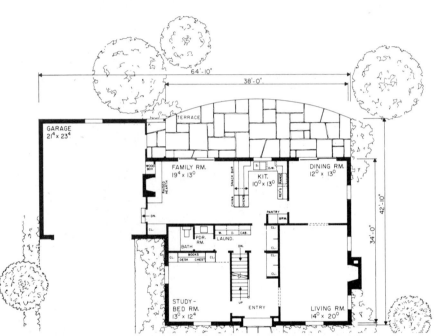

Design 11757

1,406 Sq. Ft. - First Floor
1,115 Sq. Ft. - Second Floor
36,204 Cu. Ft.

● The French Mansard style of a two-story is very popular with those seeking a design with gracious formality. Study this practical floor plan which has first floor laundry and four (optional five) bedrooms. Note two fireplaces.

Design 11951
1,346 Sq. Ft. - First Floor
1,114 Sq. Ft. - Second Floor; 39,034 Cu. Ft.

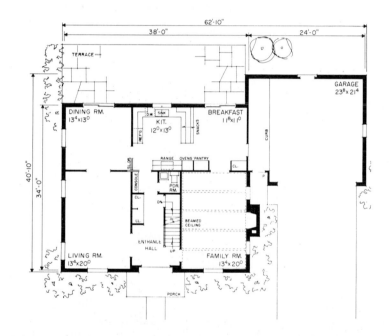

● This is surely a marvelous French home with its Mansard roof. It is equipped with all the necessary features including a large living room, dining room with access to the terrace, efficient kitchen and more.

Design 12152
1,317 Sq. Ft. - First Floor
1,111 Sq. Ft. - Second Floor; 37,198 Cu. Ft.

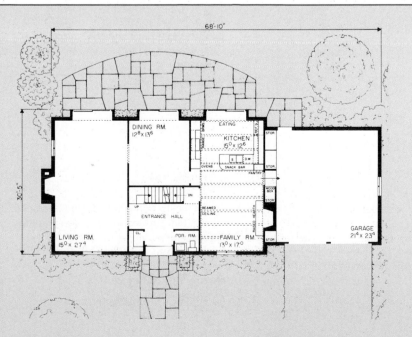

● Here is an interesting plan in which to think about living. Notice the zoning with the entrance hall and dining room dividing the formal and informal living areas. Upstairs there are four bedrooms and two full baths.

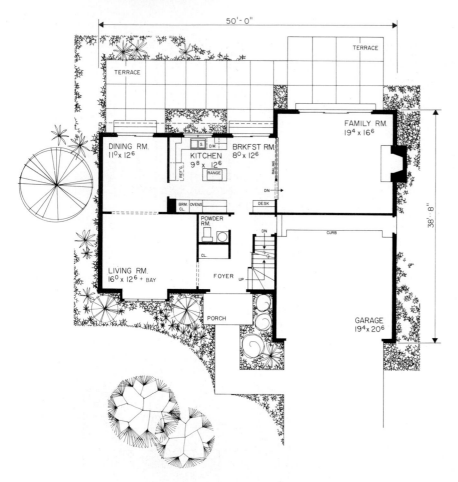

Design 12798

1,149 Sq. Ft. - First Floor
850 Sq. Ft. - Second Floor
28,450 Cu. Ft.

● An island range in the kitchen is a great feature of the work center in this two-story French designed home. The breakfast room has an open railing to the sunken family room so it can enjoy the view of the family room's fireplace.

Sliding glass doors in each of the major rear rooms, dining, breakfast and family rooms, lead to the terrace for outdoor enjoyment. The front, formal living room is highlighted by a bay window. A powder room is conven-

iently located on the first floor near all of the major areas. All of the sleeping facilities are housed on the second floor. Each of the four bedrooms will serve its occupants ideally. A relatively narrow lot can house this design.

The formality of French design is certainly impressive. This Mansard version has a notable hipped roof with a delicate nature. The exterior's architectural detailing is pleasing to behold. Double front doors are recessed and open to a center entrance hall. Note that the interior layout is practical and, indeed, efficient. The end living and dining rooms will foster formal living patterns, while the outstanding kitchen and family room with beamed ceiling will function together in a delightfully informal fashion. Both areas have the advantage to enjoy a fireplace. A woodbox is in the family room. Further, there is the quiet study or optional bedroom on the first floor. Upstairs, there are four excellent bedrooms, and two full baths.

Design 12249

1,417 Sq. Ft. - First Floor
1,171 Sq. Ft. - Second Floor
39,714 Cu. Ft.

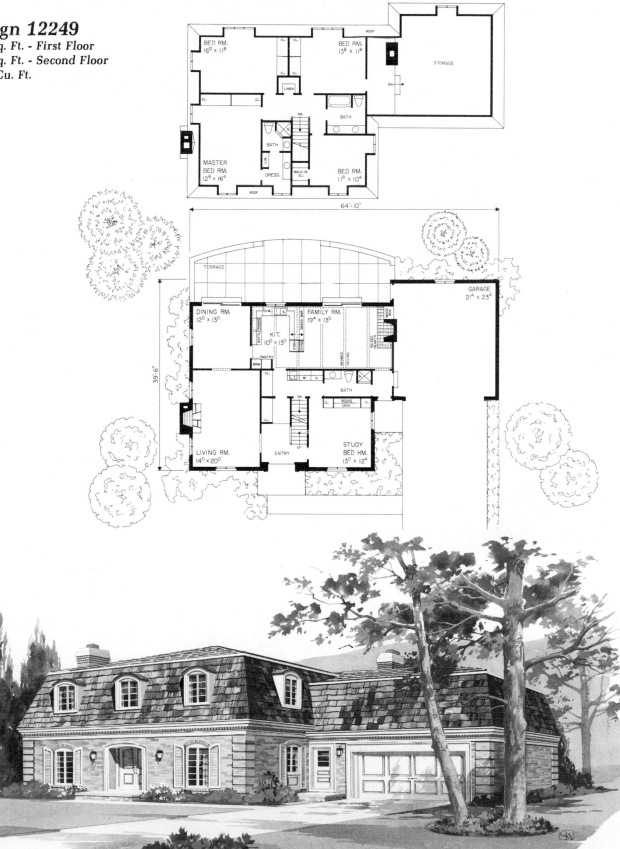

Design 12503

1,847 Sq. Ft. - First Floor
1,423 Sq. Ft. - Second Floor
50,671 Cu. Ft.

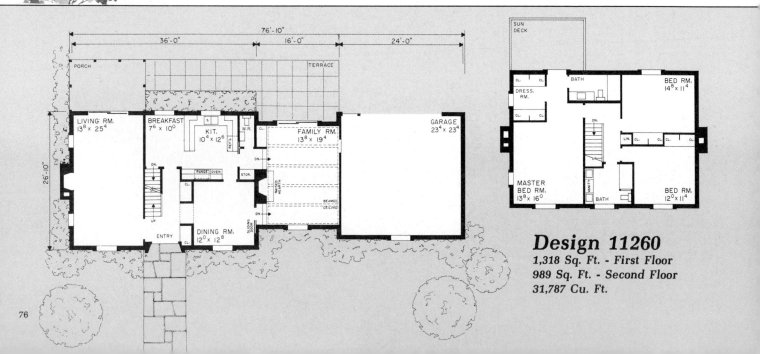

Design 11260

1,318 Sq. Ft. - First Floor
989 Sq. Ft. - Second Floor
31,787 Cu. Ft.

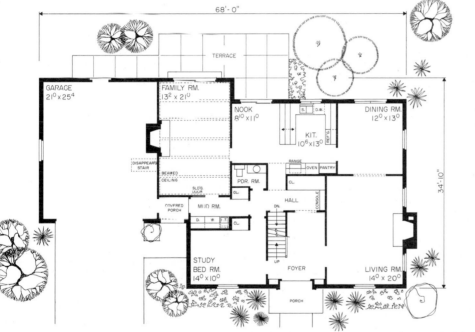

TERRACE

GARAGE
21⁰ x 25⁴

FAMILY RM.
13² x 21⁰

NOOK
8¹⁰ x 11⁰

DINING RM.
12⁰ x 13⁰

KIT.
10⁶ x 13⁰

DISAPPEARING STAIR

BEAMED CEILING

PDR. RM.

RANGE   OVEN PANTRY

COVERED PORCH

MUD RM.

HALL

STUDY
BED RM.
14⁰ x 10⁰

FOYER

LIVING RM.
14⁰ x 20⁰

PORCH

68'-0"

34'-10"

BED RM.
15⁴ x 11⁴

BED RM.
15⁸ x 11⁴

BATH

LIN.

STORAGE

BATH

SEAT

BED RM.
12⁴ x 10⁰

MASTER
BED RM.
17⁰ x 13⁰

ROOF

Design 11774

1,574 Sq. Ft. - First Floor
1,124 Sq. Ft. - Second Floor
37,616 Cu. Ft.

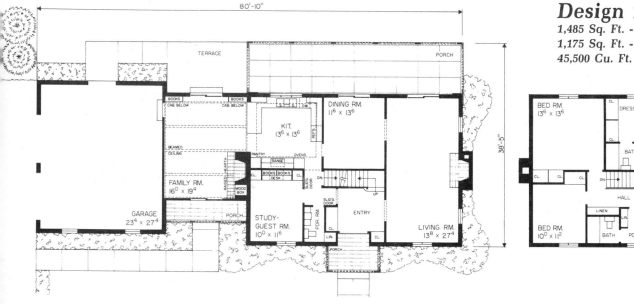

Design 12222

1,485 Sq. Ft. - First Floor
1,175 Sq. Ft. - Second Floor
45,500 Cu. Ft.

80'-10"

38'-5"

TERRACE

PORCH

BOOKS
CAB. BELOW

BOOKS
CAB. BELOW

KIT.
13⁶ x 13⁶

DINING RM.
11⁶ x 13⁶

BEAMED
CEILING

PANTRY
RANGE
OVENS

BOOKS DESK BOOKS

FAMILY RM.
16⁰ x 19⁴

WOOD
BOX

SLID'S
DOOR

DN.

UP

LIVING RM.
13⁸ x 27⁴

GARAGE
23⁴ x 27⁴

PORCH

STUDY-
GUEST RM.
10⁰ x 11⁶

PDR. RM.

SLID'S
DOOR

CL.

ENTRY

CL.

PORCH

BED RM.
13⁶ x 13⁶

DRESS. RM.

MASTER
BED RM.
17⁰ x 13⁶

CL.

CL.

BATH

CL.

CL.

CL.

DN.

HALL

BED RM.
10⁰ x 11²

LINEN

LIN.

BATH

PDR. RM.

CL.

LIN.

BED RM.
13⁰ x 13⁶

Design 12281

1,961 Sq. Ft. - First Floor
1,472 Sq. Ft. - Second Floor
49,974 Cu. Ft.

88'-10"

47'-2"

BRICK TERRACE

STORAGE
9⁶ x 10⁰

LAUND.

W. R.

CL.

DN.

DN.

BEAMED
CEILING

NOOK
8⁶ x 13⁶

KIT.
10⁰ x 13⁶

DINING RM.
13⁰ x 13⁶

OVEN RANGE PANTRY DESK

BOOKS BOOKS BOOKS

CABINETS

PDR.
RM.

DN.

UP

LIVING RM.
15⁶ x 27⁴

GARAGE
23⁴ x 21⁴

FAMILY RM.
15⁸ x 23⁴

WOOD
BOX

STUDY
11⁰ x 13⁶

ENTRANCE HALL

PORCH

BED RM.
10⁴ x 13⁶

BATH

BED RM.
13⁰ x 11⁰

BATH

VANITY

DRESSING RM.

CL.

CL.

CL.

LINEN

CL.

CL.

CL.

DN.

UP

OPEN STAIR WELL

RAILING

BED RM.
15⁰ x 11⁰

STAIR HALL

MASTER
BED RM.
15⁴ x 17⁸

CL.

CL.

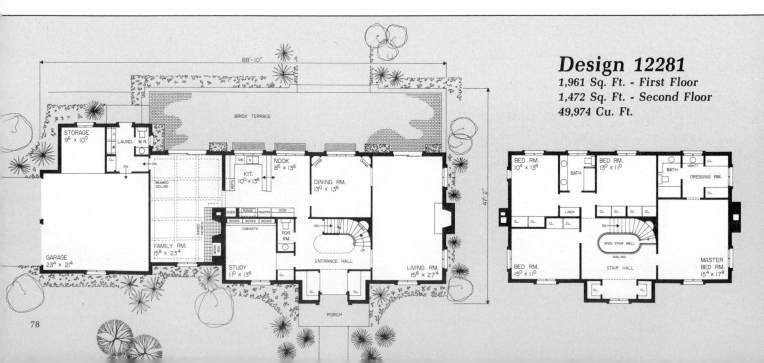

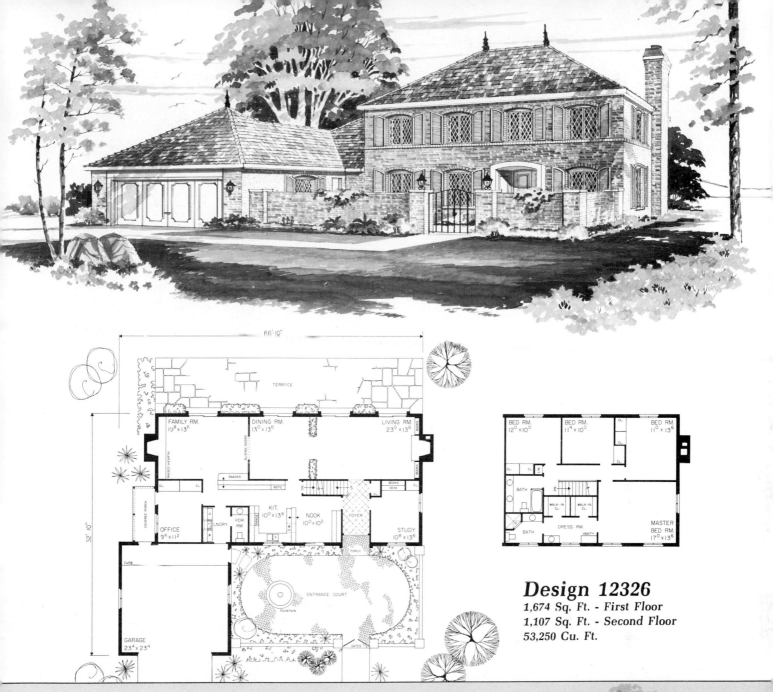

Design 12326

1,674 Sq. Ft. - First Floor
1,107 Sq. Ft. - Second Floor
53,250 Cu. Ft.

Exquisite Good Taste - French Provincial

● The elegance of pleasing proportion and delightful detailing has seldom been better exemplified than by this classic French country manor adaptation. Approaching the house across the drive court, the majesty of this multi-roofed structure is breathtaking, indeed.

While there is an aura of old world formality, there is also an accompanying feeling of contemporary livability. The graciousness with which it will unfold, will be awaiting only the arrival of the occupants; for all the elements are present to guarantee

complete livability both indoors and out. A trip through the house reveals a fine arrangement of large, spacious rooms. If necessary, the library may be called upon to become the fourth bedroom or guest room. Observe the work center of kitchen area.

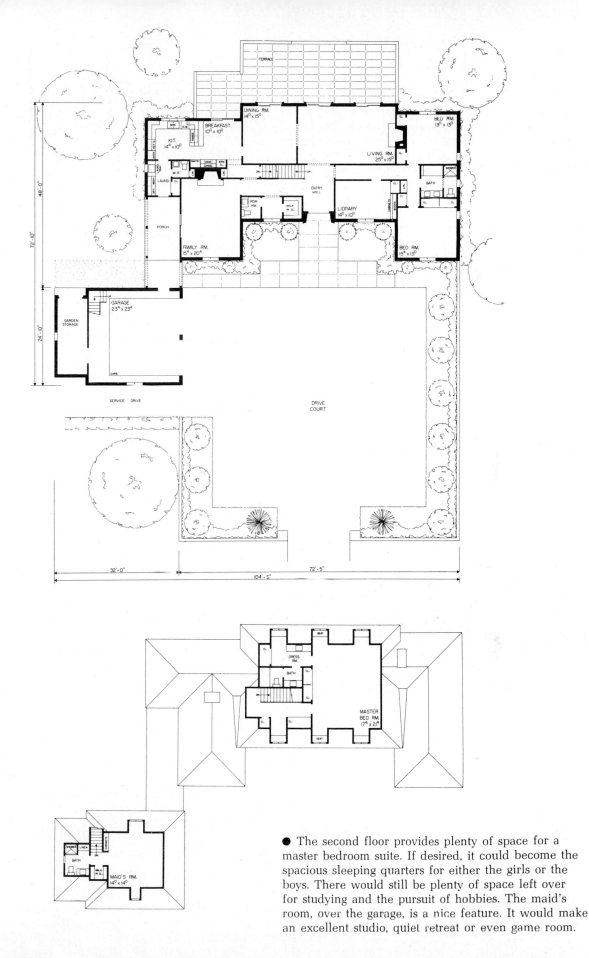

The second floor provides plenty of space for a master bedroom suite. If desired, it could become the spacious sleeping quarters for either the girls or the boys. There would still be plenty of space left over for studying and the pursuit of hobbies. The maid's room, over the garage, is a nice feature. It would make an excellent studio, quiet retreat or even game room.

Design 11993 2,658 Sq. Ft. - First Floor; 840 Sq. Ft. - Master Suite; 376 Sq. Ft. - Maid's Suite; 57,057 Cu. Ft.

Design 12543

2,345 Sq. Ft. - First Floor
1,687 Sq. Ft. - Second Floor; 76,000 Cu. Ft.

● Certainly a dramatic French adaptation highlighted by effective window treatment, delicate cornice detailing, appealing brick quoins and excellent proportion. Stepping through the double front doors the drama is heightened by the spacious entry hall with its two curving staircases to the second floor. The upper hall is open and looks down to the hall below. There is a study and a big gathering room which look out on the raised terrace. The work center is outstanding. The garage will accommodate three cars.

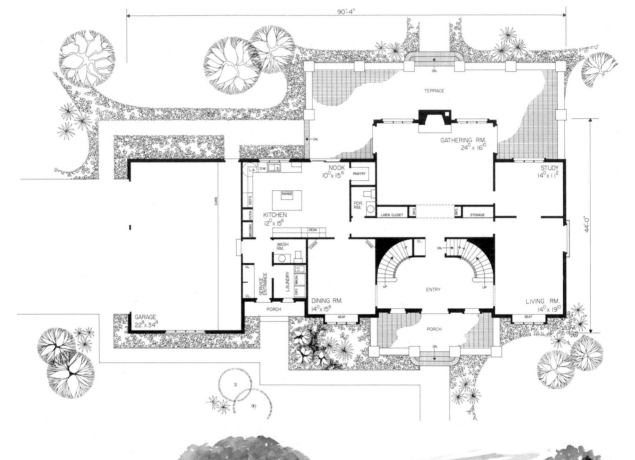

Design 12376

1,422 Sq. Ft. - First Floor
1,020 Sq. Ft. - Second Floor; 38,134 Cu. Ft.

● Make your next home one that will be truly distinctive and a reflection of your good taste. This high styled design will surely catch the eye of even the most casual of passers-by. The appealing roof lines, the window treatment, the arched openings and the stucco exterior set the charming character of this two-story. The covered front porch provides sheltered entry to the spacious foyer. From this point traffic patterns flow efficiently to all areas. Notice how the family room/laundry zone is sunken one step. The kitchen is flanked by the two eating areas and they overlook the rear yard. Each of the two large living areas feature a fireplace and functions directly through sliding glass doors with a covered porch. Upstairs there are four bedrooms, two baths and plenty of closets to serve the entire family adequately.

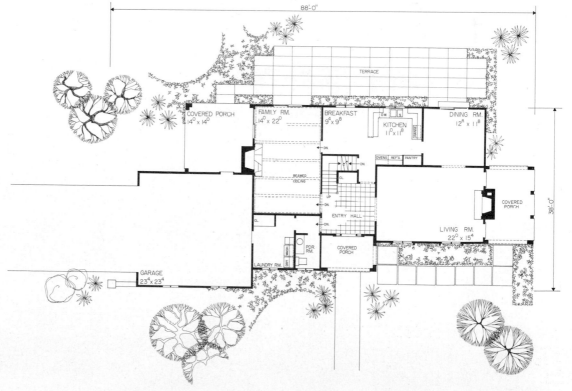

Design 12587

984 Sq. Ft. - First Floor
993 Sq. Ft. - Second Floor; 30,090 Cu. Ft.

● A traditional classic! A large living room and adjoining dining room . . . together they offer the correct setting for the most formal occasion. For casual times, a family room.

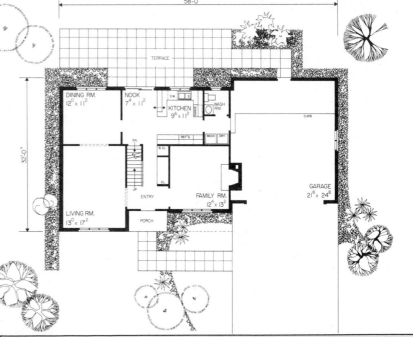

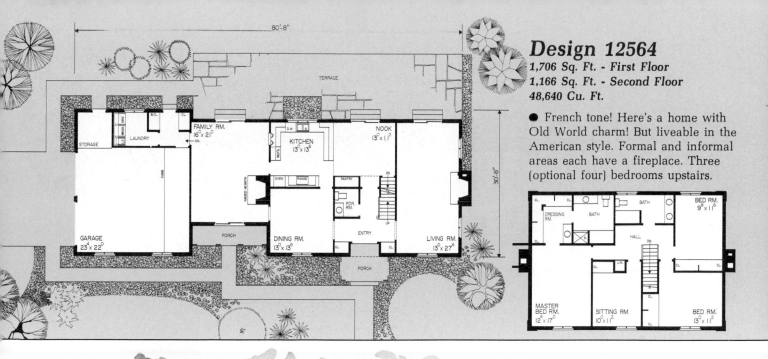

Design 12564

1,706 Sq. Ft. - First Floor
1,166 Sq. Ft. - Second Floor
48,640 Cu. Ft.

● French tone! Here's a home with Old World charm! But liveable in the American style. Formal and informal areas each have a fireplace. Three (optional four) bedrooms upstairs.

Design 12750

1,209 Sq. Ft. - First Floor
965 Sq. Ft. - Second Floor; 32,025 Cu. Ft.

● This four bedroom Mansard roof design is impressive, indeed. The covered front porch leads the way to an efficient floor plan. Includes a basement.

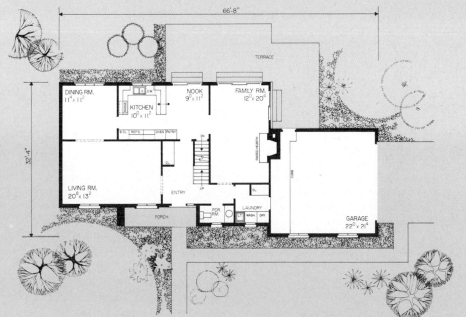

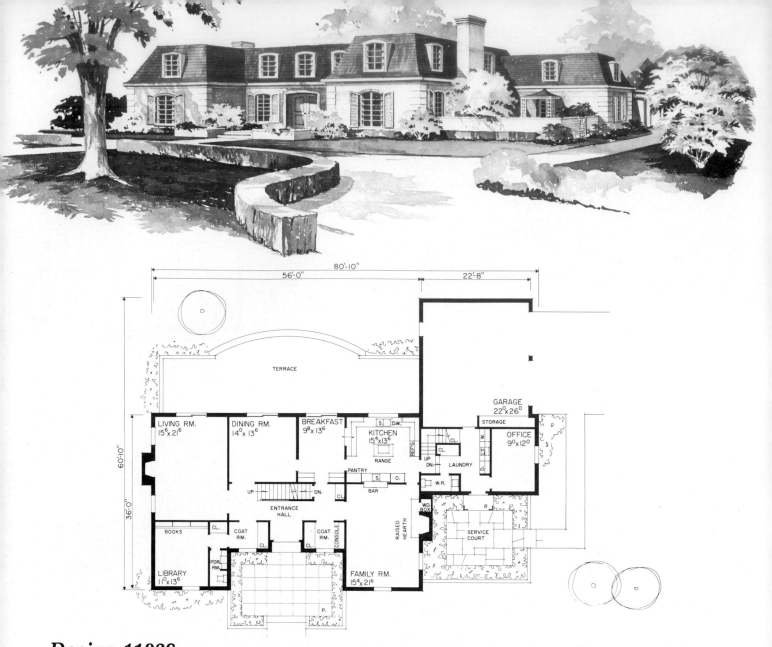

Design 11826 *2,230 Sq. Ft. - First Floor; 1,576 Sq. Ft. - Second Floor; 308 Sq. Ft. - Maid's Area; 52,852 Cu. Ft.*

● This dramatic French Mansard will provide all the livability the large, active family could possibly want. Its irregular shape results in truly captivating exterior lines. A front court and service court are the by-products of the recessed front and service entrances. A side drive leads to side-opening two-car garage. The interior features twelve (count them) major rooms. These include the quiet library, the isolated office and the private maid's room. In addition there are two coat rooms, a walk-in closet, a powder room, a wash room, a dressing room and three full baths. For family living there is the formal living room and the informal family room. For dining there is the separate dining room and breakfast room. For sleeping facilities there are four big bedrooms with plenty of closets. The first floor laundry is efficient. Three sets of sliding glass doors lead to the rear terrace.

The Quiet Dignity Of
Georgian Adaptations

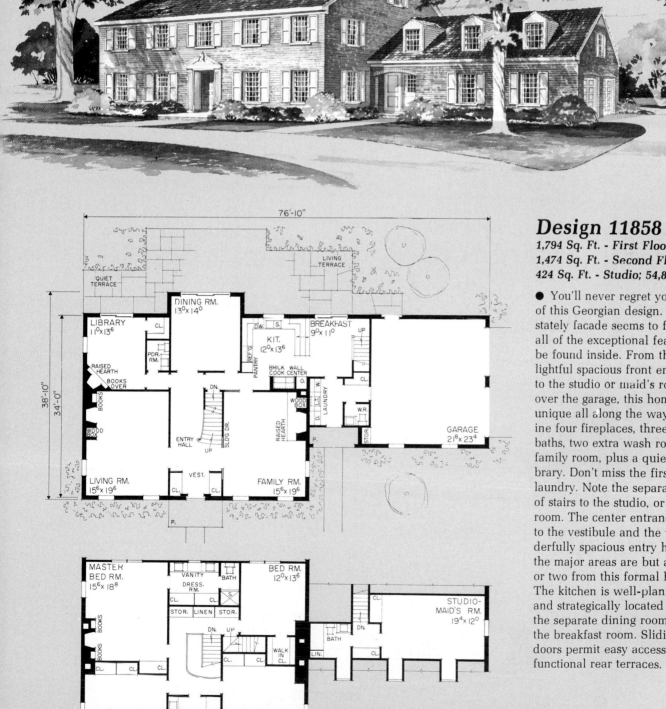

Design 11858

1,794 Sq. Ft. - First Floor
1,474 Sq. Ft. - Second Floor
424 Sq. Ft. - Studio; 54,878 Cu. Ft.

● You'll never regret your choice of this Georgian design. Its stately facade seems to foretell all of the exceptional features to be found inside. From the delightful spacious front entry hall, to the studio or maid's room over the garage, this home is unique all along the way. Imagine four fireplaces, three full baths, two extra wash rooms, a family room, plus a quiet library. Don't miss the first floor laundry. Note the separate set of stairs to the studio, or maid's room. The center entrance leads to the vestibule and the wonderfully spacious entry hall. All the major areas are but a step or two from this formal hall. The kitchen is well-planned and strategically located between the separate dining room and the breakfast room. Sliding glass doors permit easy access to the functional rear terraces.

BED RM.
15⁰ x 11⁹

BATH

MASTER
BED RM.
14⁰ x 12⁸

HALL

BATH

LINEN

DN.

WALK IN CLOSET

RAILING

LINEN

CL.

BED RM.
15⁰ x 11⁹

BED RM.
14⁰ x 11⁰

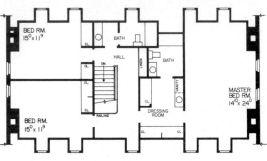

BED RM.
15⁰ x 11⁹

BATH

HALL

LINEN

BATH

DRESSING ROOM

VANITY

MASTER
BED RM.
14⁰ x 24⁰

DN.

RAILING

CL.

BED RM.
15⁰ x 11⁹

84'-6"

TERRACE

TERRACE

PORCH

LAUNDRY

COUNTRY KITCHEN
21⁸ x 15⁶

EATING

RANGE

FAMILY RM.
18⁸ x 15⁶

CABINET BOOKS

PDR. RM.

SHELVES

CAB'T.

CAB'T.

SHELVES

CL.

CABINET BOOKS

33'-6"

GARAGE
23⁴ x 23⁴

CHINA CABINET

CABINET

PANTRY

OVEN

DN.

DINING RM.
17⁴ x 15⁶

ENTRANCE HALL

LIVING RM.
20⁰ x 15⁶

SHELVES

PORCH

Design 12638

1,836 Sq. Ft. - First Floor
1,323 Sq. Ft. - Second Floor;
57,923 Cu. Ft.

● The brick facade of this two-story represents the mid-18th-Century design concept. Examine its fine exterior. It has a steeply pitched roof which is broken by two large chimneys at each end and by pedimented dormers. Inside Georgian details lend elegance. Turned balusters and a curved banister ornament the formal staircase. Blueprints include details for both three and four bedroom options.

Design 12132

1,958 Sq. Ft. - First Floor
1,305 Sq. Ft. - Second Floor
51,428 Cu. Ft.

● Another Georgian adaptation with a great heritage dating back to 18th Century America. Exquisite and symmetrical detailing set the character of this impressive home. Don't overlook such features as the two fireplaces, the laundry, the beamed ceiling, the built-in china cabinets and the oversized garage.

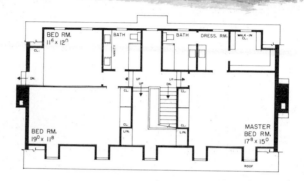

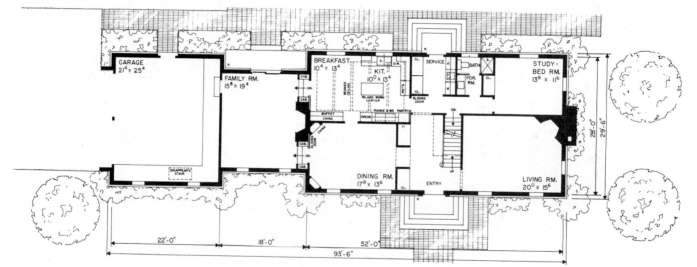

● A Georgian Colonial adaptation on the grand scale. The authentic front entrance is delightfully detailed. Two massive end chimneys, housing four fireplaces, are in keeping with the architecture of its day.

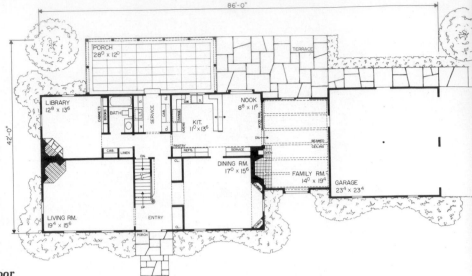

Design 12221 1,726 Sq. Ft. - First Floor
1,440 Sq. Ft. - Second Floor; 50,204 Cu. Ft.

Design 11852 1,802 Sq. Ft. - First Floor
1,603 Sq. Ft. - Second Floor; 51,361 Cu. Ft.

● This is an impressive Georgian adaptation. The front entrance detailing, the window treatment and the masses of brick help put this house in a class of its own.

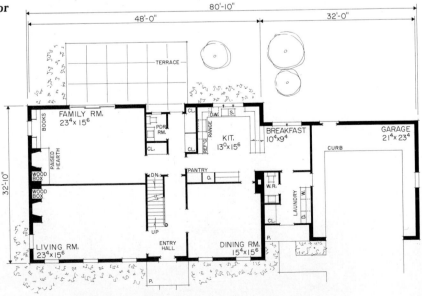

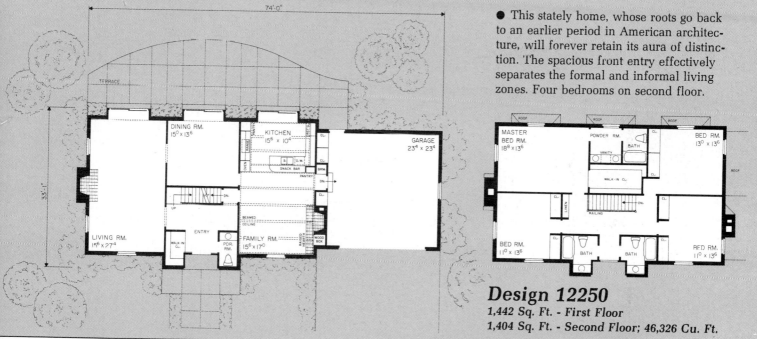

● This stately home, whose roots go back to an earlier period in American architecture, will forever retain its aura of distinction. The spacious front entry effectively separates the formal and informal living zones. Four bedrooms on second floor.

74'-0"

TERRACE

33'-1"

DINING RM.
15⁰ x 13⁶

KITCHEN
15⁶ x 10⁴

GARAGE
23⁴ x 23⁴

SNACK BAR

OVEN

PANTRY

CL.

BRM.

DN.

CL.

UP

DN.

BEAMED CEILING

LIVING RM.
15⁶ x 27⁴

WALK-IN CL.

ENTRY

PDR. RM.

FAMILY RM.
15⁶ x 17⁰

RAISED HEARTH

WOOD BOX

MASTER BED RM.
18⁸ x 13⁶

POWDER RM.

BATH

VANITY

BED RM.
13⁰ x 13⁶

WALK-IN CL.

CL.

ROOF

LINEN

RAILING

DN.

CL.

BED RM.
11⁰ x 13⁶

CL.

BATH

BATH

CL.

BED RM.
11⁰ x 13⁶

Design 12250
1,442 Sq. Ft. - First Floor
1,404 Sq. Ft. - Second Floor; 46,326 Cu. Ft.

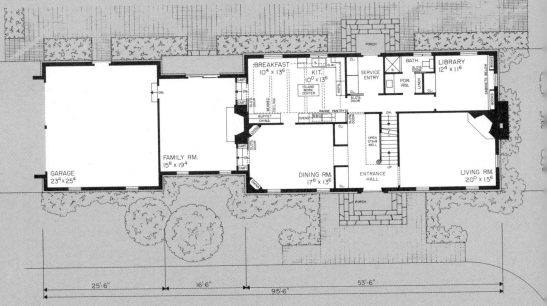

Design 12192

1,884 Sq. Ft. - First Floor
1,521 Sq. Ft. - Second Floor
58,380 Cu. Ft.

● This is surely a fine adaptation from the 18th Century when formality and elegance were by-words. The authentic detailing of this design centers around the fine proportions, the dentils, the window symmetry, the front door and entranceway, the massive chimneys and the masonry work. The rear elevation retains all the grandeur exemplary of exquisite architecture. The appeal of this outstanding home does not end with its exterior elevations. Consider the formal living room with its corner fireplace. Also, the library with its wall of bookshelves and cabinets. Further, the dining room highlights corner china cabinets. Continue to study this elegant plan.

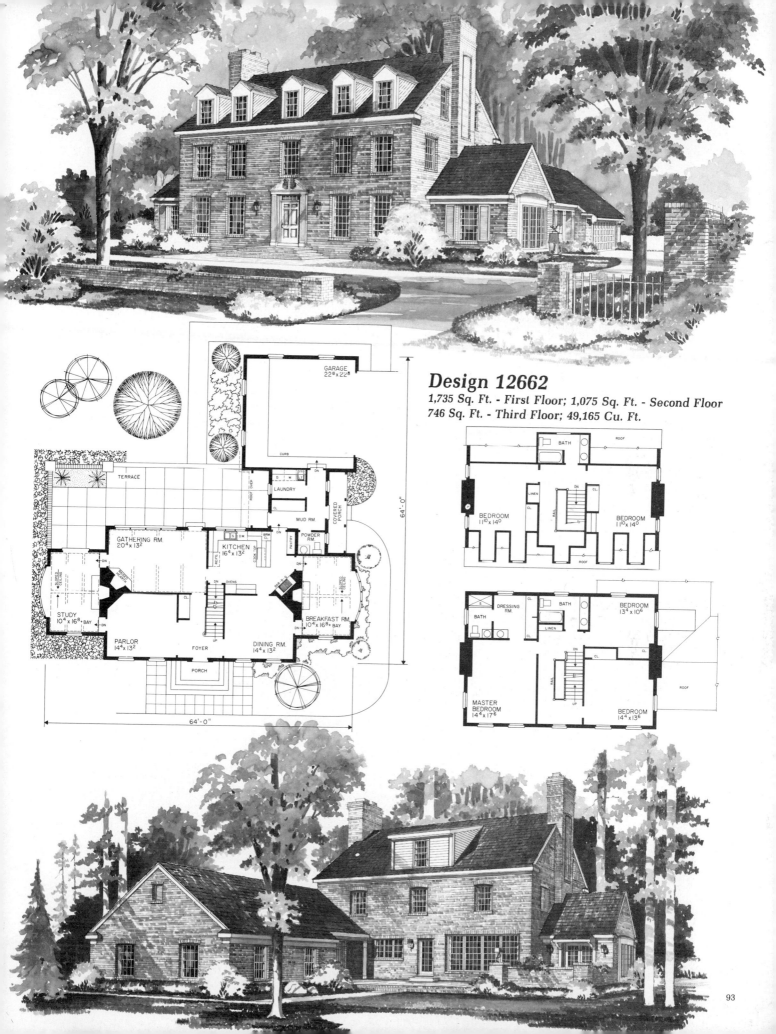

Design 12662

1,735 Sq. Ft. - First Floor; 1,075 Sq. Ft. - Second Floor
746 Sq. Ft. - Third Floor; 49,165 Cu. Ft.

GARAGE
22⁸ x 22⁸

TERRACE

LAUNDRY

MUD RM.

COVERED PORCH

POWDER RM.

GATHERING RM.
20⁴ x 13²

KITCHEN
16⁴ x 13²

PANTRY

STUDY
10⁴ x 16⁸ BAY

BREAKFAST RM.
10⁴ x 16⁸ BAY

PARLOR
14⁴ x 13²

FOYER

DINING RM.
14⁴ x 13²

OVENS

PORCH

64' - 0"

64' - 0"

BATH

ROOF

LINEN

BEDROOM
11¹⁰ x 14⁰

BEDROOM
11¹⁰ x 14⁰

RAIL

ROOF

BATH

DRESSING RM.

BATH

LINEN

BEDROOM
13⁴ x 10⁶

MASTER BEDROOM
14⁴ x 17⁶

BEDROOM
14⁴ x 13⁶

RAIL

ROOF

Design 12176

1,485 Sq. Ft. - First Floor
1,175 Sq. Ft. - Second Floor
41,646 Cu. Ft.

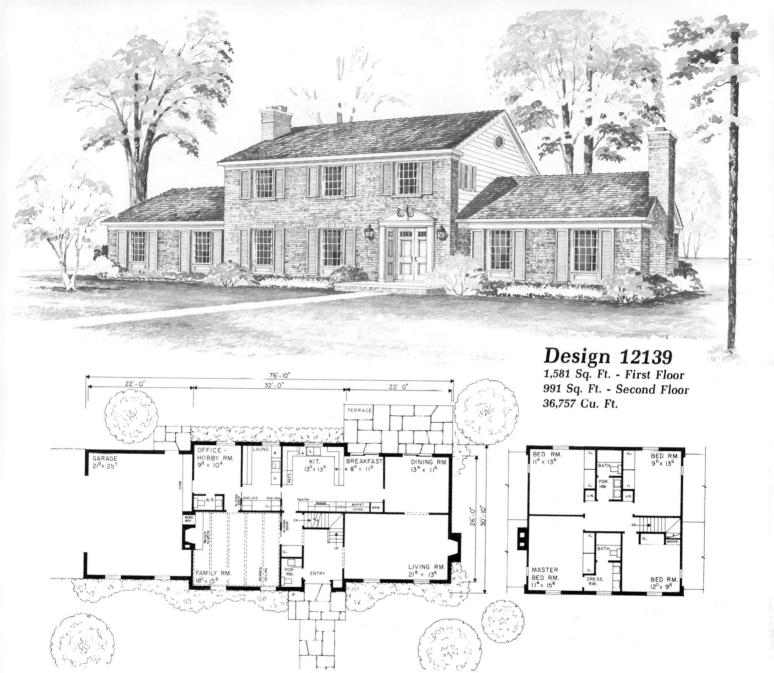

Design 12139

1,581 Sq. Ft. - First Floor
991 Sq. Ft. - Second Floor
36,757 Cu. Ft.

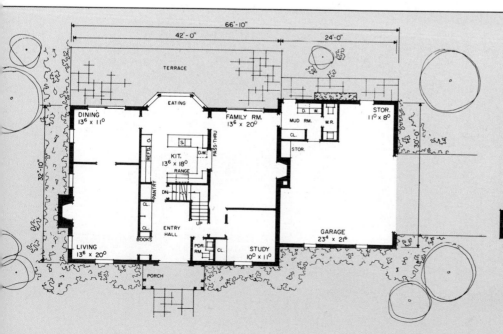

Design 11767

1,510 Sq. Ft. - First Floor
1,406 Sq. Ft. - Second Floor
42,070 Cu. Ft.

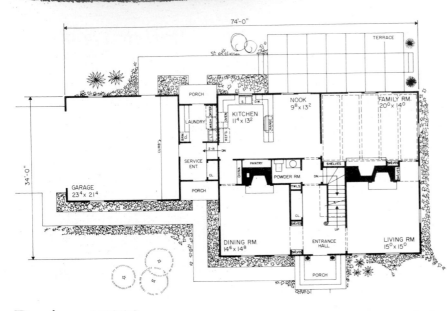

Here is a New England Georgian adaptation with an elevated doorway highlighted by pilasters and a pediment which gives way to a second-story Palladian window, capped in turn by a pediment projecting from the hipped roof. The interior is decidedly up-to-date with even an upstairs lounge.

Design 12639 1,556 Sq. Ft. - First Floor; 1,428 Sq. Ft. - Second Floor; 46,115 Cu. Ft.

Design 12283

1,559 Sq. Ft. - First Floor
1,404 Sq. Ft. - Second Floor
48,606 Cu. Ft.

● Reminiscent of the stately character of Federal architecture during an earlier period in our history, this two-story is replete with exquisite detailing. The cornice work, the pediment gable, the dentils, the brick quoins at the corners, the beautifully proportioned columns, the front door detailing, the window treatment and the massive twin chimneys are among the features which make this design so unique and appealing.

66'-10"

44'-10"

32'-10"

TERRACE

NOOK
13⁶ x 9⁰

MUD. RM.   W.R.   STORAGE

DINING RM.
13⁶ x 11⁰

FRAMED CEILING

KIT.
13⁶ x 10⁰

RANGE

FAMILY RM.
13⁶ x 20⁰

BOOKS   BOOKS

GARAGE
23⁴ x 21⁴

ENTRANCE HALL

UP   DN.

PDR. RM.

STUDY
10⁰ x 11⁰

LIVING RM.
13⁶ x 20⁰

BOOKS

PORTICO

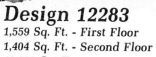

BED RM.
13⁶ x 14⁴

BATH

DRESS. RM.

WALK-IN CL.

BATH

WALK-IN CL.

CL.   LIN.

DN.

BED RM.
13⁶ x 14⁴

BED RM.
13⁸ x 10⁰

MASTER BED RM.
13⁶ x 19⁶

UPPER PORTICO

Design 12641

1,672 Sq. Ft. - First Floor
1,248 Sq. Ft. - Second Floor; 45,306 Cu. Ft.

● This Georgian adaptation is from the early 18th Century and has plenty of historical background. The classical details are sedately stated. The plan promises up-to-date livability. The size of your site need not be large, either.

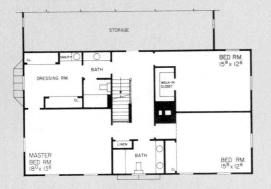

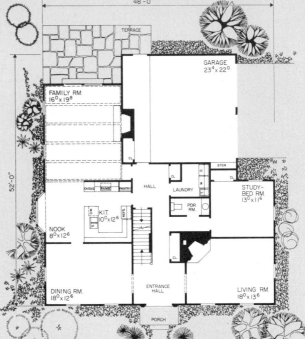

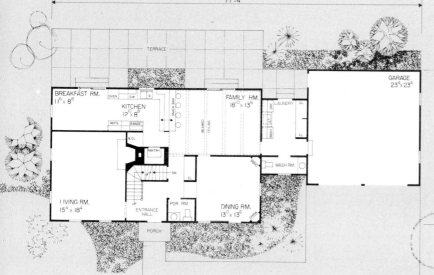

Design 12640

1,386 Sq. Ft. - First Floor
1,232 Sq. Ft. - Second Floor; 41,866 Cu. Ft.

● Here is a gracious exterior which adopts many features common to New England-style Federal homes. The symmetry and proportions are outstanding. Inside, a fine functioning plan. Note stairs to attic for additional storage and livability.

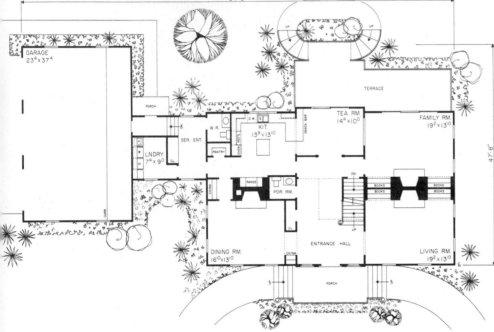

Design 12301

2,044 Sq. Ft. - First Floor
1,815 Sq. Ft. - Second Floor
69,925 Cu. Ft.

● Reminiscent of architecture with roots in the deep South, this finely detailed home is exquisite, indeed. Study the contemporary floor plan and the living patterns it offers.

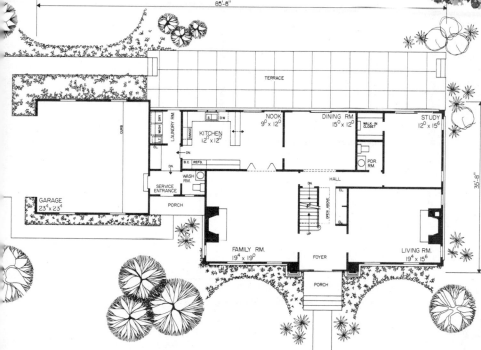

Design 12522

1,835 Sq. Ft. - *First Floor*
1,625 Sq. Ft. - *Second Floor*
58,700 Cu. Ft.

● This wood frame Georgian adaptation revives the architecture of an earlier period in New England. Its formal facade houses an abundance of spacious livability.

Design 12302

1,217 Sq. Ft. - First Floor
919 Sq. Ft. - Second Floor
29,820 Cu. Ft.

● This formal Georgian adaptation with its brick masses, its corner quoins, the delightful window treatment, the recessed front entrance, and the cornice detail, has a most interesting and efficient interior. It is most interesting to note that the two car garage is part of the main house structure. The projecting wings are the living and family rooms. Each has direct access to private outdoor terraces. Adjacent fireplaces serve each of these living areas. There will be no cross-room traffic through the kitchen. It will be easy to work in and be but an arms reach from the family room snack bar. Off the entrance hall is the formal dining room with its handy access to the kitchen. Three bedrooms and two baths comprise the second floor. Note the two built-in vanities.

The Charm Of
Early Colonial Variations

Design 12102 1,682 Sq. Ft. - First Floor; 1,344 Sq. Ft. - Second Floor; 42,960 Cu. Ft.

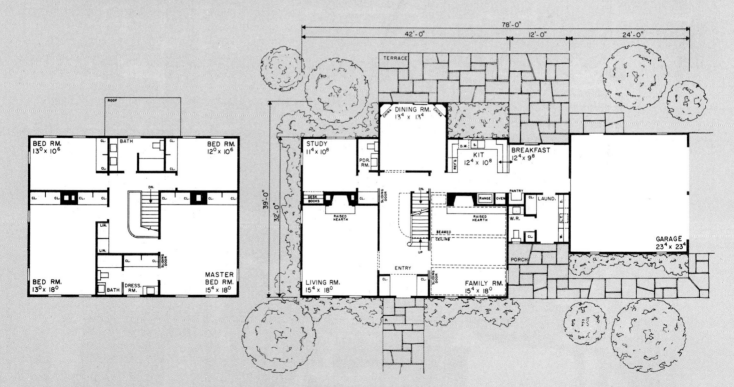

● This Early Colonial adaptation has its roots deep in the past. While it is long on history, it is equally long on 20th Century livability features. The narrow horizontal siding, the appealing window treatment, the exquisite door detailing, the hip-roof, the mas- sive chimneys and the cupola are exterior architectural features which set the character. It would certainly be difficult by today's living stand- ards to ask for more than what this floor plan offers. From the first floor laundry with its adjacent wash room to the study with its adjacent powder room, the interior is replete with con- venient living appointments. There is a wealth of "little" features such as the built-ins, the raised hearths, the pantry, the pass-thru to breakfast room and the beamed ceiling.

Design 12101
1,338 Sq. Ft. - First Floor
1,114 Sq. Ft. - Second Floor; 39,617 Cu. Ft.

● This is a modified version of one of America's most famous Colonial dwellings, the Parson Capen of Topsfield, Mass. Dating back to the 17th-Century, the English colonists built this medieval adaptation reproducing its bracketed second floor overhang, pendant drops at the corners, massive pilastered chimney and narrow clapboards. The floor plan, of course, has been updated to cater to today's living requirements.

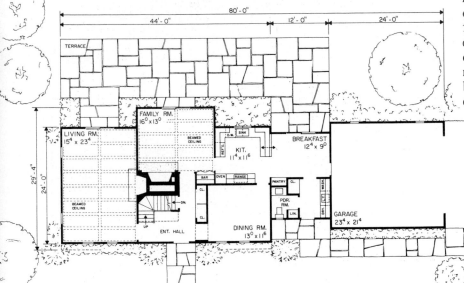

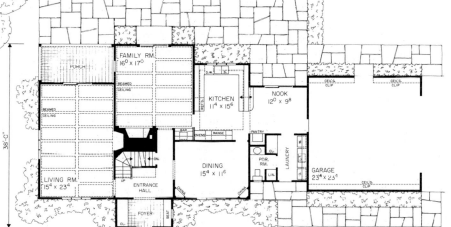

Design 12191

1,553 Sq. Ft. - First Floor
1,197 Sq. Ft. - Second Floor
47,906 Cu. Ft.

● This exquisite house reproduces the architectural details from the 17th-Century. Medieval and Tudor influences, brought to the New World by the first English colonists, distinguish this adaptation. The interior has been designed to serve today's active family.

Design 12253 1,503 Sq. Ft. - First Floor; 1,291 Sq. Ft. - Second Floor; 44,260 Cu. Ft.

● The overhanging second floor sets the character of this Early American design. Study the features, both inside and out.

Design 11179 1,378 Sq. Ft. - First Floor; 1,040 Sq. Ft. - Second Floor; 35,022 Cu. Ft.

● Loads of livability. This home could be called upon to serve as a five bedroom design. It would function admirably.

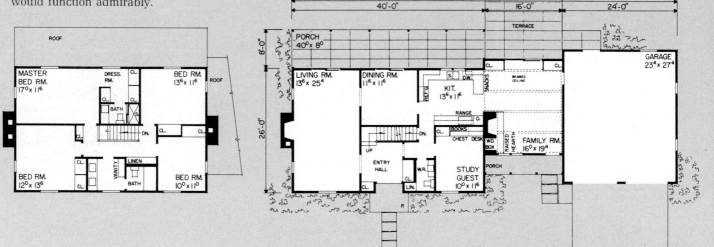

Design 11700 1,836 Sq. Ft. - First Floor; 1,232 Sq. Ft. - Second Floor; 44,660 Cu. Ft.

● Good zoning, fine traffic circulation, efficient work center, first floor laundry are among convenient living features.

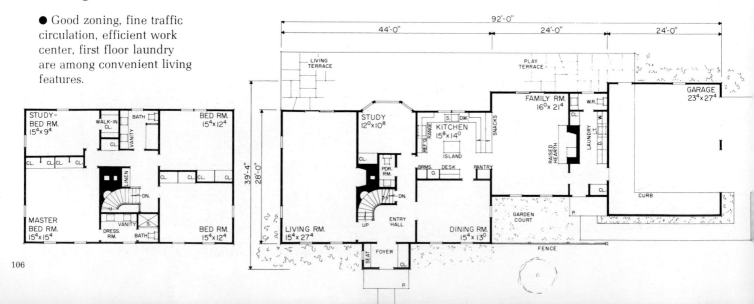

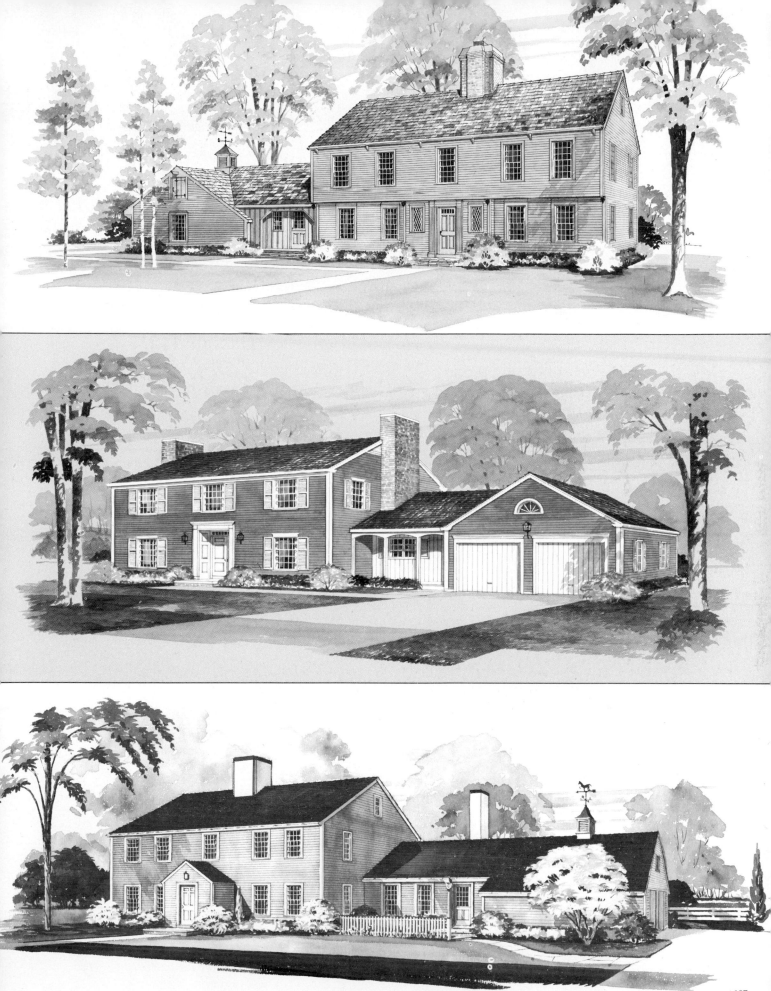

Design 11278

1,336 Sq. Ft. - First Floor
1,080 Sq. Ft. - Second Floor
34,304 Cu. Ft.

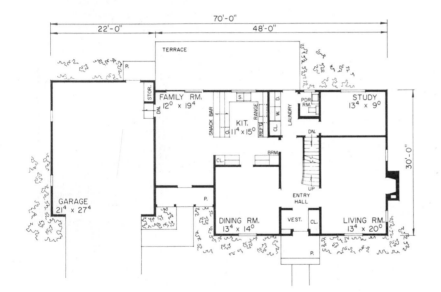

Design 11995

1,774 Sq. Ft. - First Floor
1,235 Sq. Ft. - Second Floor
44,653 Cu. Ft.

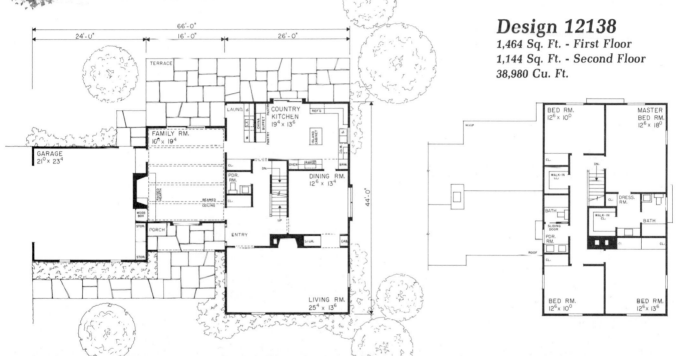

Design 12138

1,464 Sq. Ft. - First Floor
1,144 Sq. Ft. - Second Floor
38,980 Cu. Ft.

Design 12295

1,947 Sq. Ft. - First Floor
1,092 Sq. Ft. - Second Floor
43,795 Cu. Ft.

● This L-shaped two-story will make efficient use of your building site. The floor plan and how it functions is extremely interesting and practical. Study it carefully.

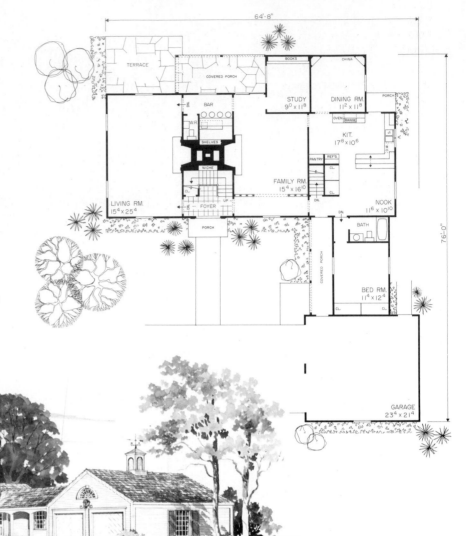

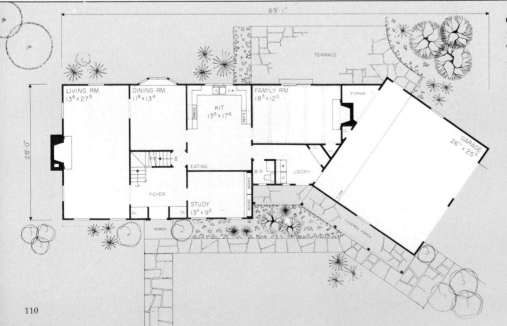

● Angular in its configuration, this inviting home offers loads of livability. There are four bedrooms, study, family room and a 27 foot long living room.

Design 12322

1,480 Sq. Ft. - First Floor
1,172 Sq. Ft. - Second Floor
41,112 Cu. Ft.

Design 12346

1,510 Sq. Ft. - First Floor
1,009 Sq. Ft. - Second Floor
36,482 Cu. Ft.

● A fine mixture of exterior materials, window treatment, and roof planes help set the character here. Envision your family enjoying all that this design has to offer.

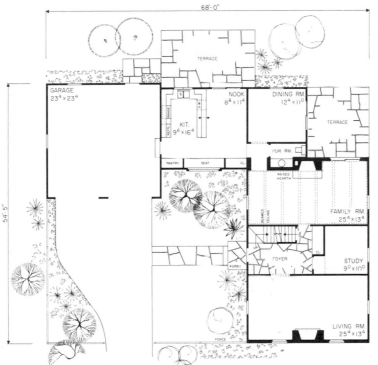

Design 12642

1,222 Sq. Ft. - First Floor
1,233 Sq. Ft. - Second Floor; 38,908 Cu. Ft.

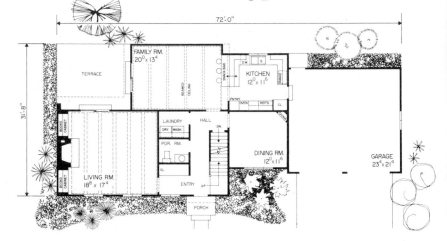

● Here is a house with plenty of history. Without the side appendages, it is reminiscent of Boston's Paul Revere House, built c. 1676. Of course, its floor plan hardly resembles any of its 17th Century forebears. Note four bedrooms. Access to storage over garage is through walk-in closet. Convenient built-ins.

Design 12651

1,404 Sq. Ft. - First Floor
1,323 Sq. Ft. - Second Floor; 45,203 Cu. Ft.

● This design is a replica of the medieval style of the housing in early New England. It is a Garrison with clapboards and sash windows highlighting the exterior. The inside has livability galore. The dramatic front entry features a curved staircase to the second floor which is open and overlooks the entry. Privacy will be enjoyed in the end-living room.

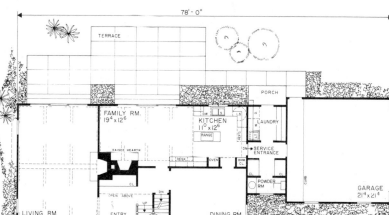

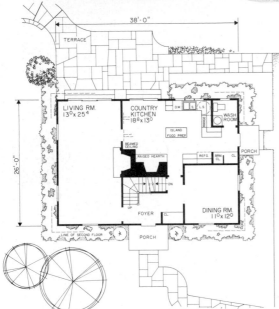

Design 12666 988 Sq. Ft. - First Floor
1,147 Sq. Ft. - Second Floor; 35,490 Cu. Ft.

● A spacious country-kitchen highlights the interior of this two-story. Its features include an island work center, fireplace, beamed ceiling and sliding glass doors leading to the rear terrace. A wash room and a side door are only steps away. A second fireplace is in the large living room. It, too, has sliding glass doors in the rear.

Design 12659
1,023 Sq. Ft. - First Floor; 1,008 Sq. Ft. - Second Floor
476 Sq. Ft. - Third Floor; 31,510 Cu. Ft.

● The facade of this three-storied, pitch-roofed house has a symmetrical placement of windows and a restrained but elegant central entrance. The central hall, or foyer, expands midway through the house to a family kitchen. Off the foyer are two rooms, a living room with fireplace and a study. The windowed third floor attic can be used as a study and studio. Three bedrooms are housed on the second floor.

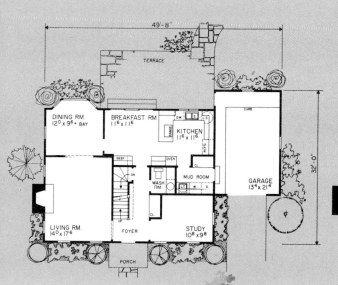

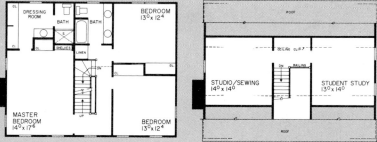

Design 12308

1,807 Sq. Ft. - First Floor
1,195 Sq. Ft. - Second Floor; 48,470 Cu. Ft.

● If yours is a corner lot you might want to give this attractive Colonial adaptation your consideration. Or, perhaps more significantly, if you have a large family this may be the design to solve your housing problem. Certainly you won't have to invest in a huge piece of property to enjoy the livability this home has to offer. In addition to the formal living room and informal family room, there is the separate dining room and kitchen eating space. Further, in addition to the three upstairs bedrooms, there is a fourth downstairs. The library could function as the fifth, if desired.

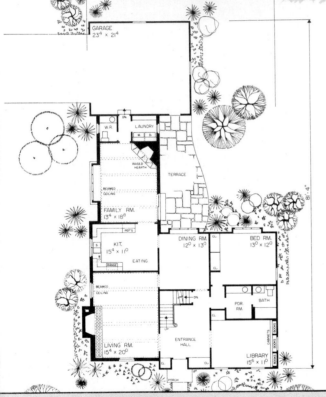

Design 12103

1,374 Sq. Ft. - First Floor
1,056 Sq. Ft. - Second Floor
36,672 Cu. Ft.

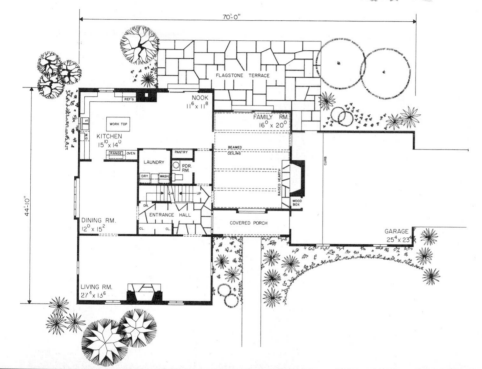

Design 12368
1,592 Sq. Ft. - First Floor
1,255 Sq. Ft. - Second Floor
54,516 Cu. Ft.

Design 12799 1,196 Sq. Ft. - First Floor
780 Sq. Ft. - Second Floor: 35,080 Cu. Ft.

● This two-story traditional design's facade with its narrow clapboards, punctuated by tall multi-paned windows, appears deceptively expansive. Yet the entire length of the house, including the garage, is 66 feet.

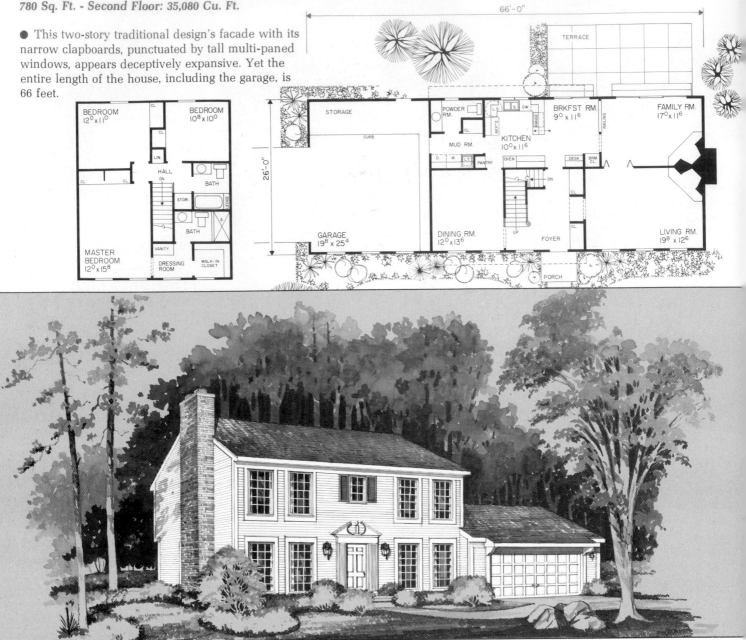

Design 12649 1,501 Sq. Ft. - First Floor
1,280 Sq. Ft. - Second Floor; 43,537 Cu. Ft.

● This design's front exterior is highlighted by four pedimented nine-over-nine windows, five second-story eyebrow windows and a massive central chimney. Note the spacious kitchen of the interior.

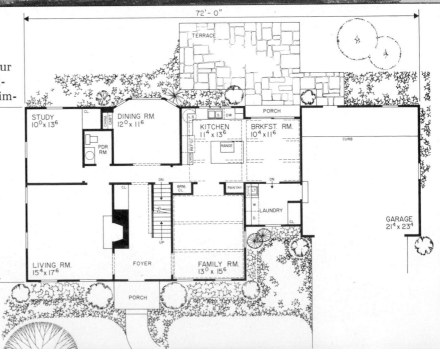

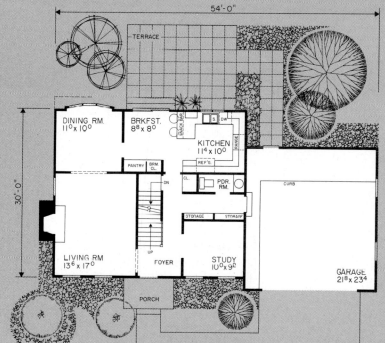

TERRACE

54'-0"

DINING RM.
11⁰ x 10⁰

BRKFST.
8⁸ x 8⁰

KITCHEN
11⁴ x 10⁰

SNACK BAR

S

DW

RANGE

30'-0"

PANTRY

BRM CL.

REF'G.

DN

CL.

PDR. RM.

CURB

UP

STORAGE

STORAGE

LIVING RM
13⁶ x 17⁰

FOYER

STUDY
10⁰ x 9²

GARAGE
21⁸ x 23⁴

PORCH

Design 12870
900 Sq. Ft. - First Floor
467 Sq. Ft. - Second Floor Left Suite
493 Sq. Ft. - Second Floor Right Suite; 35,970 Cu. Ft.

BEDROOM
13² x 10⁴

CL.

CL.

BEDROOM
13² x 10⁴

CABINET

BOOKS

CABINET

LINEN

LINEN

BATH

SUITE ENT. HALL

BATH

DN

STOR.

STOR.

CL.

CL.

MASTER
BEDROOM
11² x 13⁴

WALK-IN
CLOSET

MASTER
BEDROOM
11² x 13⁴

CL.

SHELVES

CL.

● This colonial home was designed to provide comfortable living space for two families. The first floor is the common living area, with all of the necessary living areas; the second floor has two two-bedroom-one-bath suites. Built-ins are featured in the smaller bedroom.

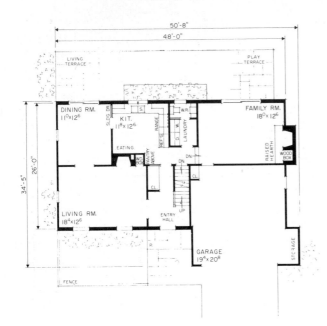

● Small house with big house features and livability. Some of the features are two full baths and extra storage upstairs; laundry, wash room and two fireplaces each with a wood box on the first floor. Two sets of sliding glass doors leading to the terrace.

Design 11856
1,023 Sq. Ft. - First Floor
784 Sq. Ft. - Second Floor; 25,570 Cu. Ft.

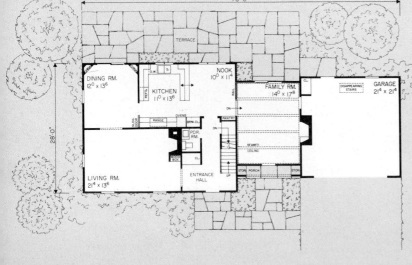

● The appeal of this Colonial home will be virtually everlasting. It will improve with age and service the growing family well. Imagine your family living here. There are four bedrooms, 2½ baths, plus plenty of first floor living space.

Design 12211
1,214 Sq. Ft. - First Floor
1,146 Sq. Ft. - Second Floor; 32,752 Cu. Ft.

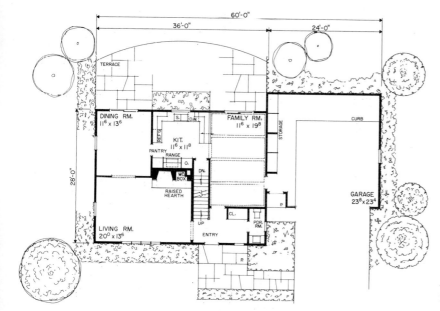

● A Garrison type adaptation that projects all the romance of yesteryear. The narrow horizontal siding, the wide corner boards, the window detailing, the overhanging second floor and the massive, centered chimney help set this home apart.

Design 11849 1,008 Sq. Ft. - First Floor
1,080 Sq. Ft. - Second Floor; 31,153 Cu. Ft.

Design 12610 *1,505 Sq. Ft. - First Floor; 1,344 Sq. Ft. - Second Floor; 45,028 Cu. Ft.*

● This full two-story traditional will be worthy of note wherever built. It strongly recalls images of a New England of yesteryear. And well it might; for the window treatment is delightful. The front entrance detail is inviting. The narrow horizontal siding and the corner boards are appealing as are the two massive chimneys. The center entrance hall is large with a handy powder room nearby. The study has built-in bookshelves and offers a full measure of privacy. The interior kitchen has a pass-thru to the family room and enjoys all that natural light from the bay window of the nook. A beamed ceiling, fireplace and sliding glass doors are features of the family room. The mud room highlights a closet, laundry equipment and an extra wash room. Study the upstairs with those four bedrooms, two baths and plenty of closets. An excellent arrangement for all.

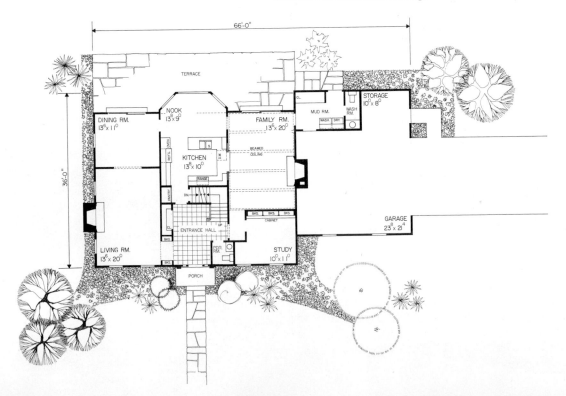

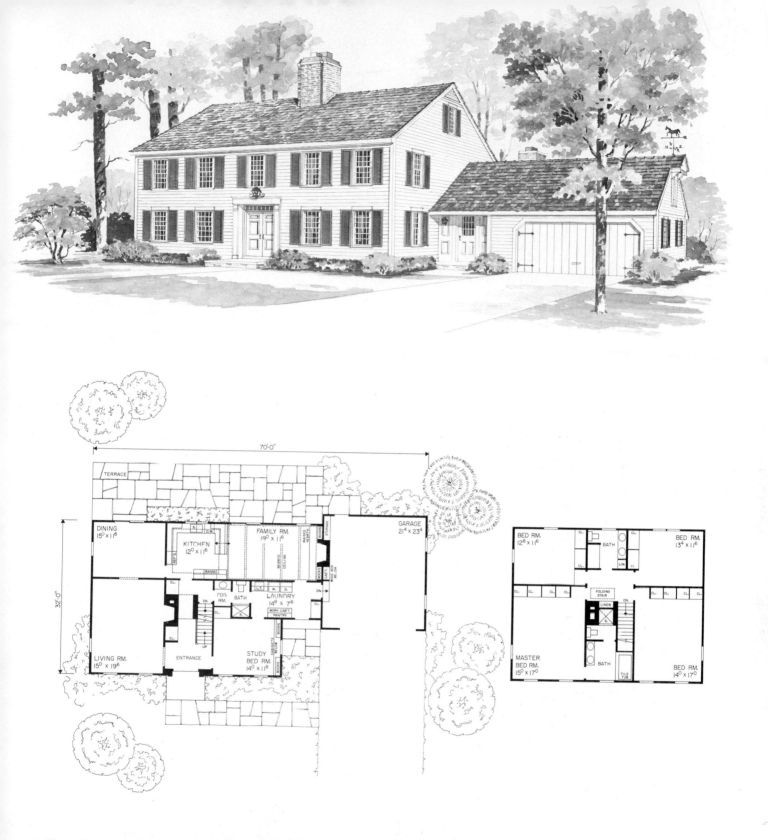

Design 12188 1,440 Sq. Ft. - First Floor; 1,280 Sq. Ft. - Second Floor; 40,924 Cu. Ft.

● This design is characteristic of early America and its presence will create an atmosphere of that time in our heritage. However, it will be right at home wherever located. Along with exterior charm, this design has outstanding livability to offer its occupants. Beginning with the first floor, there are formal and informal areas plus the work centers. Note the center bath which has direct access from three adjacent areas. Built-in book shelves are the feature of both the family room and the study/bedroom. Built-ins are also featured in the garage. Ascending up to the second floor, one will be in the private sleeping area. This area consists of the master suite, three bedrooms and full bath. Folding stairs are in the upstairs hall for easy access to the attic.

Design 12733 1,177 Sq. Ft. - First Floor; 1,003 Sq. Ft. - Second Floor; 32,040 Cu. Ft.

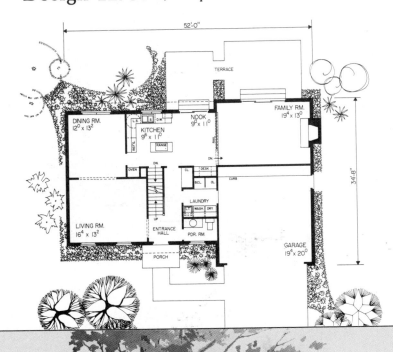

● This is definitely a four bedroom Colonial with charm galore. The kitchen features an island range and other built-ins. All will enjoy the sunken family room with fireplace, which has sliding glass doors leading to the terrace. Also a basement for recreational activities with laundry remaining on first floor for extra convenience.

Design 12598

1,016 Sq. Ft. - First Floor
890 Sq. Ft. - Second Floor; 30,000 Cu. Ft.

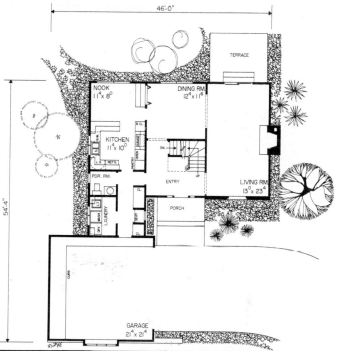

● An impressive, Early Colonial adaptation with a projecting two-car garage and front drive court. It will not demand a large, expensive piece of property. In days of high-cost building, this relatively modest-sized two-story will be a great investment. Note the huge living room. The basement lends itself to recreational facilities.

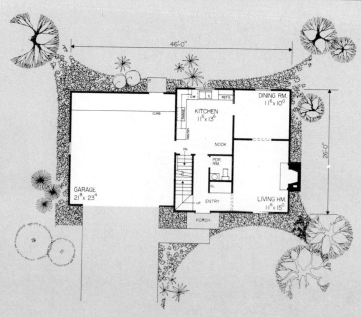

Design 12622

624 Sq. Ft. - First Floor
624 Sq. Ft. - Second Floor; 19,864 Cu. Ft.

● Appealing design can envelope little packages, too. Here is a charming, Early Colonial adaptation with an attached two-car garage to serve the young family with a modest building budget.

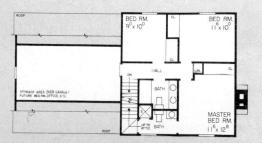

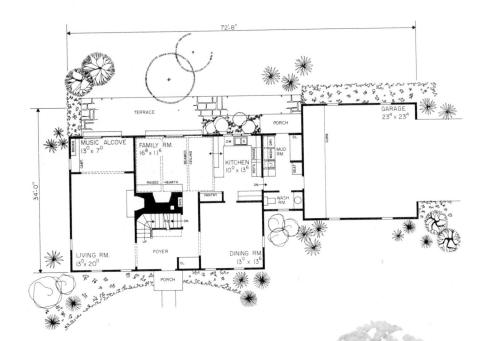

Design 12521
1,272 Sq. Ft. - First Floor
1,139 Sq. Ft. - Second Floor
37,262 Cu. Ft.

● Here is a house to remind one of the weather beaten facades of Nantucket. The active family plan is as up-to-date as tomorrow.

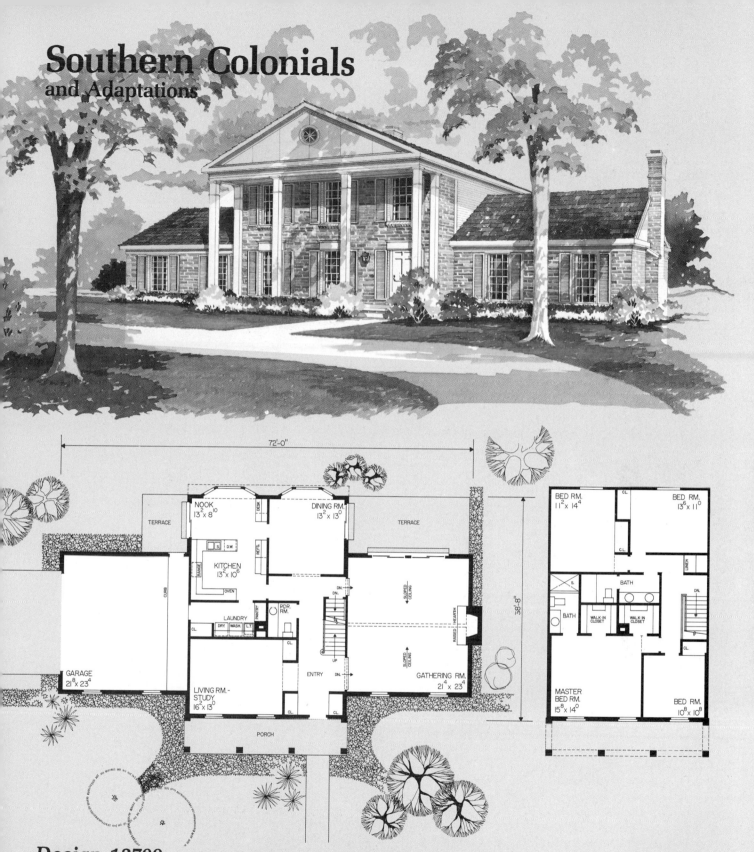

Southern Colonials
and Adaptations

Design 12700 1,640 Sq. Ft. - First Floor; 1,129 Sq. Ft. - Second Floor; 42,200 Cu. Ft.

● Southern Colonial grace! And much more. An elegant gathering room, more than 21' by 23' large. . . with sloped ceilings and a raised-hearth fireplace. Plus two sets of sliding glass doors that open onto the terrace. Correctly appointed formal rooms! A living room with full length paned windows. And a formal dining room that features a large bay window. Plus a contemporary kitchen. A separate dining nook that includes another bay window. Charming and sunny! Around the corner, a first floor laundry offers more modern conveniences. Four large bedrooms! Including a master suite with two walk-in closets and private bath. This home offers all the conveniences that make life easy! And its eminently suited to a family with traditional tastes. List your favorite features.

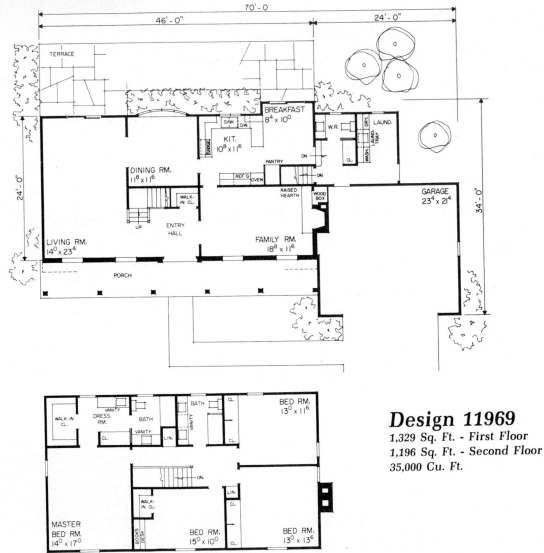

Design 11969

1,329 Sq. Ft. - First Floor
1,196 Sq. Ft. - Second Floor
35,000 Cu. Ft.

● Stately, indeed. For sheer dramatic effect it will be difficult to beat the impact of the six towering columns of this Southern Colonial adaptation. In addition to the projecting roof which forms the porch, the second floor extends out over the first floor close to two feet. This in itself is an interesting feature. The four large bedrooms upstairs are complemented by good storage and two full baths. Study the many features that this plan has to offer.

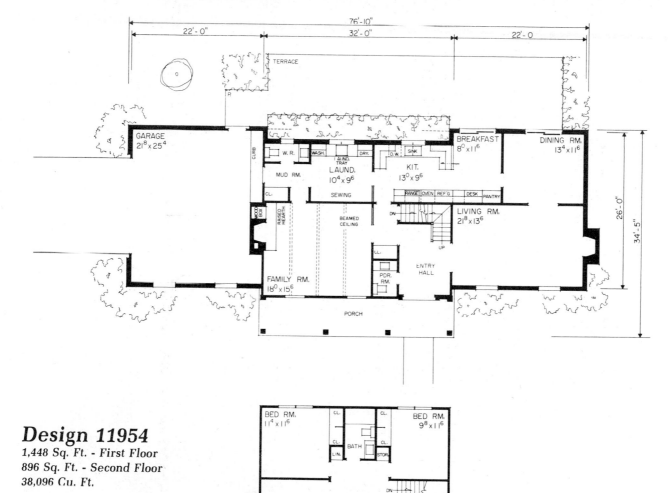

TERRACE

GARAGE
21⁸ x 25⁴

W. R. | WASH. | DRY.

MUD RM.

LAUND.
10⁴ x 9⁶

KIT.
13⁰ x 9⁶

BREAKFAST
8⁰ x 11⁶

DINING RM.
13⁴ x 11⁶

RANGE | OVEN | REF'G | DESK | PANTRY

SEWING

BEAMED CEILING

LIVING RM.
21⁸ x 13⁶

DN

UP

FAMILY RM.
18⁰ x 15⁶

RAISED HEARTH

WOOD BOX

CL.

PDR. RM.

ENTRY HALL

PORCH

22'-0"   32'-0"   22'-0

76'-10"

26'-0"

34'-5"

BED RM.
11⁴ x 11⁶

CL. | CL.

BED RM.
9⁸ x 11⁶

LIN.

BATH

STOR

DN

BOOKS

MASTER BED RM.
11⁴ x 15⁶

BATH

DRESS RM.

BED RM.
12⁰ x 10⁰

Design 11954

1,448 Sq. Ft. - First Floor
896 Sq. Ft. - Second Floor
38,096 Cu. Ft.

● Graceful porch columns of this house are reminiscent of Southern plantation homes. The first floor plan is well zoned with informal and formal living spaces definitely separated. Bedrooms are tucked away on the second floor. Added attractions are two fireplaces, a laundry with sufficient space for a sewing nook, beamed ceiling in family room, two powder rooms and two full baths. Note breakfast and dining rooms, both have access to the rear terrace.

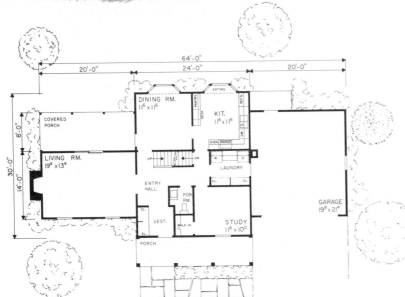

Design 12107

1,020 Sq. Ft. - First Floor
720 Sq. Ft. - Second Floor
25,245 Cu. Ft.

Design 11773

1,546 Sq. Ft. - First Floor
1,040 Sq. Ft. - Second Floor
33,755 Cu. Ft.

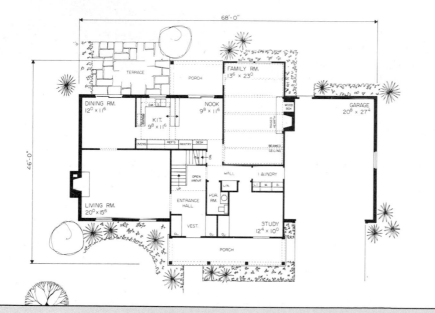

Design 11208

1,170 Sq. Ft. - First Floor
768 Sq. Ft. - Second Floor
26,451 Cu. Ft.

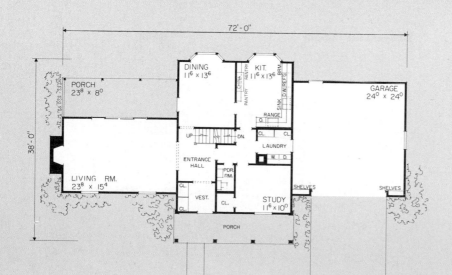

Design 12673

1,895 Sq. Ft. - First Floor
1,661 Sq. Ft. - Second Floor; 59,114 Cu. Ft.

● A two-story pillared entrance portico and tall multi-paned windows flanking the double front doors together accentuate the facade of this Southern Colonial design. This brick home is stately and classic in its exterior appeal. The three-car garage opens to the side so it does not disturb the street view. This is definitely a charming home that will stand strong for many years into the future. Not only is the exterior something to talk about, but so is the interior.

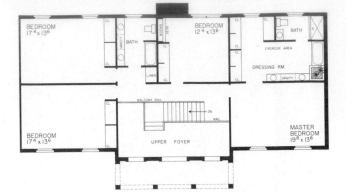

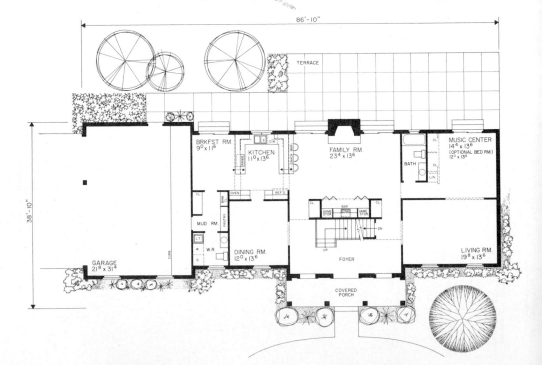

Enter into the extremely spacious foyer and begin to discover what this home has to offer in the way of livability. Front, living and dining rooms are at each end of this foyer. The living room is complimented by a music room, or close it off and make it a bedroom. A full bath is nearby. The formal dining room will be easily served by the kitchen as will the breakfast room and snack bar. The family room is spacious and features a built-in wet bar which can be closed off by doors. An open, curved staircase leads to the second floor, four bedroom sleeping area.

Design 12230

2,288 Sq. Ft. - First Floor
1,863 Sq. Ft. - Second Floor
79,736 Cu. Ft.

● The gracefulness and appeal of this southern adaptation will be everlasting. The imposing two-story portico is truly dramatic. Notice the authentic detailing of the tapered Doric columns, the balustraded roof deck, the denticulated cornice, the front entrance and the shuttered windows. The architecture of the rear is no less appealing with its formal symmetry and smaller Doric portico. The impressive exterior of this two-story houses a total of 4,151 square feet. The spacious, formal front entrance hall provides a fitting introduction to the scale and elegance of the interior.

133

Design 12572

1,258 Sq. Ft. - First Floor
1,251 Sq. Ft. - Second Floor; 42,160 Cu. Ft.

● This home offers great livability. Four bedrooms and two baths (each with a vanity) upstairs. And the first floor has features galore. Note the barbecue in the kitchen. Two fireplaces for added charm.

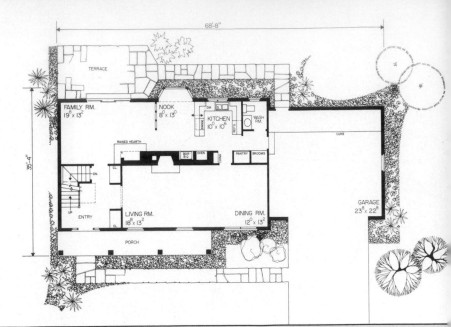

Design 12762

2,345 Sq. Ft. - First Floor
1,016 Sq. Ft. - Second Floor; 53,740 Cu. Ft.

● This home features a full apartment to the side to accommodate a live-in relative. The main house has all the features to ensure happiness for years to come. The three-car garage is sure to come in handy.

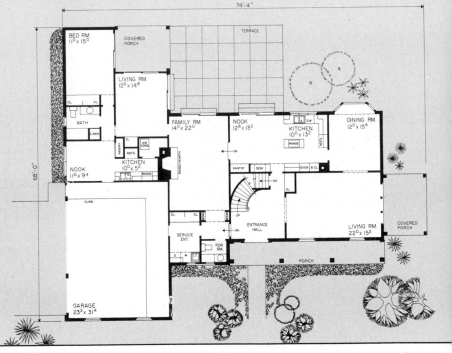

Design 12575

2,207 Sq. Ft. - First Floor
1,611 Sq. Ft. - Second Floor; 71,750 Cu. Ft.

● What a fine home this will make. Note the large entry with circular staircase. Three separate terraces. Lounge upstairs overlooking the gathering room. Extra storage space in three-car garage.

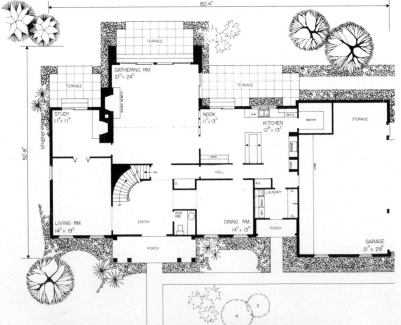

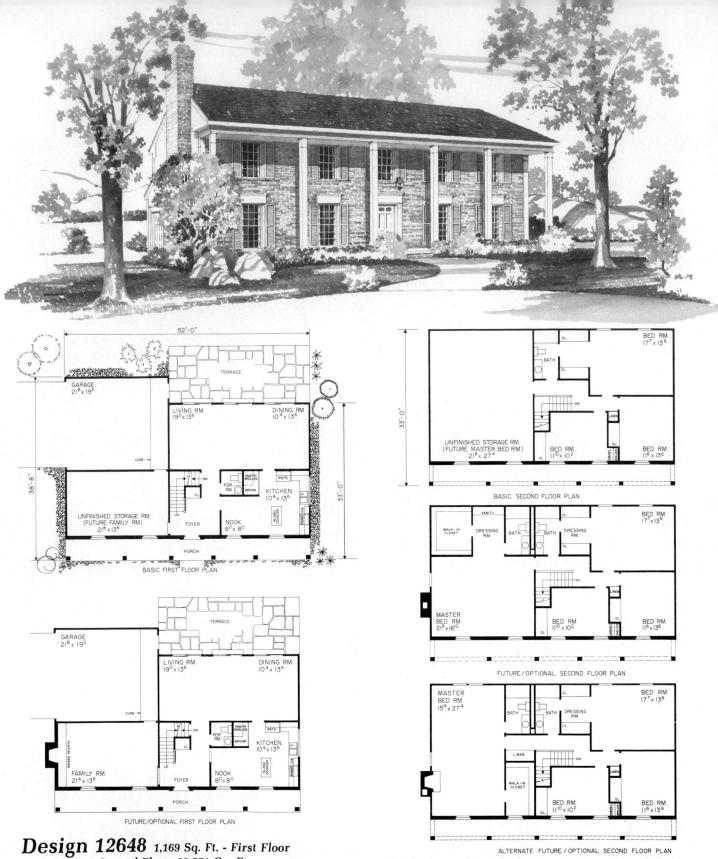

BASIC FIRST FLOOR PLAN

GARAGE 21⁸ x 19²
TERRACE
LIVING RM. 19⁰ x 13⁶
DINING RM. 10⁴ x 13⁶
CURB
UNFINISHED STORAGE RM. (FUTURE FAMILY RM.) 21⁸ x 13⁶
PANTRY SHELVES
PDR. RM.
BROOM
REFG.
KITCHEN 10⁴ x 13⁶
ISLAND COUNTER
RANGE DW
FOYER
NOOK 8⁰ x 8⁰
PORCH
52'-0"
38'-8"
33'-0"

BASIC SECOND FLOOR PLAN

BED RM. 17⁷ x 13⁶
BATH
CL
CL
DN.
UNFINISHED STORAGE RM. (FUTURE MASTER BED RM.) 21⁸ x 27⁴
LINEN
BED RM. 11¹⁰ x 10²
BED RM. 11⁶ x 13⁶
33'-0"

FUTURE/OPTIONAL FIRST FLOOR PLAN

GARAGE 21⁸ x 19²
TERRACE
LIVING RM. 19⁰ x 13⁶
DINING RM. 10⁴ x 13⁶
CURB
RAISED HEARTH
FAMILY RM. 21⁴ x 13⁶
PANTRY SHELVES
PDR. RM.
BROOM
REFG.
KITCHEN 10⁴ x 13⁶
ISLAND COUNTER
RANGE DW
FOYER
NOOK 8⁰ x 8⁰
PORCH

FUTURE/OPTIONAL SECOND FLOOR PLAN

WALK-IN CLOSET
VANITY
DRESSING RM.
BATH
BATH
DRESSING RM.
CL
BED RM. 17⁷ x 13⁶
MASTER BED RM. 21⁸ x 16¹⁰
DN.
LINEN
BED RM. 11¹⁰ x 10²
BED RM. 11⁶ x 13⁶

ALTERNATE FUTURE / OPTIONAL SECOND FLOOR PLAN

MASTER BED RM. 15⁴ x 27⁴
BATH
BATH
DRESSING RM.
BED RM. 17⁷ x 13⁶
LINEN
DN.
WALK-IN CLOSET
LINEN
BED RM. 11¹⁰ x 10²
BED RM. 11⁶ x 13⁶

Design 12648 *1,169 Sq. Ft. - First Floor*
1,473 Sq. Ft. - Second Floor; 39,551 Cu. Ft.

● If you are looking for a house to fit your present family, but also need one when it is full grown, then this is the design for you. This house appears large, but until the two unfinished rooms (one upstairs and one on the first floor), are completed it is an economical house. Later development of these rooms conserves initial construction expense. A major economy has been realized because the basic structural work is already standing. From the outside, onlookers will never know that there are unfinished rooms inside. The exterior appeal is outstanding with its two-story pillars extending from the overhanging roof and its rows of windows which cover the length of the facade. The rear elevation features three sets of sliding glass doors.

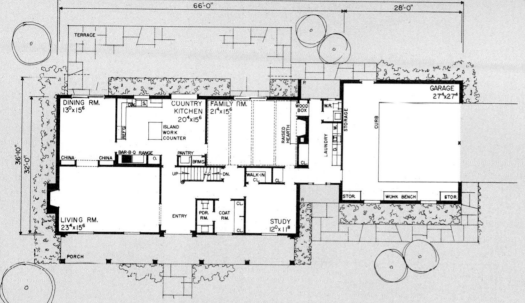

Design 11816

2,036 Sq. Ft. - First Floor
1,836 Sq. Ft. - Second Floor
55,566 Cu. Ft.

● The influence of the Colonial South is delightfully apparent in this gracious design. The stately columns of the front porch set the stage for a memorable visit. The entry hall is impressive with its open stairway. The large, country kitchen will be a sheer delight in which to work and, yes, even congregate.

Design 12627

845 Sq. Ft. - First Floor
896 Sq. Ft. - Second Floor
28,685 Cu. Ft.

● This charming, economically built, home with its stately two-story porch columns is reminiscent of the South. The efficient interior features bonus space over garage and in the third-floor attic which may be developed into another liveable room. The U-shaped kitchen offers many built-ins and is conveniently located to serve the nook and the dining room with ease. Sliding glass doors in both these eating areas lead to the terrace.

137

Design 12133 *3,024 Sq. Ft. - First Floor; 826 Sq. Ft. - Second Floor; 54,883 Cu. Ft.*

● A country-estate home which will command all the attention it truly deserves. The projecting pediment gable supported by the finely proportioned columns lends an aura of elegance. The window treatment, the front door detailing, the massive, capped chimney, the cupola, the brick veneer exterior and the varying roof planes complete the characterization of an impressive home. Inside, there are 3,024 square feet on the first floor. In addition, there is a two bedroom second floor should its development be necessary. However, whether called upon to function as one, or 1-1/2 story home it will provide a lifetime of gracious living. Don't overlook the compartment baths, the big library, the coat room, the beamed ceiling family room, the two fireplaces, the breakfast room and the efficient kitchen. Note pass-thru to breakfast room.

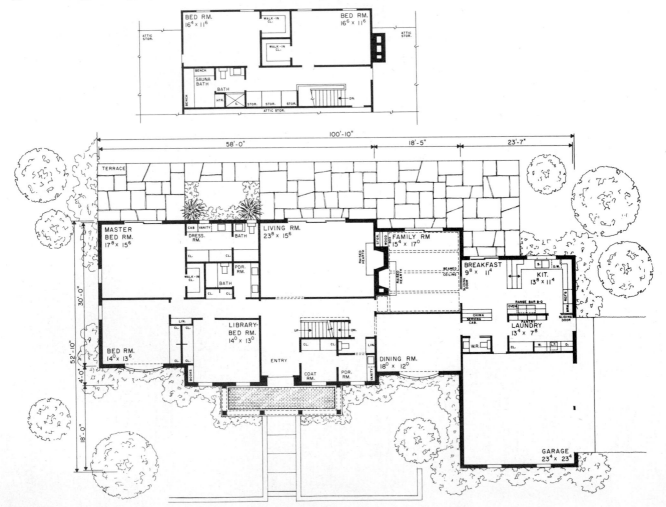

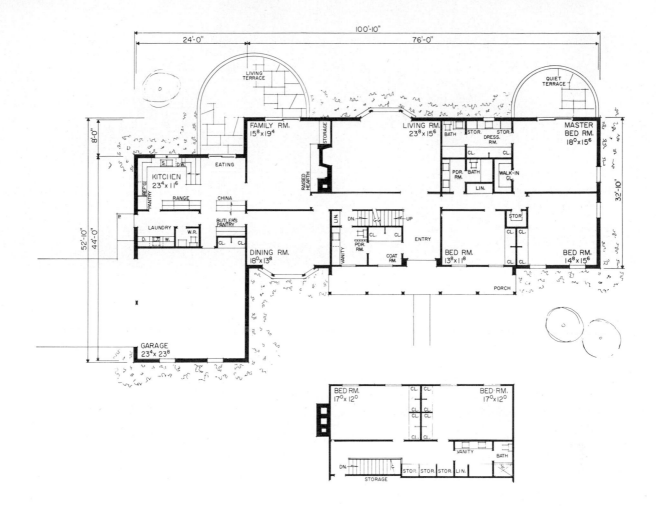

Design 11796

3,006 Sq. Ft. - First Floor
794 Sq. Ft. - Second Floor; 44,240 Cu. Ft.

● Five big bedrooms! Or make it three if you prefer not to develop the second floor. When viewing this home the initial lingering look turns into something of a studied analysis; for here is a positively outstanding design. The columned porch creates an atmosphere of charming country-estate living. Note that there is a living terrace plus a quiet terrace off the master bedroom. The floor plan will surely permit the fulfillment of such a way of life. Each and every member of the family will love the spaciousness of the interior. In addition to such big and obvious features as the delightful living, dining and family rooms, the fireplaces, kitchen and three baths, there is a multitude of little features. Be sure to list them, you'll find them most interesting.

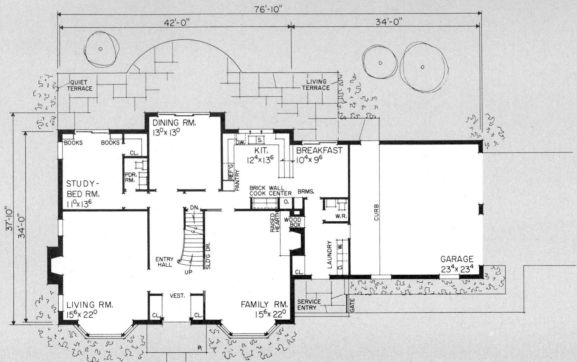

76'-10"

42'-0"   34'-0"

QUIET TERRACE

LIVING TERRACE

BOOKS   BOOKS

DINING RM.
13⁰ x 13⁰

KIT.
12⁴ x 13⁶

BREAKFAST
10⁴ x 9⁶

CL.

PDR. RM.

STUDY-BED RM.
11⁰ x 13⁶

PANTRY

REF'G

DW

S.

BRICK WALL COOK CENTER

BRMS.

RAISED HEARTH

WOOD BOX

O.

W.R.

37'-10"   34'-0"

DN.

SLD'G DR.

ENTRY HALL

UP

LAUNDRY

D.   W.

CURB

GARAGE
23⁴ x 23⁴

LIVING RM.
15⁶ x 22⁰

VEST.

CL.   CL.

FAMILY RM.
15⁶ x 22⁰

SERVICE ENTRY

CL.

GATE

P.

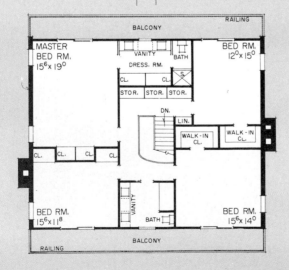

RAILING

BALCONY

MASTER BED RM.
15⁶ x 19⁰

VANITY

BATH

BED RM.
12⁰ x 15⁰

DRESS. RM.

CL.   CL.

S.

STOR.   STOR.   STOR.

DN.

LIN.

WALK-IN CL.

WALK-IN CL.

CL.   CL.   CL.   CL.

BED RM.
15⁶ x 11⁸

VANITY

BATH

BED RM.
15⁶ x 14⁰

BALCONY

RAILING

● Another gracious adaptation which is reminiscent of New Orleans. While the projecting second floor balcony sets the character, the dramatic bay windows flanking the double doors of the front entrance add a full measure of charm. The spacious center entry hall establishes most efficient traffic patterns which flow conveniently to all areas of the house. In addition to the outstanding formal living room, the wonderful, informal family room and the private, separate dining room, there is a quiet, isolated study. If desired, this room could function as a fifth bedroom or guest room. An extra powder room is nearby. The kitchen is also noteworthy. Study the exceptional second floor. Observe the use of sliding glass doors.

Design 11860 1,828 Sq. Ft. - First Floor; 1,456 Sq. Ft. - Second Floor; 51,210 Cu. Ft.

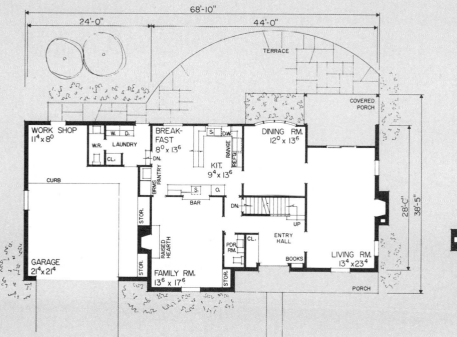

Design 11843 *1,384 Sq. Ft. - First Floor; 1,320 Sq. Ft. - Second Floor; 38,183 Cu. Ft.*

● New Orleans revisited. This adaptation is positively captivating. The recessed portion of the front exterior is highlighted by the second floor balcony with delightful wrought iron railing and posts, plus its two sets of French doors. The front entry is further recessed and features gracious double doors which are flanked by appealing carriage lamps. Inside there is space galore. There are five bedrooms, two full baths, and excellent storage facilities on the second floor. Downstairs there are two living areas (formal and informal) overlooking the front yard. Each has a fireplace. A covered rear porch functions with the formal end living room. A breakfast room and separate dining room cater to family eating patterns. See work shop.

141

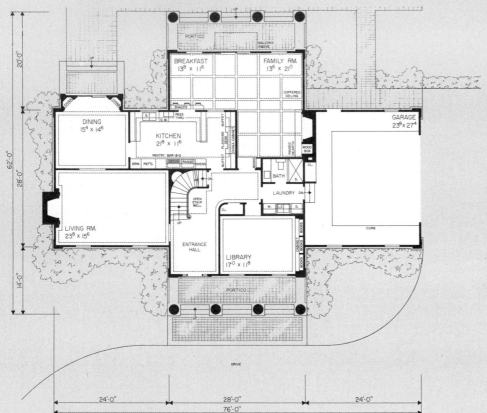

Design 12184

1,999 Sq. Ft. - First Floor
1,288 Sq. Ft. - Second Floor
58,441 Cu. Ft.

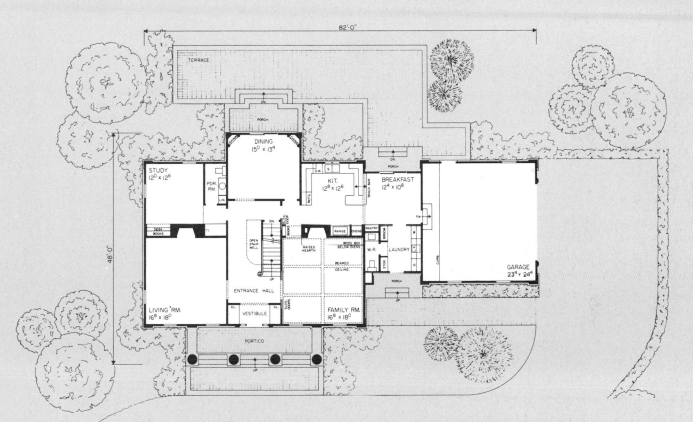

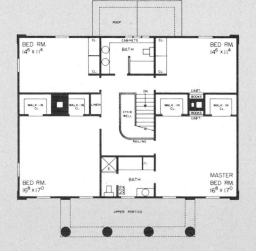

Design 12185 1,916 Sq. Ft. - First Floor
1,564 Sq. Ft. - Second Floor; 59,649 Cu. Ft.

● The elements of Greek Revival architecture when adapted to present day standards can be impressive, indeed. A study of this floor plan will reveal its similarity to that on the opposite page. There is a vestibule which leads to a wonderfully spacious entrance hall. The open stairwell is most dramatic. As it affords a view of the four bedroom, two bath second floor. The study and family room will be favorite spots for family relaxation. Both the dining and living rooms can be made to function as formally as you wish.

Design 12140 1,822 Sq. Ft. - First Floor; 1,638 Sq. Ft. - Second Floor; 52,107 Cu. Ft.

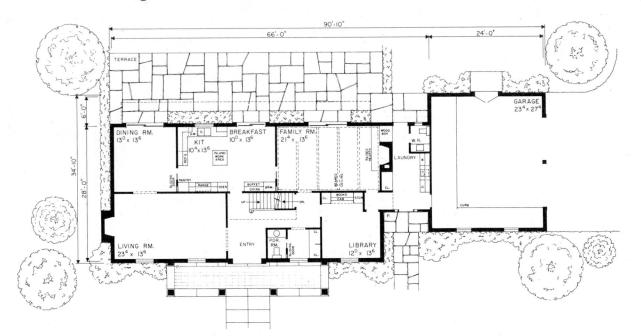

● The grandeur of this Southern Colonial adaptation is almost breathtaking. The stately columns supporting the distinctive pediment gable are truly impressive. The proportions and the symmetry of the windows and the entranceway are delightful. The double front doors enter to a spacious hall. Among the noteworthy features are the library, the powder room and the spacious kitchen area. Also, the second floor has three baths and a lounge or fifth bedroom. An outdoor balcony is accessible from each of the three rear bedrooms. What other features does your family like? Why not make a list?

● This Southern Colonial adaptation is certainly one of a kind. It will forever foster the feeling of distinctiveness as well as individuality. The second floor porches provide the shelter for the porticos. The stolidly proportioned pillars of the porticos are delightful, indeed. The center entry introduces one to a very orderly and formal interior, which is planned to assure each room its full measure of privacy. If desired, however, the family room may easily be opened up to function directly with the kitchen-nook area. The library will be a favorite spot for retreat. Four large bedrooms and three full baths are the highlights of the upstairs. Notice the complete accessibility of the two porches. The garage is attached and has a generous bulk storage area. Ideal for garden, lawn equipment.

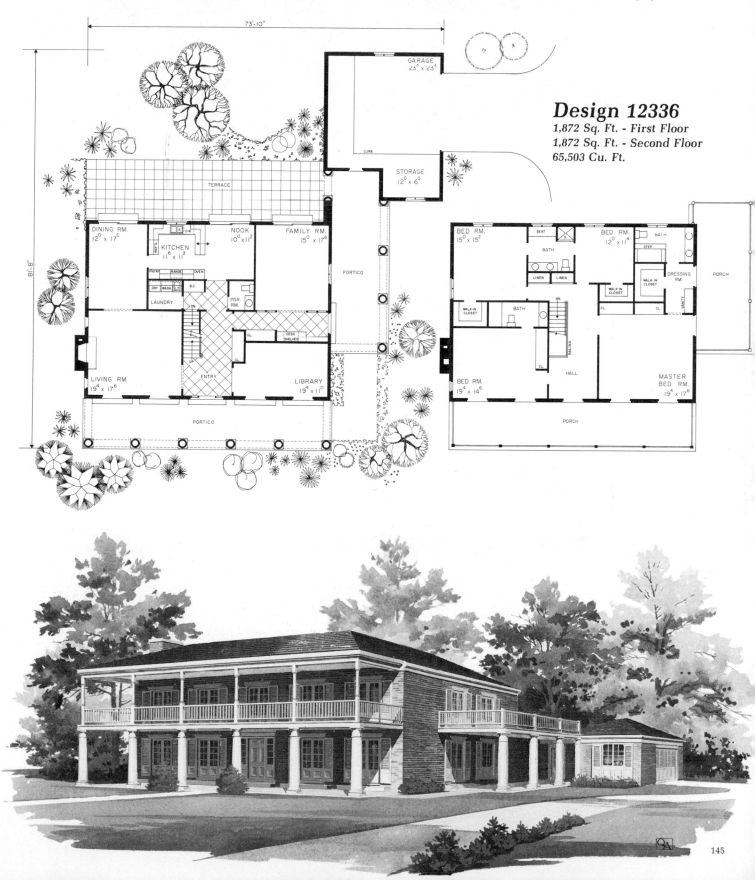

Design 12336
1,872 Sq. Ft. - First Floor
1,872 Sq. Ft. - Second Floor
65,503 Cu. Ft.

Design 12555

1,701 Sq. Ft. - First Floor
1,240 Sq. Ft. - Second Floor
44,025 Cu. Ft.

● Here is an interesting and delightful use of contrasting exterior materials. A curving, open stairway leads to the second floor with its dramatic balcony effect over the vestibule. Imagine, a 22 foot square gathering room!

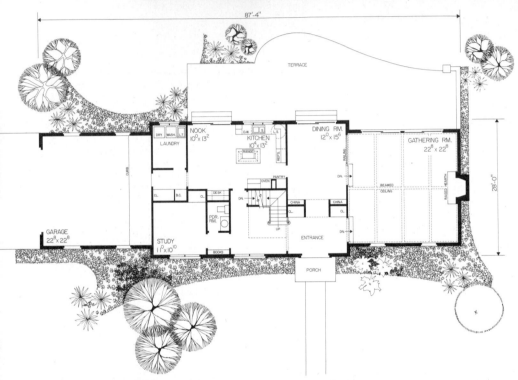

Design 12524

994 Sq. Ft. - First Floor
994 Sq. Ft. - Second Floor; 32,937 Cu. Ft.

● This small two-story, with a modest investment, will result in an impressive exterior and an outstanding interior which will provide exceptional livability. Your list of features will be long and surely impressive.

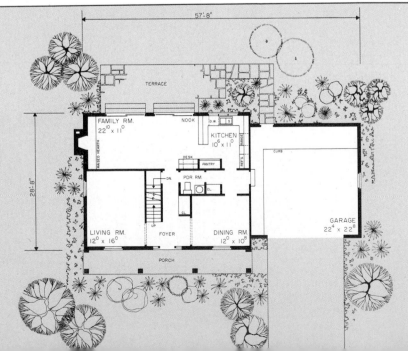

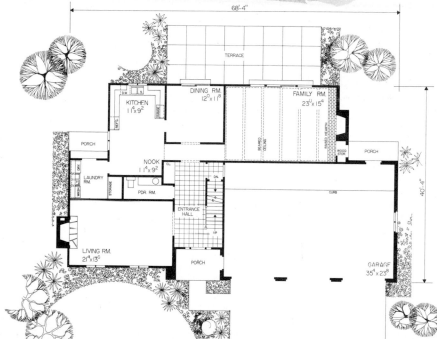

Design 12388
1,441 Sq. Ft. - First Floor
1,187 Sq. Ft. - Second Floor; 36,466 Cu. Ft.

● It isn't very often that you see an attached three-car garage. But, this isn't the only practical feature of this design. There are many others. Don't miss sun deck, laundry room, two fireplaces and sliding doors to terrace.

Design 12553
2,065 Sq. Ft. - First Floor
1,612 Sq. Ft. - Second Floor; 65,772 Cu. Ft.

● A stately Southern Colonial that could hardly be more impressive, or offer more pleasureable livability. The massive columns and the pediment gable are dramatic. No less so, is the open ceiling of the large gathering room. The second floor lounge area looks down on this favorite family living area. The two-story front entrance has its special appeal, also. Observe the quiet living room and its adjacent study. The bedroom bath arrangement of the second floor is particularly noteworthy. The oversized garage will accommodate three cars.

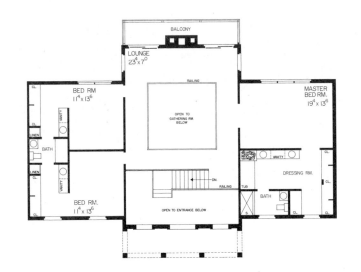

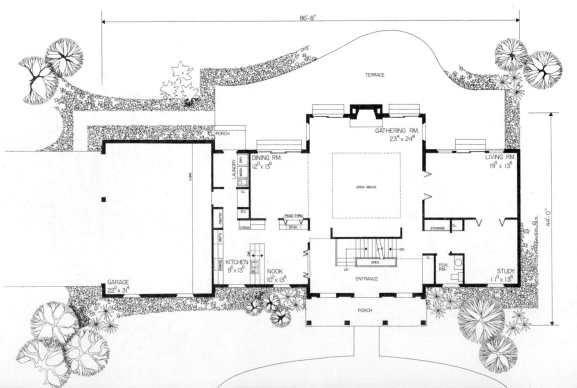

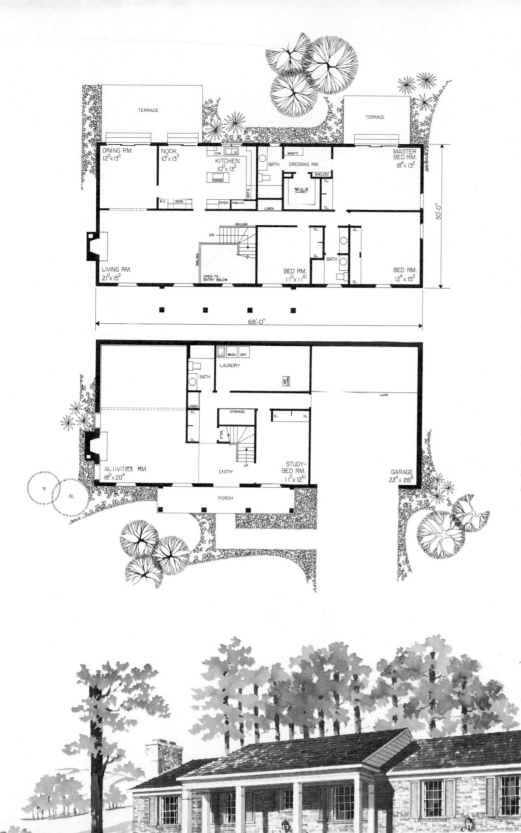

Design 12547
1,340 Sq. Ft. - First Floor
1,946 Sq. Ft. - Second Floor
40,166 Cu. Ft.

● Here are living patterns that are decidedly different for two-story living. In fact, since it is built into a sloping site, it may also be characterized as a bi-level adaptation. It is the exposure of the first floor in the front that creates that two story effect. With the activities room and the study (or fourth bedroom) there is significant livability on this level. Of course, upstairs there is the complete living unit. Its access to outdoor living is through sliding glass doors to the rear yard terraces. The master bedroom with all that space and storage, is outstanding. The living room is spacious and enjoys the open view of the high ceilinged entry. There are two fireplaces, three full baths and a fine laundry room. Note garage storage space.

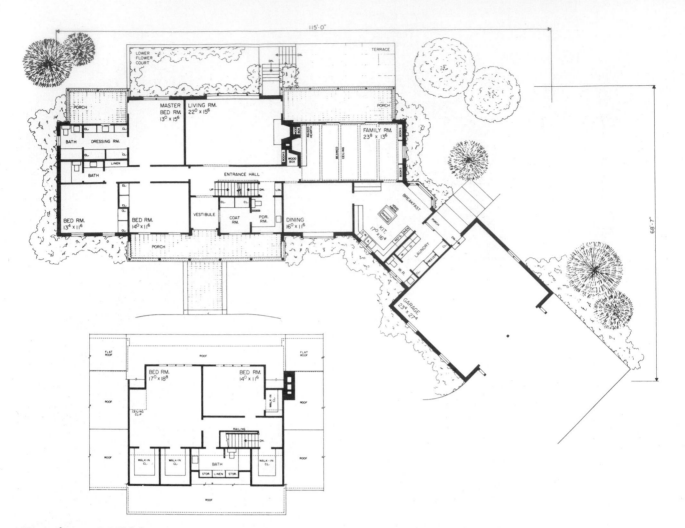

Design 11711 *2,580 Sq. Ft. - First Floor; 938 Sq. Ft. - Second Floor; 46,788 Cu. Ft.*

● If the gracious charm of the Colonial South appeals to you, this may be just the house you've been waiting for. There is something solid and dependable in its well-balanced facade and wide, pillared front porch. Much of the interest generated by this design comes from its interesting expanses of roof and angular projection of its kitchen and garage. The feeling of elegance is further experienced upon stepping inside, through double doors, to the spacious entrance hall where there is the separate coat room. Adjacent to this is the powder room, also convenient to the living areas. The work area of the kitchen and laundry room is truly outstanding. Designed as a five bedroom house, each is large. Storage and bath facilities are excellent.

The Farmhouse Theme
and Variations

Design 12223 1,266 Sq. Ft. - First Floor; 1,232 Sq. Ft. - Second Floor; 34,286 Cu. Ft.

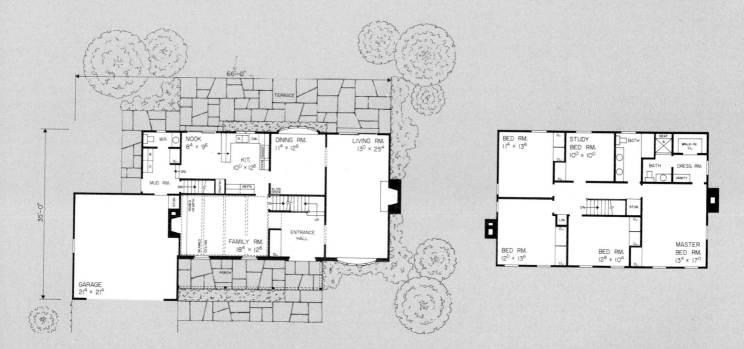

● The appealing double front doors of this home open wide to fine livability for the large, growing family. The spacious entrance hall is flanked by the formal, end living room and the all-purpose, beamed ceiling family room. Both rooms have a commanding fire-place. The U-shaped kitchen overlooks the rear yard and is but a step, or two, from the breakfast nook and the formal dining room. The mud room controls the flows of traffic during the inclement weather. Observe the laundry equipment and the wash room. Five bedrooms, two full baths, and plenty of closets are what make the second floor truly outstanding. There are a number of other convenient living features that make this design distinctive. How many of these can you list?

Design 12775

1,317 Sq. Ft. - First Floor
952 Sq. Ft. - Second Floor
47,795 Cu. Ft.

● This front porch Farmhouse adaptation is characteristic of the rolling hills of Pennsylvania. Warm summer evenings will be a delight when the outdoors can be enjoyed in such an impressive manner. You will also be impressed by the interior after the floor plan is reviewed. Double front doors lead the way into this interior. Both the formal and informal areas are outstandingly spacious. There are two eating areas: the formal dining room and the nook with sliding glass doors to a dining terrace. Many built-ins will be found in the nook-kitchen area; including a desk, pantry and more. Notice pass-thru counter. Make special note, there is a covered porch to the side of the family room for more outside enjoyment. Three family bedrooms, bath and master bedroom suite are on the second floor. Years of pleasurable living will be enjoyed in this home.

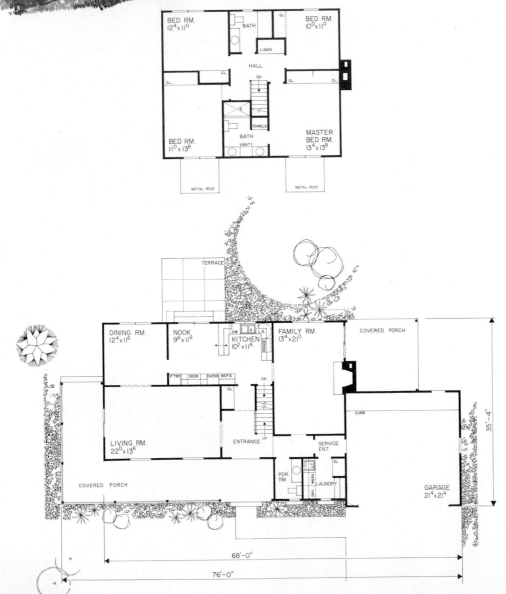

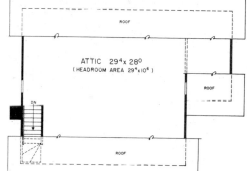

ATTIC 29⁴ x 28⁰
(HEADROOM AREA 29⁴x10⁶)

ROOF

ROOF

ROOF

DN

BED RM.
STUDY
11⁰x13²

BATH

DRESSING RM.

VANITY

MASTER
BED RM.
13⁰x13²

BATH

CL

CL

LIN

CL CL

BED RM.
10⁰x10⁶

CL

BED RM.
13⁰x10⁶

UP

Design 12774

1,370 Sq. Ft. - First Floor
969 Sq. Ft. - Second Floor
38,305 Cu. Ft.

● Another Farmhouse adaptation with all the most up-to-date features expected in a new home. Beginning with the formal areas, this design offers pleasures for the entire family. There is the quiet corner living room which has an opening to the sizeable dining room. This room will enjoy plenty of natural light from the delightful bay window overlooking the rear yard. It is also conveniently located with the efficient U-shaped kitchen just a step away. The kitchen features many built-ins with pass-thru to the beamed ceiling nook. Sliding glass doors to the terrace are fine attractions in both the sunken family room and nook. The service entrance to the garage has a storage closet on each side, plus there is a secondary entrance through the laundry area. Recreational activities and hobbies can be pursued in the basement area. Four bedrooms, two baths upstairs.

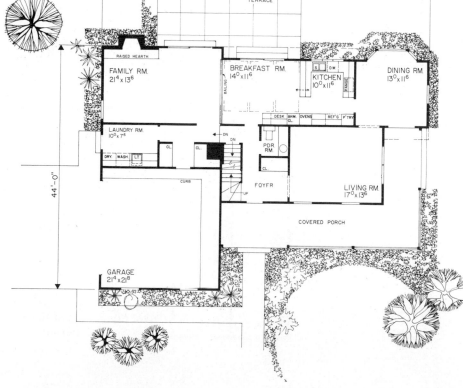

59'-8"

44'-0"

TERRACE

RAISED HEARTH

FAMILY RM.
21⁴ x 13⁶

LAUNDRY RM.
10⁰ x 7⁶

DRY. WASH. LT.

CL CL

CURB

BREAKFAST RM.
14⁰ x 11⁶

KITCHEN
10⁰ x 11⁶

S D.W.

RANGE

DESK. BRM. OVENS

CL

REF'G P'TRY

DN

DN

PDR. RM.

CL

FOYER

UP

DINING RM.
13⁰ x 11⁶

LIVING RM.
17⁰ x 13⁶

COVERED PORCH

GARAGE
21⁴ x 21⁸

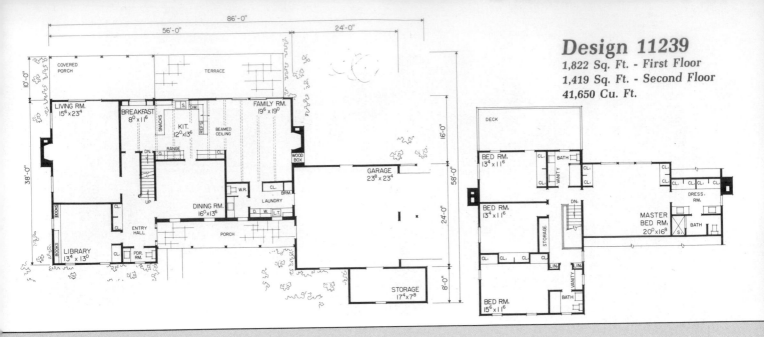

Design 11239
1,822 Sq. Ft. - First Floor
1,419 Sq. Ft. - Second Floor
41,650 Cu. Ft.

Design 11955
1,192 Sq. Ft. - First Floor
1,192 Sq. Ft. - Second Floor
32,408 Cu. Ft.

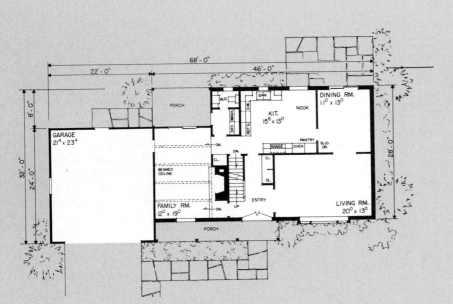

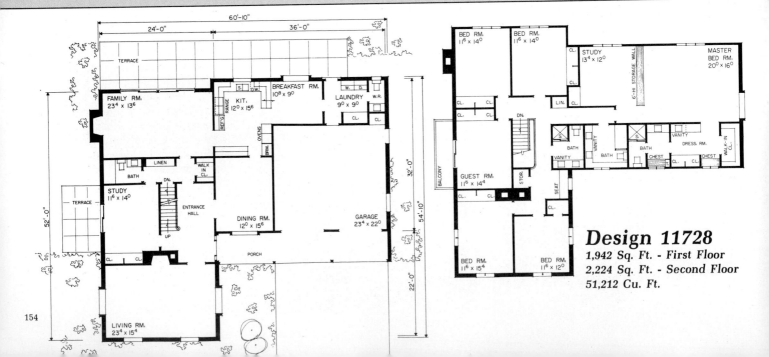

Design 11728
1,942 Sq. Ft. - First Floor
2,224 Sq. Ft. - Second Floor
51,212 Cu. Ft.

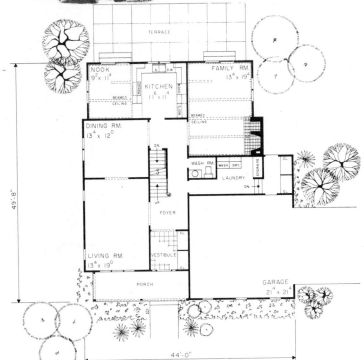

Design 12333
1,411 Sq. Ft. - First Floor
1,152 Sq. Ft. - Second Floor
31,825 Cu. Ft.

Design 12172
1,618 Sq. Ft. - First Floor
1,205 Sq. Ft. - Second Floor
42,667 Cu. Ft.

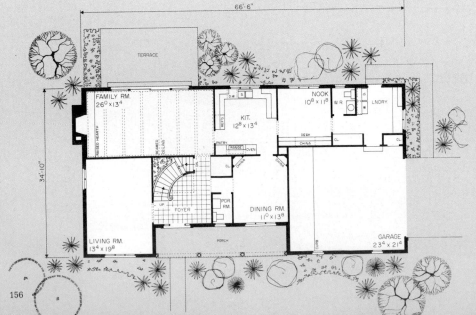

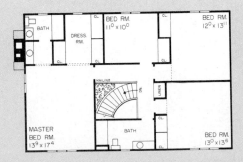

Design 12344

1,516 Sq. Ft. - First Floor
1,794 Sq. Ft. - Second Floor
44,219 Cu. Ft.

GARAGE
21⁸ x 23⁸

COVERED PORCH

WORK BENCH

FAMILY RM.
13⁸ x 25⁴

UP

CURB

DN.

DINING RM.
11⁸ x 10⁰

LAUNDRY

MUD RM.

WASH DRY.

CL.

REF'G RANGE

KITCHEN
13⁴ x 11⁶

NOOK

UP

BOOKS BOOKS

CABINETS

LIBRARY-STUDY
9⁰ x 9⁸

PDR. RM.

CL.

ENTRANCE HALL

CL.

COVERED PORCH

LIVING RM.
27⁴ x 13⁴

56'-0"

64'-0"

WALK-IN CLOSET

CL.

BED RM.
11⁴ x 11⁸

CL.

LIN.

DN.

HALL

BED RM.
19⁴ x 11⁸

CL.

BATH

CL.

BATH

BED RM.
13⁴ x 11⁰

STUDY-LOUNGE
10⁰ x 10⁰

BATH

DN.

STAIR HALL

DRESS RM.

STOR.

CL.

ROOF

LOUNGE
9⁰ x 9⁸

MASTER BED RM.
18⁰ x 13⁴

CL.

157

Design 11868

1,190 Sq. Ft. - First Floor
1,300 Sq. Ft. - Second Floor
32,327 Cu. Ft.

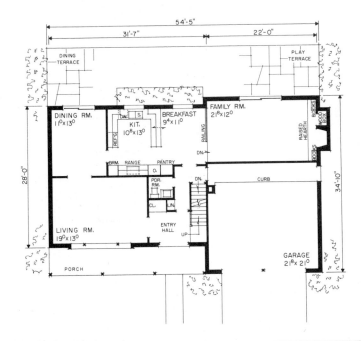

● A five bedroom Farmhouse adaptation that is truly a home for family living. The big family room will be everyone's favorite area. Note the master bedroom suite located over the garage.

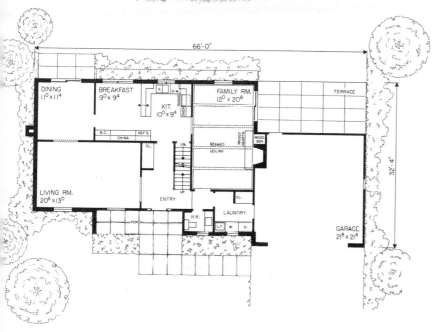

Design 11285

1,202 Sq. Ft. - First Floor
896 Sq. Ft. - Second Floor
27,385 Cu. Ft.

● Laundry, extra powder room, two full baths, four bedrooms, separate dining room, breakfast room and beamed ceiling family room are among the features of this two-story traditional design.

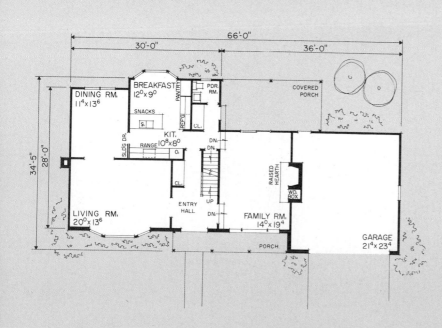

Design 11875

1,200 Sq. Ft. - First Floor
1,186 Sq. Ft. - Second Floor
30,734 Cu. Ft.

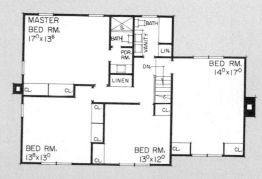

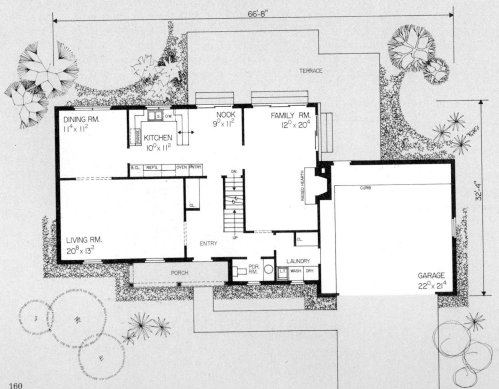

Design 12752

1,209 Sq. Ft. - First Floor
960 Sq. Ft. - Second Floor
34,725 Cu. Ft.

● This impressive two-story home is sure to catch the eye of even the most casual of on-lookers. The extended one-story wing adds great appeal to the exterior. The covered porch with pillars also is a charming feature. Now take a walk through the efficient floor plan. The living/dining room is L-shaped with the dining room being convenient to the kitchen. The U-shaped kitchen has a pass-thru to the breakfast nook plus has many built-ins to help ease kitchen duties. The nook, along with the family room, has sliding glass doors to the terrace. Also on the first floor is a powder room and laundry. The second floor houses the three family bedrooms, bath and the master bedroom suite with all the extras. Note the extra curb area in the garage.

Design 12585

990 Sq. Ft. - First Floor
1,011 Sq. Ft. - Second Floor
30,230 Cu. Ft.

● An elegant Colonial! This is a version of a front porch type house. The exterior is highlighted with seven large paned-glass windows and pillars. Note that the second floor overhangs in the front to extend the size of the master bedroom. After entering through the front door one can either go directly to the formal area of the living room and dining room or to the informal area which is the front family room with fireplace. No matter which direction you choose, satisfaction will be found. The U-shaped kitchen will serve the nook area orderly and is just a step away from the wash room. Upstairs one will find all of the sleeping facilities.

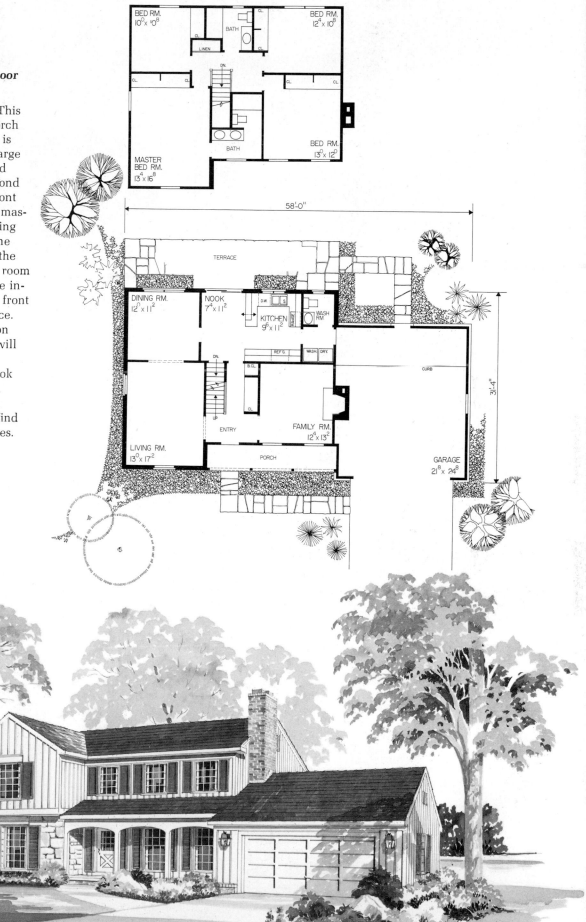

Design 11318
854 Sq. Ft. - First Floor
896 Sq. Ft. - Second Floor
24,420 Cu. Ft.

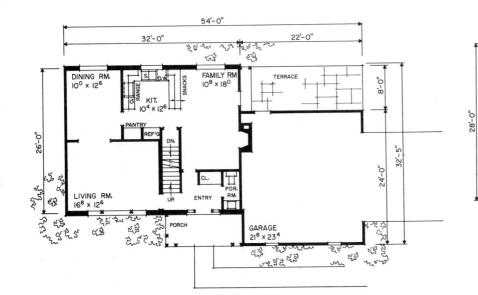

● Imagine! Five bedrooms, 2½ baths, informal family room, formal living and dining rooms, excellent kitchen, snack bar and a big two-car garage.

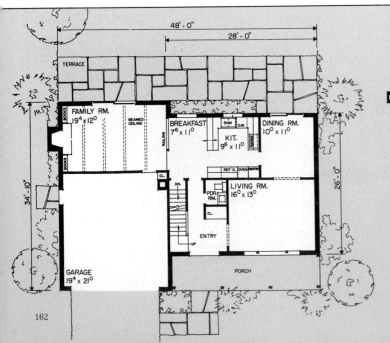

OPTIONAL 3 BEDROOM PLAN

Design 11956
990 Sq. Ft. - First Floor
728 Sq. Ft. - Second Floor
23,703 Cu. Ft.

● The blueprints for this home include details for both the three bedroom and four bedroom options. The first floor livability does not change.

Design 11719
864 Sq. Ft. - First Floor
896 Sq. Ft. - Second Floor
26,024 Cu. Ft.

● What an appealing low-cost Colonial adaptation. Most of the livability features generally found in the largest of homes are present to cater to family needs.

Design 11354

644 Sq. Ft. - First Floor
572 Sq. Ft. - Second Floor
11,490 Cu. Ft.

● Livability galore for the 50 foot building site. The homemaker will enjoy the U-shaped work center with the extra wash room, laundry equipment nearby.

OPTIONAL BASEMENT

Design 11913

740 Sq. Ft. - First Floor
728 Sq. Ft. - Second Floor
20,860 Cu. Ft.

● With or without a basement this will be a great low-cost two-story home for the large family. Note first floor laundry, wash room.

OPTIONAL NON-BASEMENT

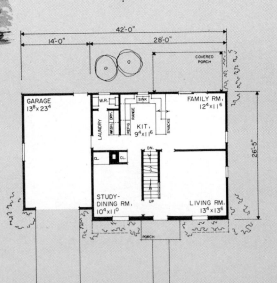

Design 11723

888 Sq. Ft. - First Floor
970 Sq. Ft. - Second Floor
19,089 Cu. Ft.

● You'll not need a large parcel of property to accommodate this home. Neither will you need too large a building budget. Note fourth bedroom.

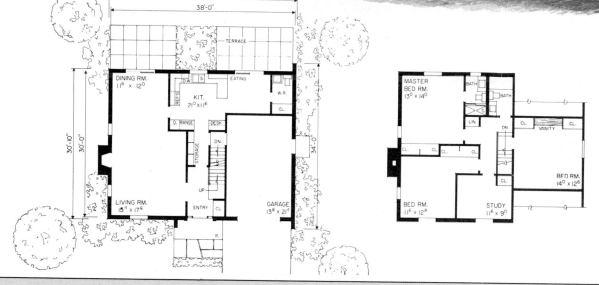

Design 11368

728 Sq. Ft. - First Floor
728 Sq. Ft. - Second Floor
20,020 Cu. Ft.

● Similar in plan to 11913 on the opposing page, this home features an entirely different exterior. Which do you prefer? Note covered rear porches.

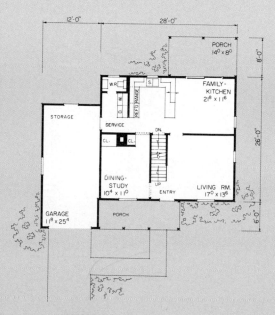

OPTIONAL NON-BASEMENT

165

Design 11996

1,056 Sq. Ft. - First Floor
1,040 Sq. Ft. - Second Floor
29,071 Cu. Ft.

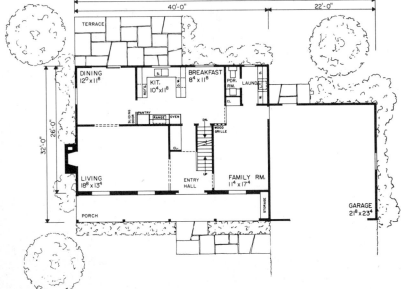

Design 11304

1,120 Sq. Ft. - First Floor
1,120 Sq. Ft. - Second Floor
31,920 Cu. Ft.

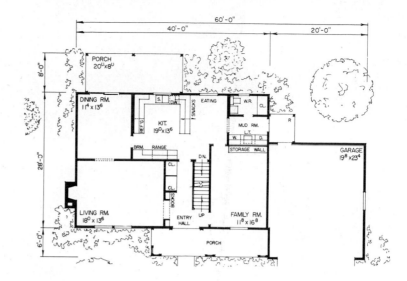

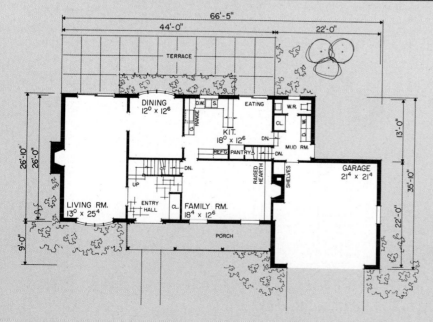

Design 11339

1,292 Sq. Ft. - First Floor
1,232 Sq. Ft. - Second Floor
34,706 Cu. Ft.

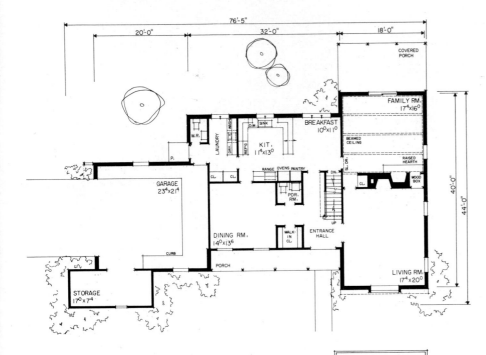

Design 11905

1,596 Sq. Ft. - First Floor
1,574 Sq. Ft. - Second Floor
48,700 Cu. Ft.

● A pleasing Farmhouse adaptation that just looks like it should be catering to the needs of a big, active family. What makes this house so interesting are the various roof lines and projecting wings. The covered front porch and the double front doors add their full measure of charm, too. The traffic patterns of this plan will be a favorite feature for a long time. One whole wing is devoted to living activities. Off the formal entrance hall is the quiet living room. Behind, and functioning with the covered rear porch, is the beamed ceiling family room. It has fine blank wall space and a raised hearth fireplace. The kitchen looks out upon the rear yard and efficiently serves the eating areas. Observe the laundry area with the powder room. Upstairs, four bedrooms!

Design 11857

1,654 Sq. Ft. - First Floor
1,536 Sq. Ft. - Second Floor
44,457 Cu. Ft.

● If ever there was a house of modest size designed for the large and active family, this has to be one of those houses. It would be difficult to decide which floor plan - the first or second - is the most outstanding. The first floor highlights a formal living room and an informal family room. Each has a fireplace. The outstanding kitchen is but a step or two from the formal dining room and the informal breakfast room. Then, there is the separate laundry room with a wash room nearby. But that's not all. In addition, there is the quiet library with an extra powder room next to it. An extremely practical feature are the two flights of stairs to the basement. Note their location. The second floor has six bedrooms! There are two full baths and loads of closets.

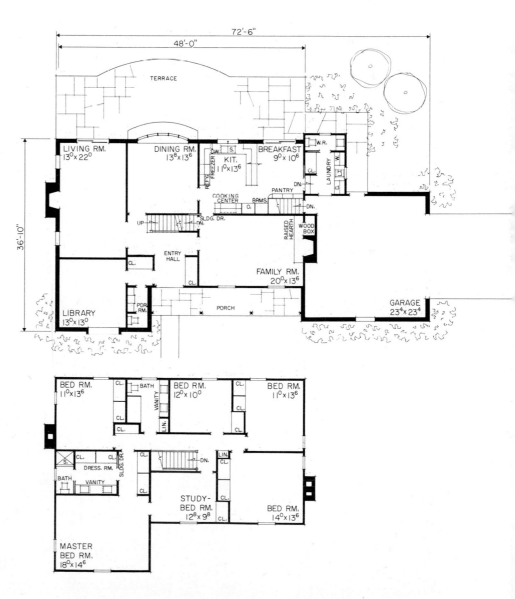

Design 11933

1,184 Sq. Ft. - First Floor
884 Sq. Ft. - Second Floor
27,976 Cu. Ft.

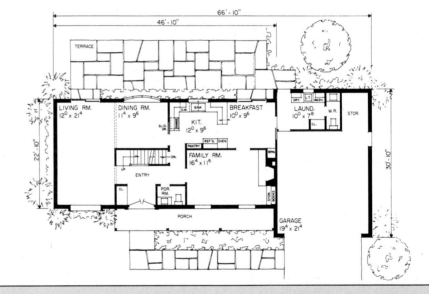

Design 11269

1,232 Sq. Ft. - First Floor
1,232 Sq. Ft. - Second Floor
33,344 Cu. Ft.

Design 11082

1,254 Sq. Ft. - First Floor
1,096 Sq. Ft. - Second Floor
37,239 Cu. Ft.

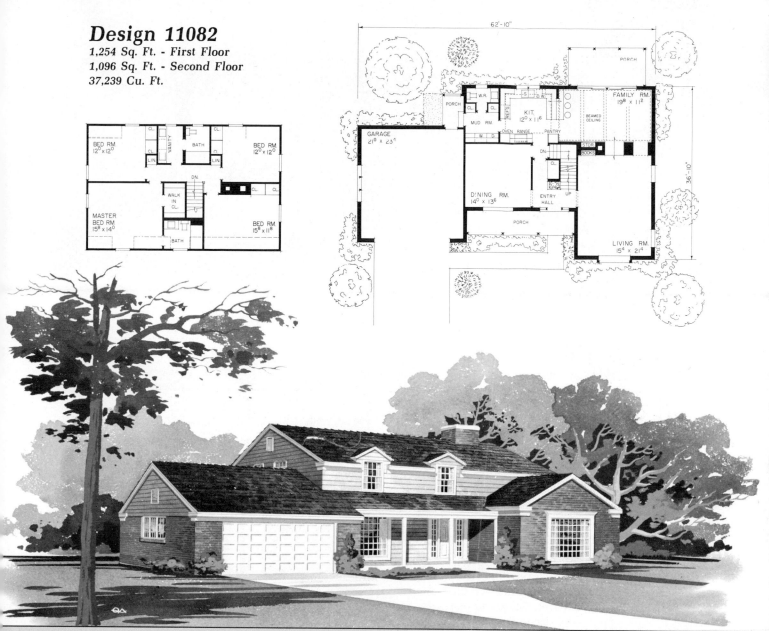

BED RM. 12⁰ x 12⁰ · CL. · VANITY · BATH · CL. · BED RM. 12⁰ x 12⁰ · LIN. · LIN.

DN. · CL. · CL.

MASTER BED RM. 15⁸ x 14⁰ · WALK IN CL. · BATH · BED RM. 15⁸ x 11⁸

62'-10"

PORCH

GARAGE 21⁰ x 23⁷ · PORCH · W.R. · CL. · CL. · KIT. 12⁰ x 11⁶ · MUD RM. · S. · D.W. · REF'G. · FAMILY RM. 19⁸ x 11² · BEAMED CEILING

OVEN RANGE · W D · PANTRY · STOR. · BOOKS

DN. · UP · B'K'ST.

DINING RM. 14⁰ x 13⁶ · ENTRY HALL · CL.

PORCH

LIVING RM. 15⁴ x 21⁴

36'-10"

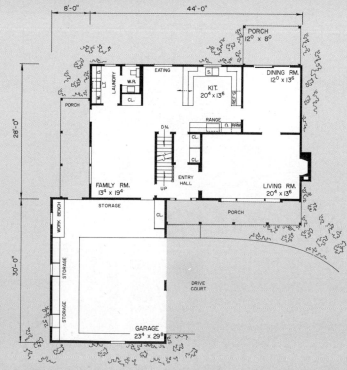

8'-0" · 44'-0"

PORCH 12⁰ x 8⁰

LAUNDRY · W.R. · CL. · EATING · S. · KIT. 20⁴ x 13⁶ · REF'G. · DINING RM. 12⁰ x 13⁶

PORCH

28'-0"

RANGE · O. RM.

DN. · CL. · CL.

FAMILY RM. 13⁴ x 19⁴ · ENTRY HALL · UP · LIVING RM. 20⁴ x 13⁶

30'-0"

WORK BENCH · STORAGE · CL. · PORCH · STORAGE · STORAGE

GARAGE 23⁴ x 29⁸ · DRIVE COURT

DECK

BED RM. 10⁰ x 13⁶ · BATH · BED RM. 10⁴ x 10⁰ · CL. · BED RM. 12⁰ x 13⁶ · VANITY · LIN. · CL. · CL.

CL. · CL. · DN. · WALK IN CL. · CL.

BED RM. 13⁴ x 11⁰ · BATH · LIN. · MASTER BED RM. 18⁰ x 13⁶

● Here are three homes of modest size each one completely capable of catering most successfully to the living requirements of the large family. There is no lack of sleeping space. Bath facilities are excellent. Eating potential is outstanding. Formal and informal living space is exceptional. As for exterior design appeal - unsurpassed. Don't miss the laundries, fireplaces, number of closets and oversized garages. Each design has a big basement.

Design 12542 2,025 Sq. Ft. - First Floor
1,726 Sq. Ft. - Second Floor; 61,315 Cu. Ft.

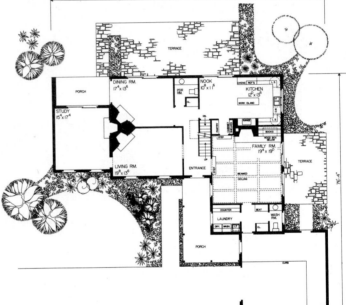

● Here is a fieldstone Farmhouse that has its roots in the rolling countryside of Pennsylvania. In addition to its stone exterior, the charm of such a house is characterized by the various appendages. These additions, of course, came into being as the size of the family fortune increased. The living potential offered by this Farmhouse adaptation can hardly be topped. Imagine, five fireplaces! Study the outstanding livability offered in this house from the past. Surely its floor plan has been up-dated to serve today's contemporary family.

Design 12633

1,338 Sq. Ft. - First Floor
1,200 Sq. Ft. - Second Floor
506 Sq. Ft. - Third Floor
44,525 Cu. Ft.

● This is certainly a pleasing Georgian. Its facade features an atypical porch with a roof supported by simple wooden posts. The garage wing has a sheltered service entry and brick facing which complements the design. Sliding glass doors link the terrace and family room, providing an indoor/outdoor area for entertaining as pictured in the rear elevation. The floor plan has been designed to serve the family efficiently. The stairway in the foyer leads to four second-floor bedrooms. The third floor is windowed and can be used as a studio and study.

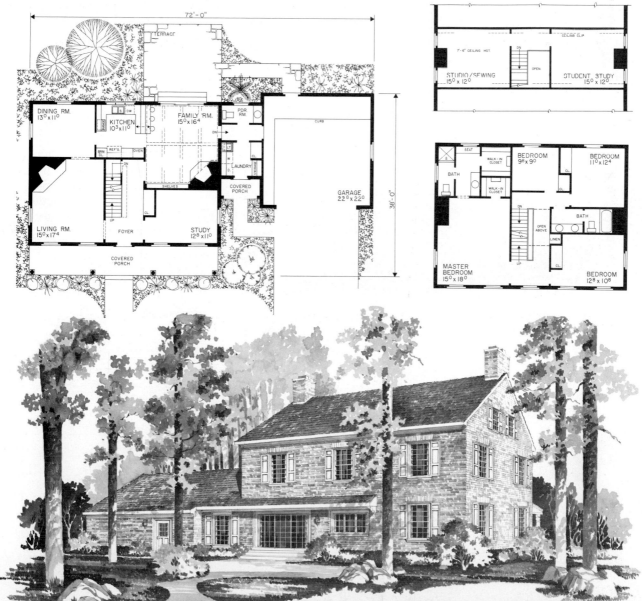

Design 12325

1,154 Sq. Ft. - First Floor
1,188 Sq. Ft. - Second Floor; 29,621 Cu. Ft.

● Here is a modest package which will build economically on a relatively small site. All the elements are present to guarantee tremendous livability. Your family is not likely to outgrow this house. Imagine, four bedrooms, 2½ baths!

● What an appealingly different type of two-story home! It is one whose grace and charm project an aura of welcome. The large entry hall routes traffic efficiently to all areas. Don't miss the covered porch.

Design 11972

1,286 Sq. Ft. - First Floor; 960 Sq. Ft. - Second Floor
30,739 Cu. Ft.

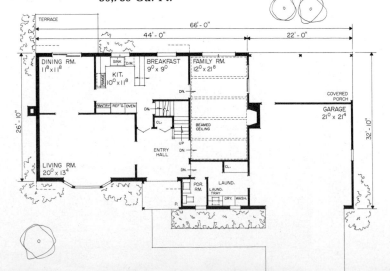

Traditional Design
As You Like It

Design 11715 1,276 Sq. Ft. - First Floor; 1,064 Sq. Ft. - Second Floor; 31,295 Cu. Ft.

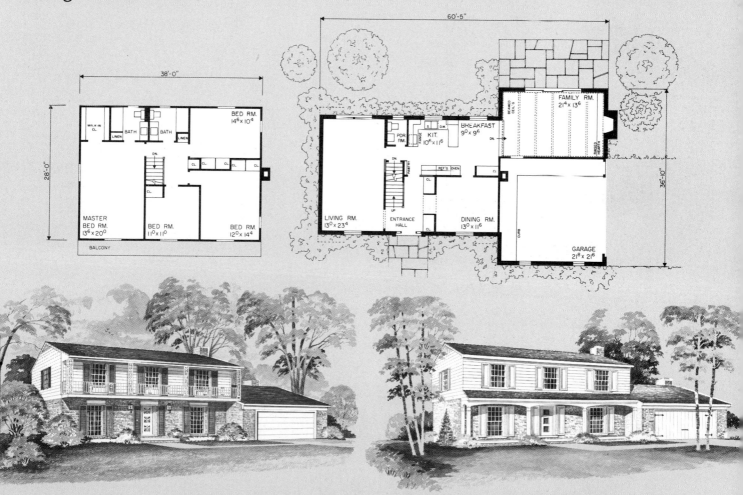

● The blueprints you order for this design show details for building each of these three appealing exteriors. Which do you like best? Whatever your choice, the interior will provide the growing family with all the facilities for fine living.

Design 11831 1,108 Sq. Ft. - First Floor; 992 Sq. Ft. - Second Floor; 31,075 Cu. Ft.

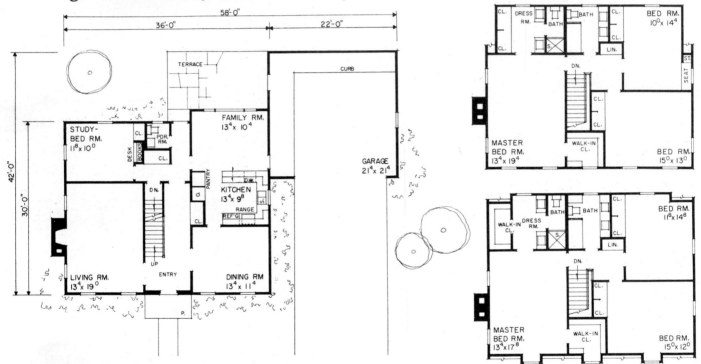

Design 11832 1,108 Sq. Ft. - First Floor; 1,018 Sq. Ft. - Second Floor; 31,342 Cu. Ft.

Design 11833 1,152 Sq. Ft. - First Floor; 958 Sq. Ft. - Second Floor; 31,386 Cu. Ft.

Four Authentic Exteriors Go With This Practical Family Living Plan . . .

● . . . which one do you prefer? Each of these delightful exteriors - the New England Salt Box, Design 11831; the Connecticut Gambrel, Design 11832; the French Mansard, Design 11833; the Georgian, Design 11834 - will provide you with a proud link with the past. Pride of ownership will be yours forever! The efficient first floor plan is common to each of these four designs. The second floor, however, varies with each exterior style. While each house features three sizeable bedrooms, excellent bath facilities and fine storage potential, a study of the various bedroom dimensions reveals difference in sizes. This is due to the varying characteristics of the roof structures. Observe the center entrance and how the main hall effectively routes traffic to all areas. The efficient work center is strategically located between the separate dining room and the informal family room. The formal living room will be entirely free of unnecessary traffic. Note the fireplace and all that blank space for flexible furniture placement. Don't miss the extra room which may be used as a study or fourth bedroom.

Design 11834 1,150 Sq. Ft. - First Floor; 1,120 Sq. Ft. - Second Floor; 34,460 Cu. Ft.

Floor Plans

First Floor

- PLAY TERRACE
- DINING TERRACE
- FAMILY RM. 19⁴ x 12⁰ — BEAMED CEILING
- BOOKS
- BREAKFAST 8⁰ x 11⁰
- KIT. 10⁰ x 11⁰
- SINK
- D.W.
- RANGE
- DINING RM. 11⁰ x 11⁰
- GARAGE 19⁴ x 21⁰
- DN.
- CL.
- REF'G
- OVEN
- PANTRY
- PDR. RM.
- CL.
- DN
- ENTRY
- UP
- LIVING RM. 18⁰ x 13⁰
- PORCH
- 50'-0"
- 20'-8"
- 29'-4"
- 26'-0"
- 34'-10"

Second Floor

- BED RM. 10⁴ x 9⁴
- SHOWER
- BATH
- MASTER BED RM. 11⁰ x 15⁰
- CL.
- BATH
- DN
- CL.
- CL.
- LIN.
- CL.
- CL.
- BED RM. 9⁴ x 10⁰
- BED RM. 14⁴ x 10⁰
- 30'-0"
- 26'-0"

Design 11957 1,042 Sq. Ft. - First Floor; 780 Sq. Ft. - Second Floor; 24,982 Cu. Ft.

● When you order your blueprints for this design you will receive details for the construction of each of the three charming exteriors pictured above. Whichever the exterior you finally decide to build, the floor plan will be essentially the same except the location of the windows. This will be a fine home for the growing family. It will serve well for many years. There are four bedrooms and two full baths (one with a stall shower) upstairs.

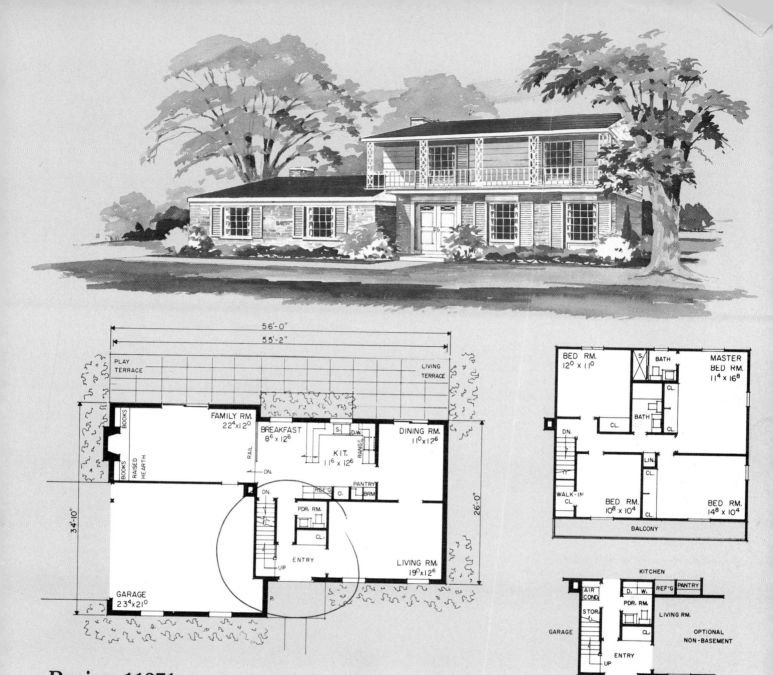

Design 11371 1,172 Sq. Ft. - First Floor; 896 Sq. Ft. - Second Floor; 28,726 Cu. Ft.

First floor plan labels: PLAY TERRACE, LIVING TERRACE, 56'-0", 55'-2", FAMILY RM. 22⁴ x 12⁰, BREAKFAST 8⁶ x 12⁶, KIT. 11⁶ x 12⁶, DINING RM. 11⁰ x 12⁶, BOOKS, RAISED HEARTH, RAIL, DN., REF'G, PANTRY, BRM, PDR. RM., CL., O., ENTRY, UP, DN., 34'-10", 26'-0", GARAGE 23⁴ x 21⁰, LIVING RM. 19⁰ x 12⁶, P.

Second floor plan labels: BED RM. 12⁰ x 11⁰, BATH, MASTER BED RM. 11⁴ x 16⁸, CL., BATH, DN., LIN., WALK-IN CL., BED RM. 10⁸ x 10⁴, BED RM. 14⁸ x 10⁴, BALCONY, S.

Optional non-basement plan labels: KITCHEN, AIR COND., D., W., REF'G, PANTRY, STOR., PDR. RM., LIVING RM., GARAGE, CL., ENTRY, UP, OPTIONAL NON-BASEMENT.

● If you like traditional charm and the tried and true living patterns of the conventional two-story idea, you'll not go wrong in selecting this design as your next home. In fact, when you order blueprints for Design 11371 you'll receive details for building all three optional elevations. So, you needn't decide which front exterior is your favorite right now. Any one of these will surely add a touch of class to your new neighborhood.

Design 12149

988 Sq. Ft. - First Floor
952 Sq. Ft. - Second Floor; 30,438 Cu. Ft.

● Any one of these three traditional exteriors can be built with the same basic floor plan. If you like the traditional version above order blueprints for 12149; if you prefer the Farmhouse adaptation below order 12150; should your choice be for the Tudor variation on the opposing page order 12151. Whatever your selection you'll be thrilled to know that your new home will be a finely proportioned, well-detailed one. In each case the attached two-car garage adds to the appeal as its roof continues to provide shelter for the front doors. A professional builder could hardly do better than to find a place for these charming houses in his sub-division. The basically rectangular shape of the main house will mean economical construction.

Design 12150

991 Sq. Ft. - First Floor
952 Sq. Ft. - Second Floor; 27,850 Cu. Ft.

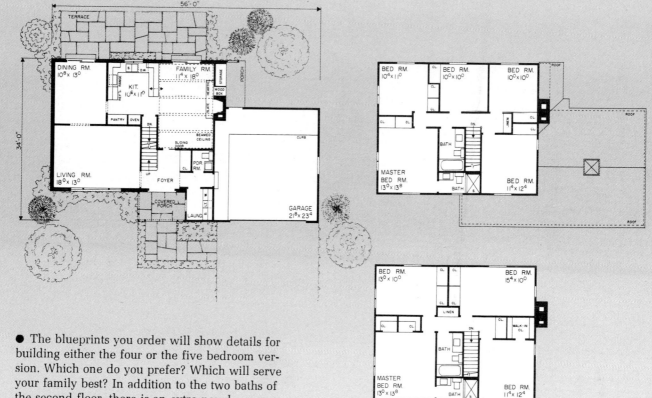

● The blueprints you order will show details for building either the four or the five bedroom version. Which one do you prefer? Which will serve your family best? In addition to the two baths of the second floor, there is an extra powder room downstairs. Further, there is a laundry, a separate dining room, a beamed ceiling family room, a U-shaped kitchen and a basement. A great plan for the modest budget.

OPTIONAL 4 BEDROOM PLAN

Design 12151
991 Sq. Ft. - First Floor
952 Sq. Ft. - Second Floor; 28,964 Cu. Ft.

Hacienda From The Old West

● This authentic Spanish Colonial adaptation has its roots in the past. Here is a design whose exterior captures the romance of a bygone era, while its floor plan offers all the up-to-date conveniences of today's living. Space is obviously the byword. For there are over 3,300 square feet on both floors together. The rustic theme of the exterior is carried into the delightful interior where beam ceilings create the aura of warmth and friendliness. Both living areas - the informal family room and the formal living room - feature a raised hearth fireplace. The large kitchen will be a wonderful place in which to work. The laundry is nearby, as is the extra wash room. Eating facilities (formal or informal) could hardly be improved upon. Upstairs there are four huge bedrooms, a pleasant lounge and two large baths. Note that each bath features both a tub and a stall shower.

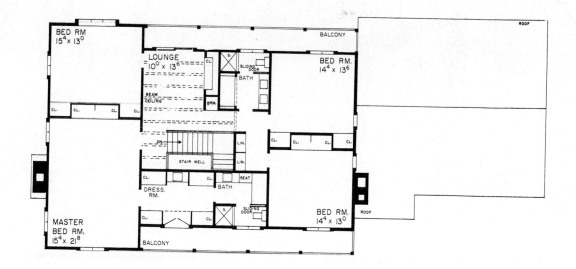

BED RM
15⁴ x 13⁰

LOUNGE
10⁰ x 13⁶

BALCONY

BED RM.
14⁴ x 13⁶

ROOF

CL.

S.

SLIDING DOOR

BATH

BEAM CEILING

CL.

CL.

CL.

BRM.

DN.

STAIR WELL

LIN.

LIN.

CL.

CL.

CL.

MASTER BED RM.
15⁴ x 21⁸

DRESS. RM.

CL.

SEAT

BATH

S.

CL.

CL.

SLIDING DOOR

BED RM.
14⁴ x 13⁰

ROOF

BALCONY

Design 12136 1,688 Sq. Ft. - First Floor; 1,688 Sq. Ft. - Second Floor; 50,353 Cu. Ft.

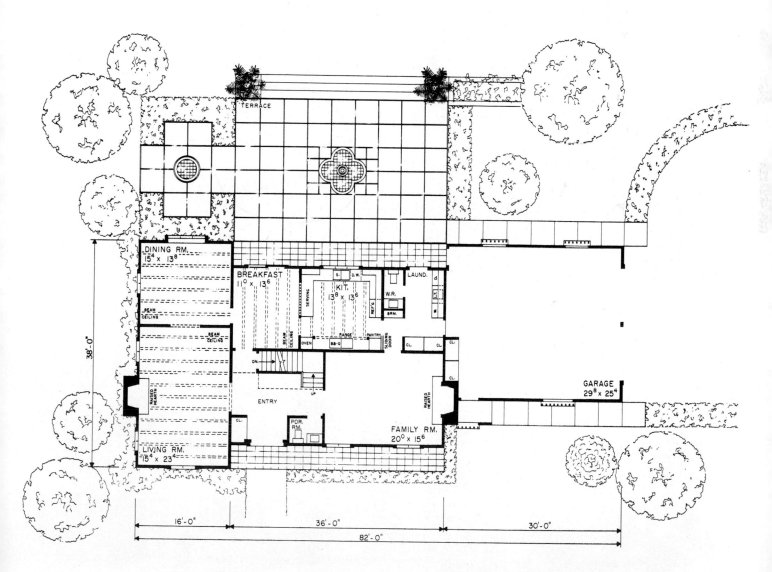

TERRACE

DINING RM.
15⁴ x 13⁸

BREAKFAST
11⁰ x 13⁶

LAUND.

BEAM CEILING

SERVING

S.   D.W.

KIT.
13⁸ x 13⁶

W.R.

REF'G.

BRM.

BEAM CEILING

BEAM CEILING

OVEN

BB-Q

RANGE

PANTRY

SLIDING DOOR

CL.

CL.

DN.

RAISED HEARTH

ENTRY

UP

CL.

PDR. RM.

RAISED HEARTH

FAMILY RM.
20⁰ x 15⁶

GARAGE
29⁸ x 25⁴

LIVING RM.
15⁴ x 23⁴

38'-0"

16'-0"

36'-0"

30'-0"

82'-0"

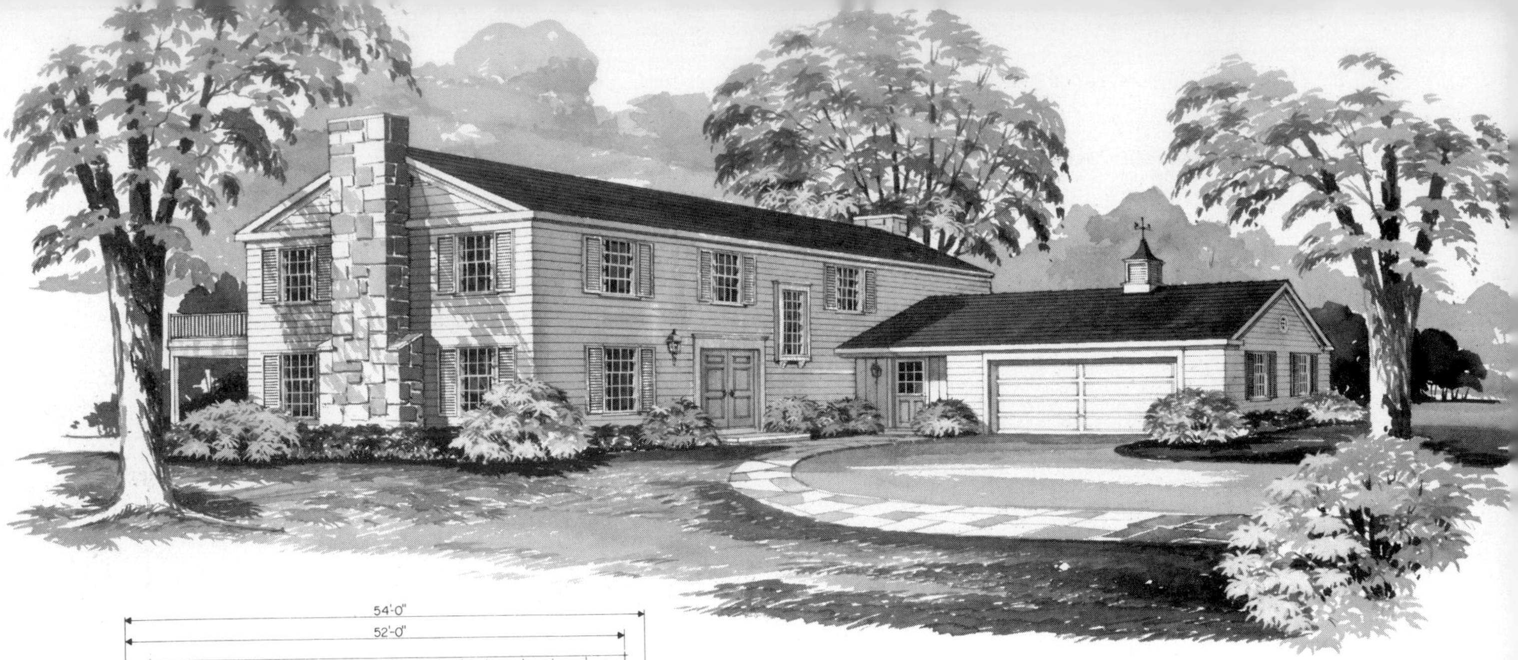

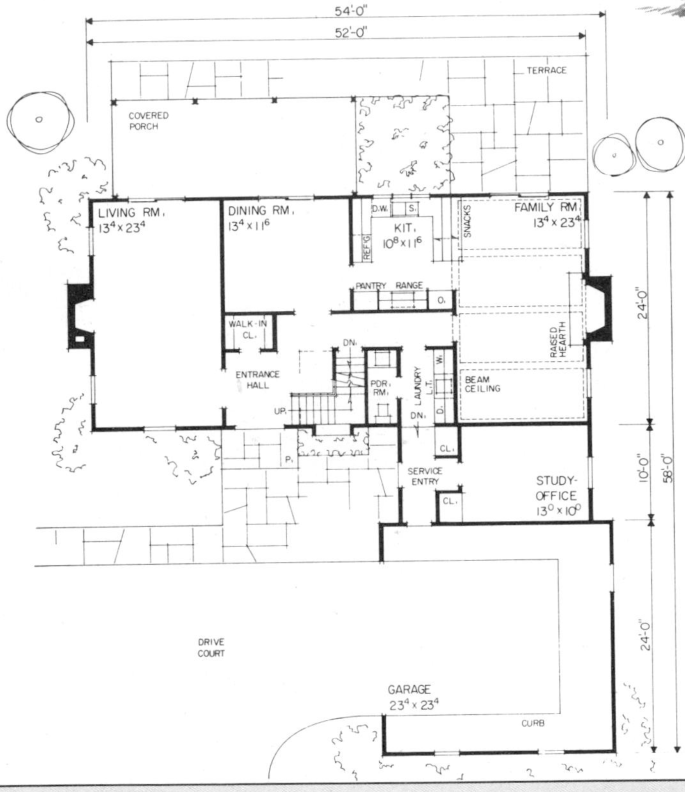
54'-0"
52'-0"
TERRACE
COVERED PORCH
LIVING RM. 13⁴ x 23⁴
DINING RM. 13⁴ x 11⁶
D.W.
S.
KIT. 10⁸ x 11⁶
REF'G.
SNACKS
FAMILY RM. 13⁴ x 23⁴
PANTRY RANGE
O.
WALK-IN CL.
DN.
ENTRANCE HALL
UP.
PDR. RM.
LAUNDRY
L.T.
W.
D.
DN.
RAISED HEARTH
BEAM CEILING
CL.
P.
SERVICE ENTRY
CL.
STUDY-OFFICE 13⁰ x 10⁰
24'-0"
10'-0"
58'-0"
24'-0"
DRIVE COURT
GARAGE 23⁴ x 23⁴
CURB

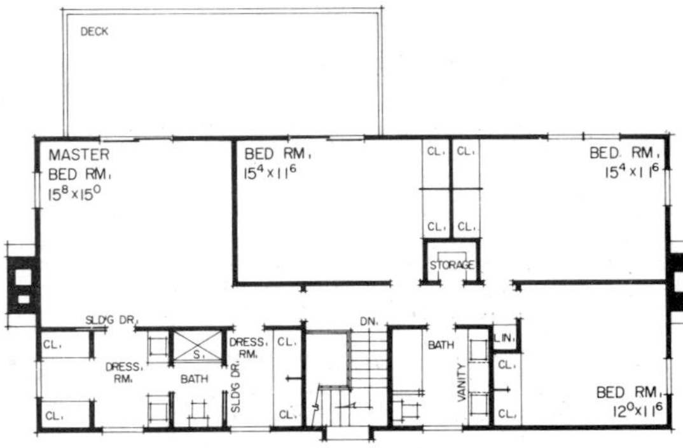
DECK
MASTER BED RM. 15⁸ x 15⁰
BED RM. 15⁴ x 11⁶
CL.
CL.
CL.
CL.
BED RM. 15⁴ x 11⁶
STORAGE
SLDG. DR.
CL.
DRESS. RM.
S.
BATH
DRESS. RM.
SLDG. DR.
CL.
CL.
DN.
BATH
VANITY
LIN.
CL.
CL.
BED RM. 12⁰ x 11⁶
CL.

Design 11907

1,448 Sq. Ft. - First Floor
1,248 Sq. Ft. - Second Floor
37,768 Cu. Ft.

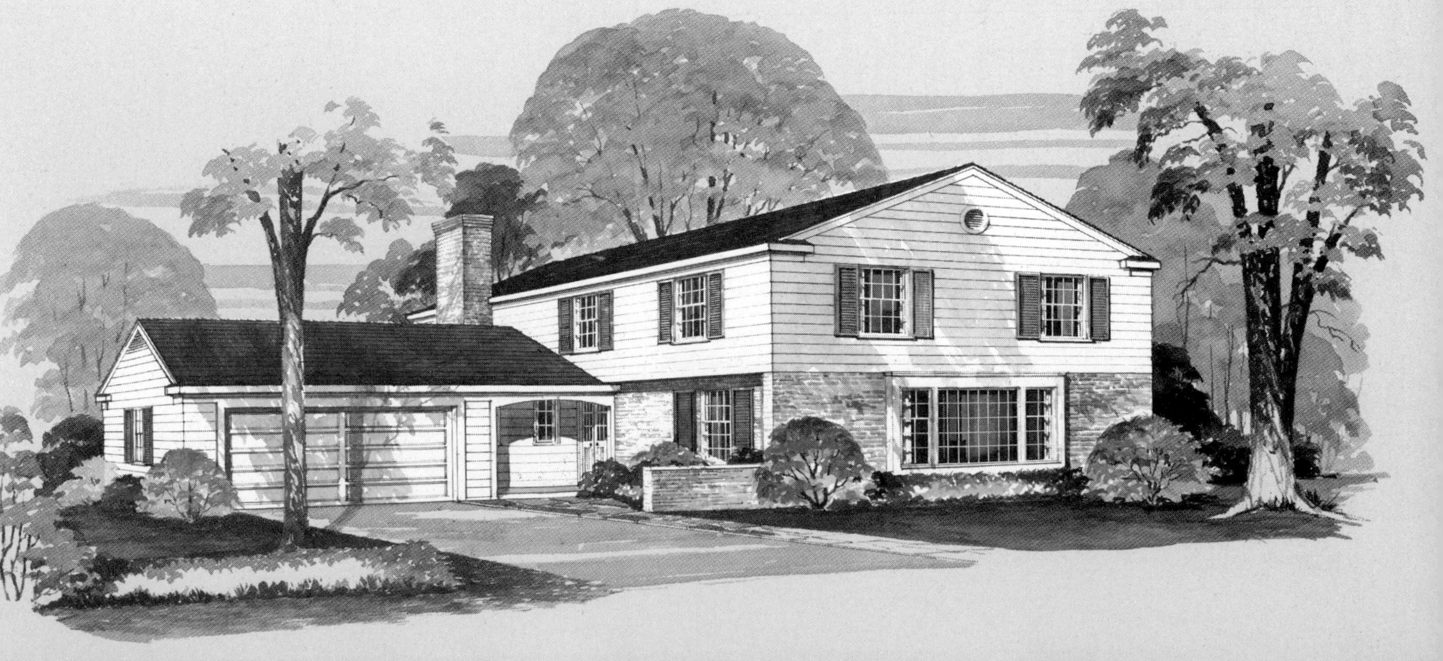

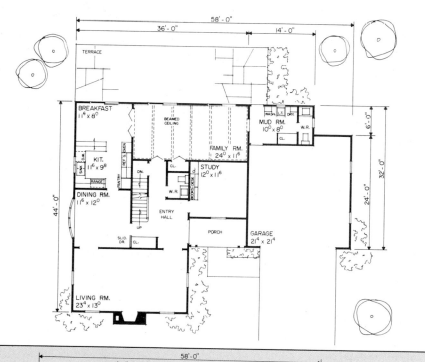

Design 11971
1,460 Sq. Ft. - First Floor
1,056 Sq. Ft. - Second Floor
34,726 Cu. Ft.

58' - 0"
36' - 0"
14' - 0"
44' - 0"
6' - 0"
32' - 0"
24' - 0"

TERRACE

BREAKFAST
11⁶ x 8⁰

BEAMED CEILING

MUD RM.
10⁰ x 8⁰

WASH L.T. DRY.

W.R.

CL.

KIT.
11⁶ x 9⁸

REF'G & OVEN

FAMILY RM.
24⁰ x 11⁶

DN.

STUDY
12⁰ x 11⁶

RANGE

DINING RM.
11⁶ x 12⁰

W.R.

ENTRY HALL

UP

SLID. DR.

CL.

PORCH

GARAGE
21⁴ x 21⁴

LIVING RM.
23⁴ x 13⁰

MASTER BED RM.
11⁶ x 17⁰

BED RM.
11⁶ x 11⁶

CL.

DN.

WALK IN CL.

CL.

VANITY

PDR. RM.

BATH

DRESS. RM.

LIN.

BATH

SHOWER

CL.

CL.

CL.

BED RM.
11⁶ x 14⁴

BED RM.
11⁶ x 11⁰

Design 11966
1,244 Sq. Ft. - First Floor
1,232 Sq. Ft. - Second Floor
34,014 Cu. Ft.

58' - 0"
32' - 0"
24' - 0"
22' - 0"
44' - 0"

TERRACE

GARAGE
21⁴ x 21⁴

FAMILY RM.
11⁶ x 19⁰

BREAKFAST
9⁶ x 8⁰

CL.

DRY. WASH.

LAUND.

LAUND. TRAY

BEAMED CEILING

REF'G OVEN

KIT.
11⁶ x 10⁰

PDR. RM.

RANGE

D.W.

SINK

PORCH

DN.

DINING RM.
11⁶ x 11⁰

ENTRY

UP

CL.

LIVING RM.
23⁴ x 13⁰

BED RM.
13⁶ x 13⁰

BED RM.
13⁶ x 13⁰

CL.

CL.

BRM.

LINEN

CL.

CL.

BATH

ROOF

STUDY-BED RM.
10⁰ x 11⁸

DN.

STOR.

SHOWER

VANITY

BATH

CL.

CHEST

CL.

WALK IN CL.

MASTER BED RM.
23⁰ x 13⁴

WALK IN CL.

Design 12599

2,075 Sq. Ft. - First Floor
1,398 Sq. Ft. - Second Floor
55,000 Cu. Ft.

● This traditional two-story
with its projecting one-story
wings is delightfully proportioned. The symmetrical window
treatment is most appealing.
The massive field-stone arch
projects from the front line of
the house providing a sheltered
front entrance. Inside, there
is the large foyer with the
curving, open staircase to the
second floor. Flexibility will be
the byword to describe the living patterns. Not only are there
the formal living and informal
family rooms, but there is the
quiet study and the upstairs
sitting room. As for eating, there
is a sizeable breakfast nook and
a separate dining room. The
second floor offers the option
to function as either a three,
or four, bedroom sleeping zone.
That's a fine master bedroom
suite when the sitting room
is included.

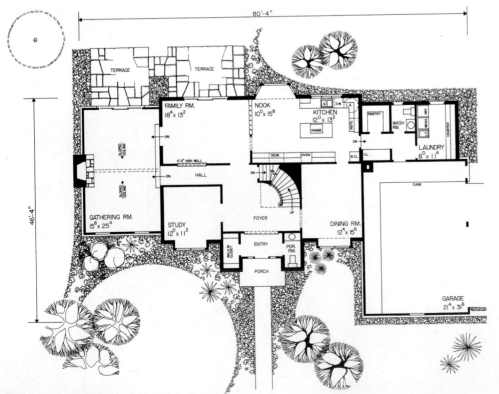

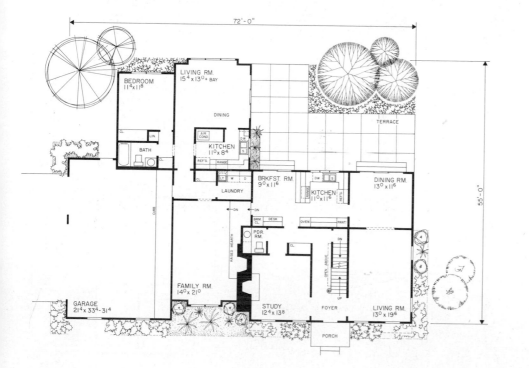

Design 12808

1,540 Sq. Ft. - First Floor
1,117 Sq. Ft. - Second Floor
605 Sq. Ft. - Apartment
48,075 Cu. Ft.

● A complete apartment is tucked in the back of this Colonial home. This apartment would be ideal for a live-in relative or supplement your income by becoming a landlord and rent out the apartment. Whatever you choose, the occupants will be served by an L-shaped kitchen, living room with bay and dining area, bedroom and bath. A complete unit in itself. The rest of this house will serve a larger family with great ease. There is a formal living room and an informal family room plus a good-sized study. Every family member will have a place to go in this home. Sliding glass doors in the two eating areas, the informal breakfast room and the formal dining room, open to a large terrace. All of the sleeping facilities are on the efficiently planned second floor.

Design 12518
1,630 Sq. Ft. - First Floor
1,260 Sq. Ft. - Second Floor
43,968 Cu. Ft.

● For those who have a predilection for the Spanish influence in their architecture. Outdoor oriented, each of the major living areas on the first floor have direct access to the terraces. Traffic patterns are excellent.

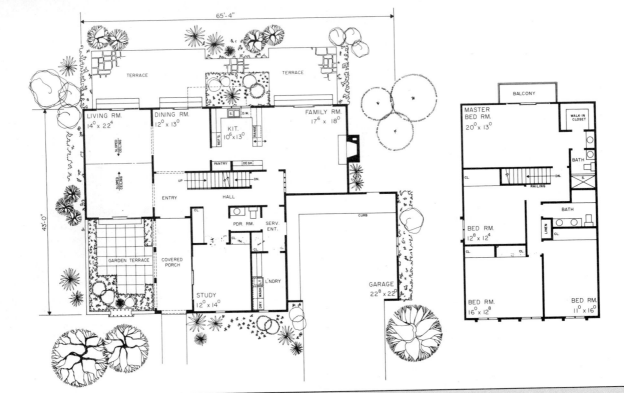

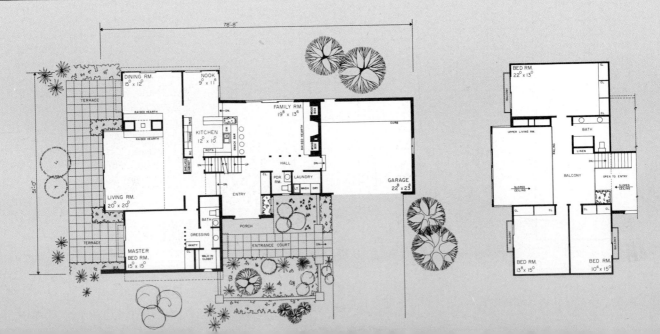

Design 12517

1,767 Sq. Ft. - First Floor
1,094 Sq. Ft. - Second Floor
50,256 Cu. Ft.

● Wherever built - north, east, south, or west - this home will surely command all the attention it deserves. And little wonder with such a well-designed exterior and such an outstanding interior. List your favorite features.

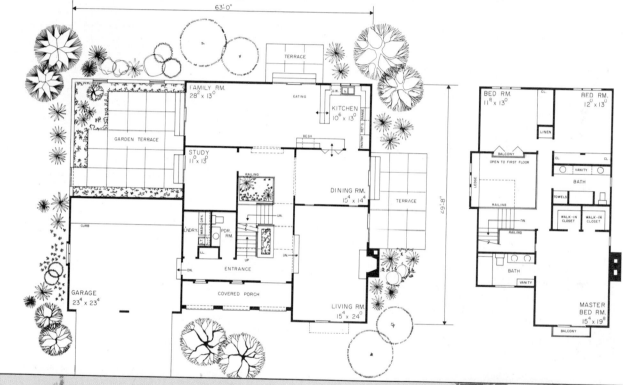

Design 12512

2,074 Sq. Ft. - First Floor
1,116 Sq. Ft. - Second Floor
41,500 Cu. Ft.

Design 12619

1,269 Sq. Ft. - First Floor
1,064 Sq. Ft. - Second Floor
29,195 Cu. Ft.

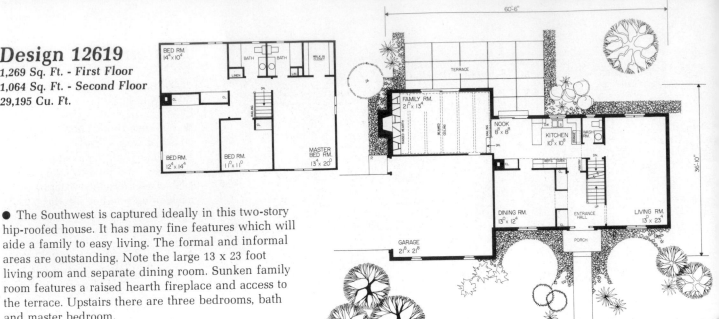

● The Southwest is captured ideally in this two-story hip-roofed house. It has many fine features which will aide a family to easy living. The formal and informal areas are outstanding. Note the large 13 x 23 foot living room and separate dining room. Sunken family room features a raised hearth fireplace and access to the terrace. Upstairs there are three bedrooms, bath and master bedroom.

Design 11753

1,580 Sq. Ft. - First Floor
1,008 Sq. Ft. - Second Floor
26,484 Cu. Ft.

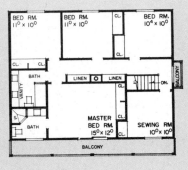

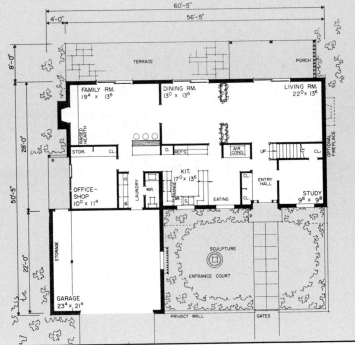

● The charm of the old Spanish Southwest is captured by the rugged individualism characterized by this design. The family, dining and living rooms will cater to the family's informal and formal group activities most adequately. This non-basement home has separate laundry, wash room and office on the first floor.

Design 12214

3,011 Sq. Ft. - First Floor
2,297 Sq. Ft. - Second Floor; 78,585 Cu. Ft.

● A Spanish hacienda with all the appeal and all the comforts one would want in a new home. This is a house that looks big and really is big. Measuring 100 feet across the front with various appendages and roof planes.

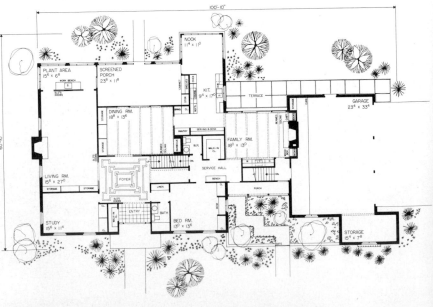

Design 12367

1,356 Sq. Ft. - First Floor
780 Sq. Ft. - Second Floor
31,230 Cu. Ft.

● This attractively proportioned two-story is a good study in effective zoning. Observe how the various areas function independently as well as together.

Design 12634 1,308 Sq. Ft. - First Floor
1,047 Sq. Ft. - Second Floor; 32,600 Cu. Ft.

● The second floor of this fine home overhangs the first floor. Four bedrooms and two baths are located here. This home will be an outstanding investment.

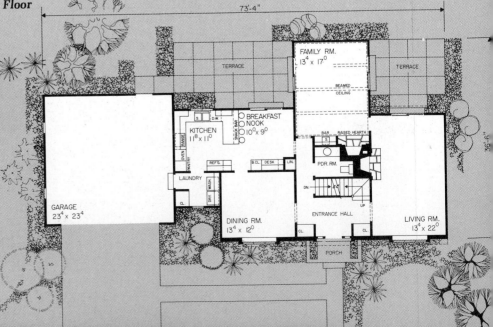

Design 12108
1,188 Sq. Ft. - First Floor
720 Sq. Ft. - Second Floor; 27,394 Cu. Ft.

● This design features a full two-story section flanked by one-story wings. The livability offered in this home is interesting and practical. It has separated the functions to assure convenient living.

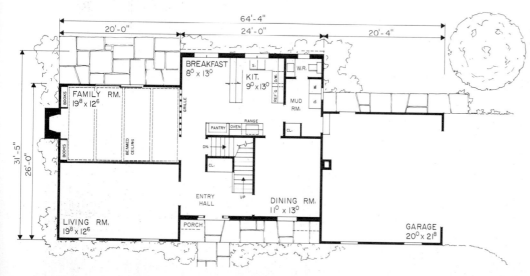

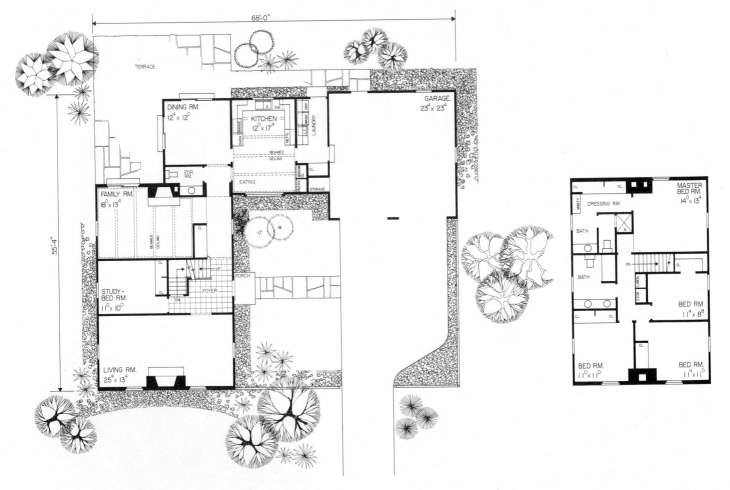

Design 12609 *1,543 Sq. Ft. - First Floor; 1,005 Sq. Ft. - Second Floor; 36,800 Cu. Ft.*

● Here is a picturesque L-shaped two-story with a variety of features that help recall the architectural charm of Colonial America. Observe the massive twin chimneys, the attractive contrasting exterior materials, the delightful window and door treatment, the cupola and the picket fence. The front court yard is a pleasant feature. The interior is designed for real family living. Four bedrooms, two full baths and plenty of closets provide excellent sleeping facilities. The large, formal end living room will enjoy its privacy. A study provides that often sought-after haven for the enjoyment of peace and quiet. Beamed ceilings are a highlight of the family room and kitchen. Don't miss the breakfast eating area, the separate dining room, the laundry and the stairs to the basement. Notice the bank of closets near the entrance from the garage. Of interest is the configuration of the rear terrace.

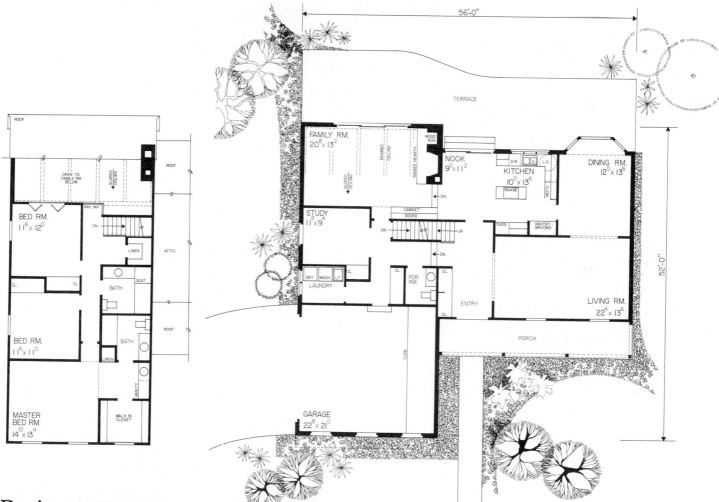

Design 12561 *1,655 Sq. Ft. - First Floor; 943 Sq. Ft. - Second Floor; 41,738 Cu. Ft.*

● A convenient living plan housed in a distinctively appealing exterior. This L-shaped design places the one-story portion at right angles to the two-story section. With the overhanging second floor and the large covered front porch, the result is noteworthy, indeed. Passing through the double front doors one immediately observes a fine functioning interior. Traffic patterns are efficient, but also flexible. The family room/study area is sunken a couple of steps below the level of the breakfast nook and entry. The open planning of the kitchen area, and between the living and dining rooms add to the spaciousness. Note the bay window of the dining room. The laundry and the strategically placed powder room are adjacent to the garage entrance. Study the upstairs and how it is open to the family room below. Those are folding doors that provide the bedroom with privacy.

Design 12535

986 Sq. Ft. - First Floor
1,436 Sq. Ft. - Second Floor; 35,835 Cu. Ft.

● What a great package this is! An enchanting Colonial exterior and an exceptional amount of interior livability. Utilizing the space over the garage results in a fifth bedroom with bath.

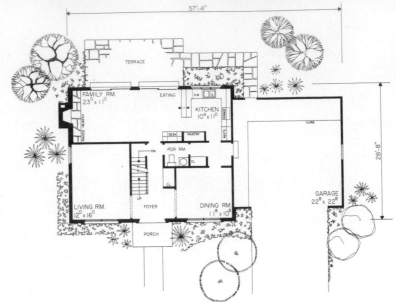

Design 12558

1,030 Sq. Ft. - First Floor
840 Sq. Ft. - Second Floor; 27,120 Cu. Ft.

● This relatively low-budget house is long on exterior appeal and interior livability. It has all the features to assure years of convenient living. Make a list of your favorite features.

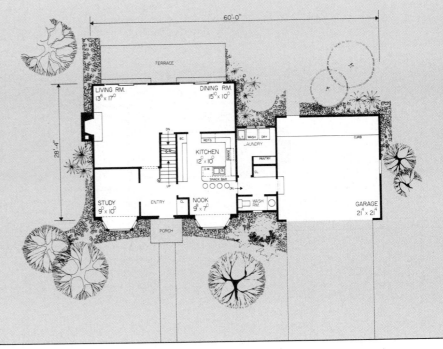

Design 12540

1,306 Sq. Ft. - First Floor
1,360 Sq. Ft. - Second Floor; 57,792 Cu. Ft.

● This efficient Colonial abounds in features. A spacious entry flanked by living areas. A kitchen flanked by eating areas. Upstairs, four bedrooms including a sitting room in the master suite.

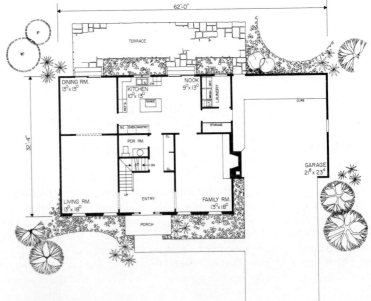

Design 12646
1,274 Sq. Ft. - First Floor
1,322 Sq. Ft. - Second Floor; 42,425 Cu. Ft.

● What a stylish departure from today's usual architecture. This refreshing exterior may be referred to as Neo-Victorian. Its vertical lines, steep roofs and variety of gables remind one of the old Victorian houses of yesteryear. Inside, there is an efficiently working floor plan that is delightfully spacious.

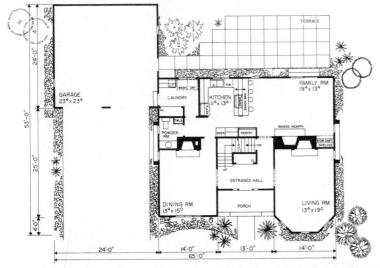

Design 12647 2,104 Sq. Ft. - First Floor; 1,230 Sq. Ft. - Second Floor; 56,395 Cu. Ft.

● Another Neo-Victorian, and what an impressive and unique design it is. Observe the roof lines, the window treatment, the use of contrasting exterior materials and the arched, covered front entrance.

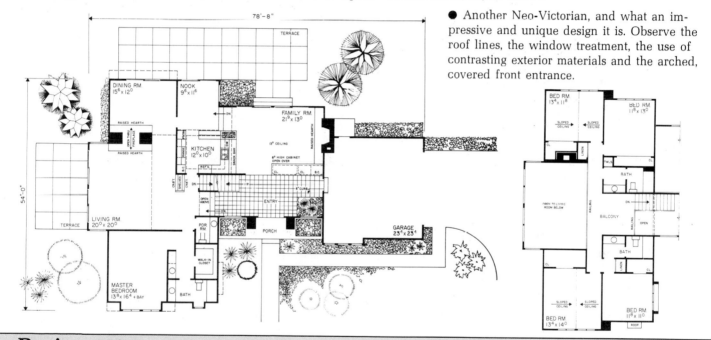

Design 12645 1,600 Sq. Ft. - First Floor; 1,305 Sq. Ft. - Second Floor
925 Sq. Ft. - Third Floor; 58,355 Cu. Ft.

● Reminiscent of the Gothic Victorian style of the mid-19th Century, this delightfully detailed, three-story house has a wrap-around veranda for summertime relaxing. The parlor and family room, each with fireplaces, provide excellent formal and informal living facilities. The third floor houses two more great areas plus bath.

● Here are three optional elevations that function with the same basic floor plan. No need to decide now which is your favorite since the blueprints for this design include details for each optional exterior.

If yours is a restricted building budget, your construction dollar could hardly return greater dividends in the way of exterior appeal and interior livability. Also, you won't need a big, expensive site on which to build.

In addition to the four bedrooms and 2½ baths, there are two living areas, two places for dining, a fireplace and a basement. Notice the fine accessibility of the rear outdoor terrace.

Design 12366
1,078 Sq. Ft. - First Floor
880 Sq. Ft. - Second Floor
27,242 Cu. Ft.

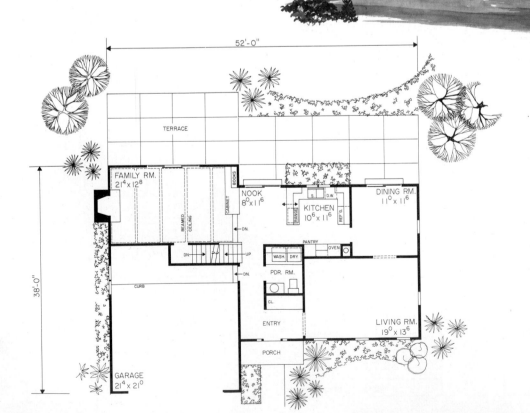

52'-0"

38'-0"

TERRACE

FAMILY RM.
21⁴ x 12⁸

BEAMED CEILING

CABINET

BOOKS

NOOK
8⁰ x 11⁶

KITCHEN
10⁶ x 11⁶

RANGE S DW

REF S

DINING RM.
11⁰ x 11⁶

DN.

DN. UP

DN.

PANTRY

WASH DRY

OVEN

PDR. RM.

CL

CURB

ENTRY

PORCH

LIVING RM.
19⁰ x 13⁶

GARAGE
21⁴ x 21⁰

BED RM.
10⁶ x 11⁴

BED RM.
10⁶ x 11⁴

CL

CL

CL

LINEN

DN.

BED RM.
10⁶ x 9⁰

BATH

S

BATH

MASTER
BED RM.
13¹⁰ x 13⁸

WALK-IN CLOSET

1½-Story Designs
An Optimum Return On Investment

Design 12174
1,506 Sq. Ft. - First Floor
1,156 Sq. Ft. - Second Floor
37,360 Cu. Ft.

● Your building budget could hardly buy more charm, or greater livability. The appeal of the exterior is wrapped up in a myriad of design features. They include: the interesting roof lines; the effective use of brick and horizontal siding; the delightful window treatment; the covered front porch; the chimney and dove-cote detailing. The livability of the interior is represented by a long list of convenient living features. There is a formal area consisting of a living room with fireplace and dining room. The family room has a raised hearth fireplace, wood box and beamed ceiling. Also on the first floor is a kitchen, laundry and bedroom with adjacent bath. Three bedrooms, lounge and two baths upstairs plus plenty of closets and bulk storage over garage. Don't overlook the sliding glass doors, the breakfast area and the basement. An excellent plan.

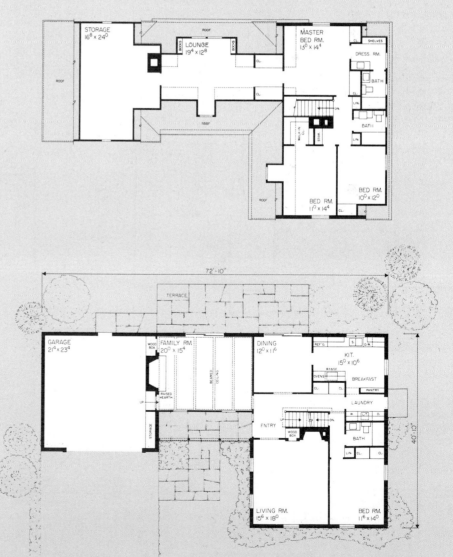

Design 12145

1,182 Sq. Ft. - First Floor
708 Sq. Ft. - Second Floor
28,303 Cu. Ft.

● Historically referred to as a "half house", this authentic adaptation has its roots in the heritage of New England. With completion of the second floor, the growing family doubles its sleeping capacity. Notice that the overall width of the house is only 44 feet. Take note of the covered porch leading to the garage and the flower court.

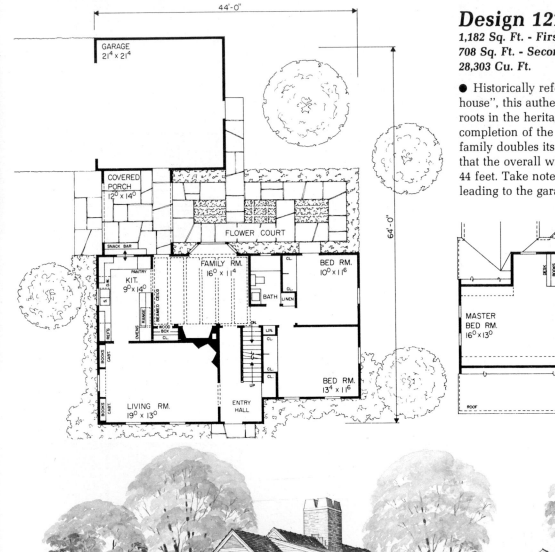

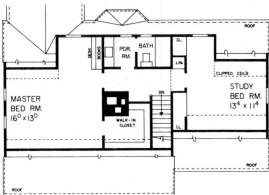

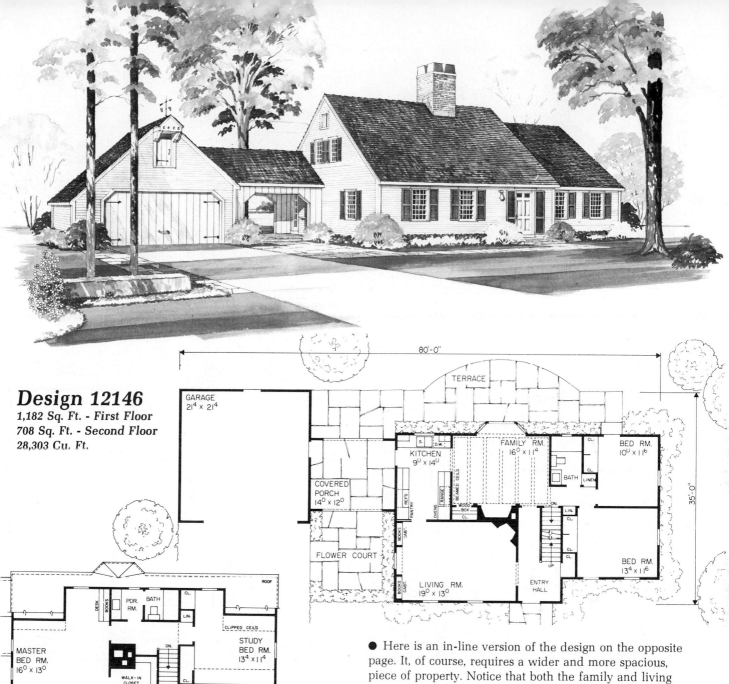

Design 12146

1,182 Sq. Ft. - First Floor
708 Sq. Ft. - Second Floor
28,303 Cu. Ft.

GARAGE 21⁴ x 21⁴

TERRACE

KITCHEN 9⁰ x 14⁰

FAMILY RM. 16⁰ x 11⁴

BED RM. 10⁰ x 11⁶

COVERED PORCH 14⁰ x 12⁰

BATH

LINEN

80'-0"

35'-0"

REFG

OVENS

RANGE

BEAMED CEIL'G

WOOD BOX

CL.

LIN.

CL.

UP

DN.

BED RM. 13⁴ x 11⁶

FLOWER COURT

BOOKS CAB'T

PANTRY

BOOKS CAB'T

LIVING RM. 19⁰ x 13⁰

ENTRY HALL

DESK

BOOKS

PDR. RM.

BATH

CL.

LIN.

ROOF

CLIPPED CEIL'G

MASTER BED RM. 16⁰ x 13⁰

WALK-IN CLOSET

DN.

CL.

STUDY BED RM. 13⁴ x 11⁴

ROOF

ROOF

● Here is an in-line version of the design on the opposite page. It, of course, requires a wider and more spacious, piece of property. Notice that both the family and living rooms have a fireplace. Don't overlook the many built-in units featured throughout the plan.

Design 11242 1,872 Sq. Ft. - First Floor
982 Sq. Ft. - Second Floor; 29,221 Cu. Ft.

● Here are three long, low one-and-a-half story designs with all the traditional charm one would wish for a new home. The floor plans offer all the livability an active family would want. Which is your favorite design?

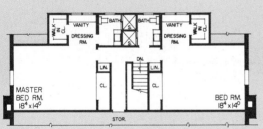

OPTIONAL NON-BASEMENT

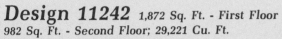

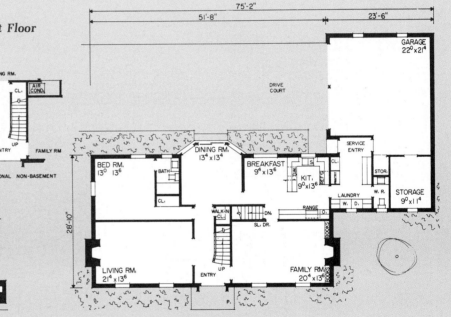

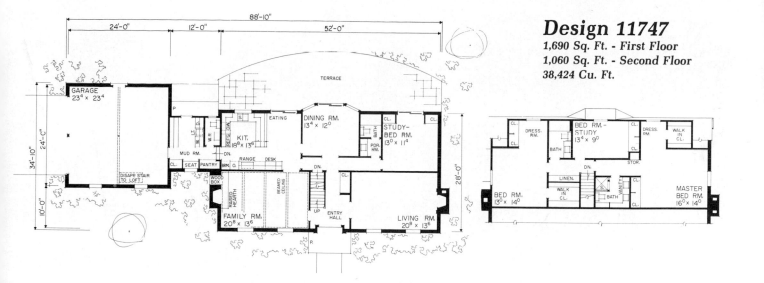

Design 11747

1,690 Sq. Ft. - First Floor
1,060 Sq. Ft. - Second Floor
38,424 Cu. Ft.

Design 11906

1,514 Sq. Ft. - First Floor
992 Sq. Ft. - Second Floor
37,311 Cu. Ft.

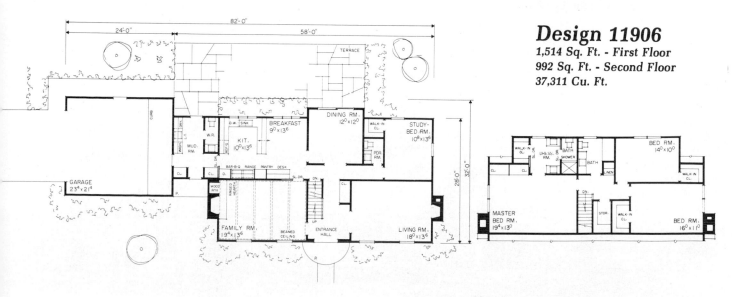

Design 12615
2,563 Sq. Ft. - First Floor
552 Sq. Ft. - Second Floor; 59,513 Cu. Ft.

● The exterior detailing of this design recalls 18th-Century New England architecture. Enter by way of the centered front door and you are greeted into the foyer. Directly to the right is the study or optional bedroom or to the left is the living room. This large formal room features sliding glass doors to the sun-drenched solarium. The beauty of the solarium will be appreciated from the master bedroom and the dining room along with the living room.

● Can't you picture this dramatic home sitting on your property? The curving front drive is impressive as it passes the walks to the front door and the service entrance. The roof masses, the centered masonry chimney, the window symmetry and the 108 foot expanse across the front are among the features that make this a distinctive home. Of interest arc thc living and family rooms — both similar in size and each having its own fireplace.

Floor plan labels

108'-0"
24'-0" 20'-0" 36'-0" 28'-0"
16'-0"
16'-0"
64'-5"
28'-0"

POOL 36⁰ x 20⁰

TERRACE

STOR
COOKING
POOL HOUSE
STOR.
GATE

STORAGE

BED RM. 11⁸ x 12⁰   BED RM. 11⁰ x 15⁸
CL   CL

BATH   BED RM. 11⁰ x 13⁶
BATH

CL   LAUNDRY   BREAKFAST 11⁰ x 10⁰
W   D

KIT. 11⁴ x 15⁰
DW   S
REFG.

FAMILY RM. 23⁸ x 14⁴

UP
CL

LIN   CL   CHEST   CL
CL
CL

PDR. RM.
DN   PORCH   STOR

PANTRY
BAR-B-Q   RANGE
O
CHINA   WOOD BOX   RAISED HEARTH   STORAGE

ENTRY HALL

BED RM. 17⁰ x 11⁴

GARAGE 23⁴ x 27⁴

DINING RM. 11⁸ x 14⁴   LIVING RM. 23⁴ x 14⁰   PORCH

Second floor plan

STUDY - LOUNGE 16⁴ x 12⁴

BOOKS
DN.
LIN.

STORAGE

MASTER BED RM. 15⁰ x 21⁶   DRESSING RM.   BATH
CL   CL

Design 11787
2,656 Sq. Ft. - First Floor
744 Sq. Ft. - Second Floor
51,164 Cu. Ft.

207

Design 12520
1,419 Sq. Ft. - First Floor
1,040 Sq. Ft. - Second Floor
39,370 Cu. Ft.

● From Tidewater Virginia comes this historic adaptation, a positive reminder of the charm of Early American architecture. Note how the center entrance gives birth to fine traffic circulation. List the numerous features.

Design 11970

1,664 Sq. Ft. - First Floor
1,116 Sq. Ft. - Second Floor
41,912 Cu. Ft.

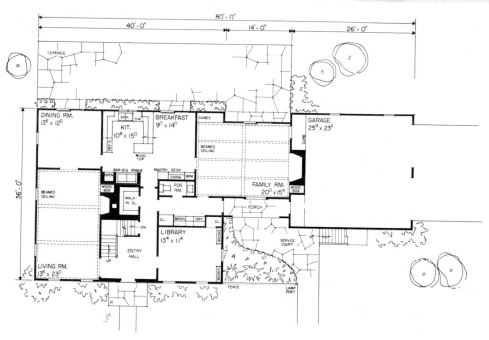

● The prototype of this Colonial house was an integral part of the 18th-Century New England landscape; the updated version is a welcome addition to any suburban scene. The main entry wing, patterned after a classic Cape Cod cottage design, is two stories high but has a pleasing groundhugging look. The steeply pitched roof, triple dormers, and a massive central chimney anchor the house firmly to its site. Entry elevation is symmetrically balanced; doorway, middle dormer, and chimney are in perfect alignment. The one story wing between the main house and the garage is a spacious, beam-ceilinged family room with splay-walled entry porch at the front elevation and sliding glass windows at the rear opening to terrace, which is the full length of the house.

● A versatile plan, wrapped in a pleasing traditional facade, to cater to the demands of even the most active of families. There is plenty of living space for both formal and informal activities. With two bedrooms upstairs and two down, sleeping accommodations are excellently planned to serve all.

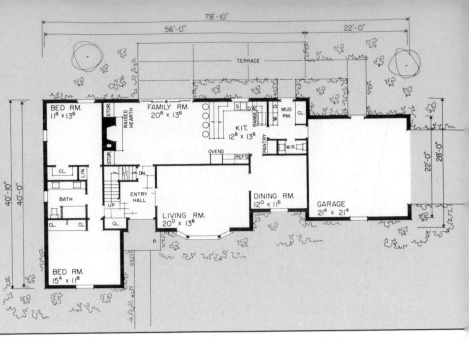

● A great plan! The large family will find its living requirements satisfied admirably all throughout those active years of growing up. This would make a fine expansible house. The upstairs may be finished off as the size of the family increases and budget permits. Complete living requirements can be obtained on the first floor.

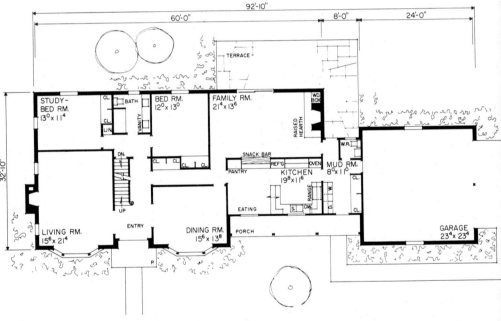

● A study of the first and second floors of this charming design will reveal that nothing has been omitted to assure convenient living. List your family's living requirements and then observe how this house will proceed to satisfy them. Features galore.

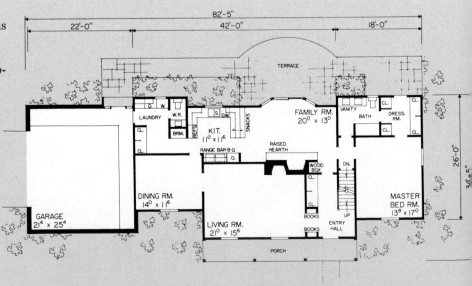

Design 11790 1,782 Sq. Ft. - First Floor; 920 Sq. Ft. - Second Floor; 37,359 Cu. Ft.

Design 11793 1,986 Sq. Ft. - First Floor; 944 Sq. Ft. - Second Floor; 35,800 Cu. Ft.

Design 11736 1,618 Sq. Ft. - First Floor; 952 Sq. Ft. - Second Floor; 34,106 Cu. Ft.

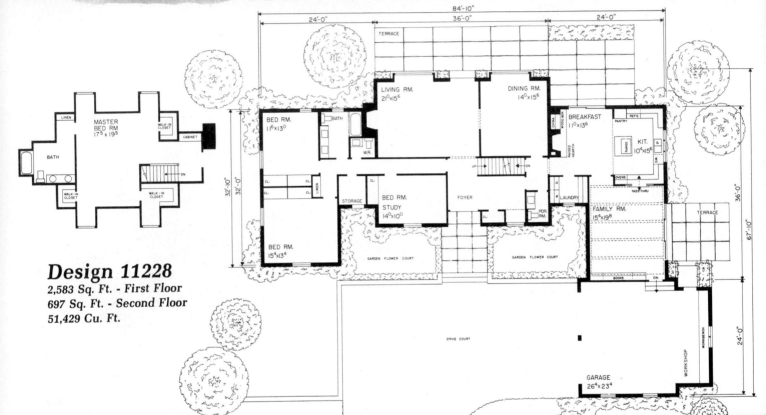

TERRACE

84'-10"

24'-0" 36'-0" 24'-0"

LIVING RM.
21⁰x15⁶

DINING RM.
14⁰x15⁶

BREAKFAST
11⁰x13⁶

PANTRY

REF'G

CHINA

KIT.
10⁴x15⁶

BED RM.
11⁶x13⁰

BATH

W.R.

RANGE

WOOD BOX

RAISED HEARTH

UP

DN

OVENS

PASS-THRU

DW.

32'-0"

CL.

CL.

LINEN

STORAGE

BED RM. STUDY
14⁰x10⁰

FOYER

CL.

CL.

LAUNDRY

PDR. RM.

FAMILY RM.
15⁴x19⁸

TERRACE

36'-0"

67'-10"

BED RM.
15⁴x13⁴

GARDEN FLOWER COURT

GARDEN FLOWER COURT

BOOKS

DN.

MASTER BED RM.
17⁵x19⁵

LINEN

WALK-IN CLOSET

CABINET

BATH

WALK-IN CLOSET

DN

WALK-IN CLOSET

DRIVE COURT

WORKSHOP

WORKBENCH

24'-0"

GARAGE
26⁴x23⁴

Design 11228

2,583 Sq. Ft. - First Floor
697 Sq. Ft. - Second Floor
51,429 Cu. Ft.

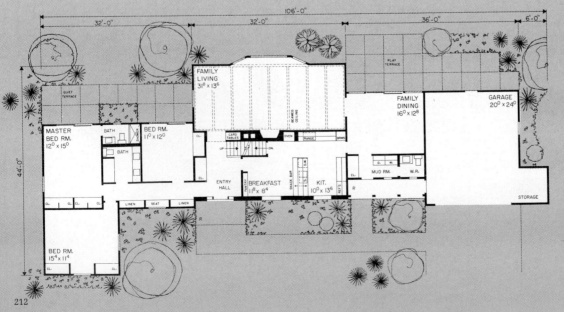

106'-0"

32'-0" 32'-0" 36'-0" 6'-0"

PLAY TERRACE

QUIET TERRACE

FAMILY LIVING
31⁸x13⁶

BEAMED CEILING

FAMILY DINING
16⁰x12⁸

GARAGE
20⁰x24⁰

MASTER BED RM.
12⁰x15⁰

BATH

BATH

BED RM.
11⁰x12⁰

CL.

CARD TABLES

OVEN

RANGE

BRM.

MUD RM.

W.R.

44'-0"

UP

DN

D.

W.

CL.

ENTRY HALL

PANTRY

BREAKFAST
11⁸x8⁴

SNACK BAR

D.W.

KIT.
10⁰x13⁶

REF'G

R

STORAGE

CL.

CL.

CL.

LINEN

SEAT

LINEN

R

BED RM.
15⁴x11⁴

CL.

CL.

STUDIO BED RM.
16⁴x11⁶

ALCOVE

CL.

CL.

DN

LINEN

DRESSING

BATH

ATTIC STORAGE

Design 11106

1,997 Sq. Ft. - First Floor
498 Sq. Ft. - Second Floor
37,678 Cu. Ft.

212

First floor plan (labels)

100'-10"

72'-10"

PORCH

AREAWAY FOR BASEMENT WINDOWS

PORCH

FAMILY RM.
21⁴ x 15⁶

LIVING RM.
24⁰ x 15⁶

MASTER
BED RM.
15⁸ x 15⁶

CHEST

VANITY

DRESSING RM.

BATH

OVEN

KIT.
16⁰ x 14⁸

RANGE

WOOD BOX

RAISED HEARTH

WOOD BOX

BATH

VANITY

SNACK BAR

LINEN

ENTRANCE HALL

LINEN

REF'G   FREEZER

DESK   PANTRY

CL.

BATH

POWDER ROOM

COAT ROOM

VESTIBULE

BED RM.-
STUDY
15⁸ x 11⁰

BED RM.
15⁰ x 12⁸

DINING RM.
17⁸ x 13⁶

D. W.

MAID'S RM.
9⁶ x 13⁶

LAUNDRY
11⁰ x 8⁰

IRONER

PORCH

GARAGE
23⁴ x 26⁴

Design 11060
3,190 Sq. Ft. - First Floor
1,024 Sq. Ft. - Second Floor
52,189 Cu. Ft.

Second floor plan (labels)

LOUNGE
15⁸ x 13⁴

BOOKS

BOY'S
DORM
15⁸ x 20⁰

STUDY
8⁰ x 9⁶

GAMES

STORAGE

BOOKS

HI FI

STORAGE
15⁸ x 8⁰

BOOKS

VANITY

BATH

LINEN

WALK-IN CL.

WALK-IN CL.

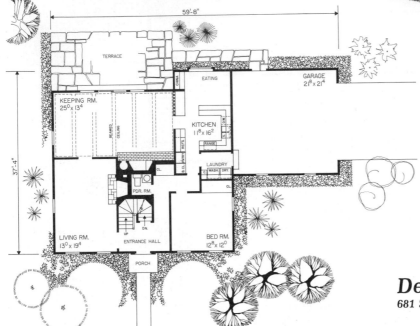

● From the island of Nantucket comes this unique 1¾-story cottage. This updated version of a style that was popular in the early 1700's has a charm all its own. The modern floor plan offers outstanding livability.

Design 12635 1,317 Sq. Ft. - First Floor
681 Sq. Ft. - Second Floor; 35,014 Cu. Ft.

● Another 1¾-story home - a type of house favored by many of Cape Cod's early whalers. The compact floor plan will be economical to build and surely an energy saver. An excellent house to finish-off in stages.

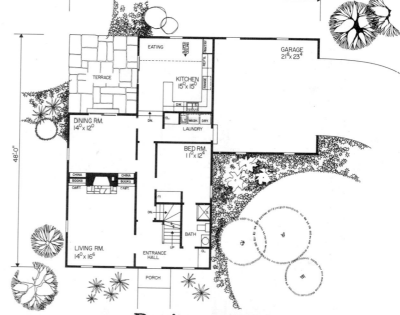

Design 12636 1,211 Sq. Ft. - First Floor
747 Sq. Ft. - Second Floor; 28,681 Cu. Ft.

Design 12718
1,941 Sq. Ft. - First Floor
791 Sq. Ft. - Second Floor; 49,895 Cu. Ft.

● You and your family will just love the new living patterns you'll experience in this story-and-a-half home. Livability will be equally as great on the second floor as well as the first.

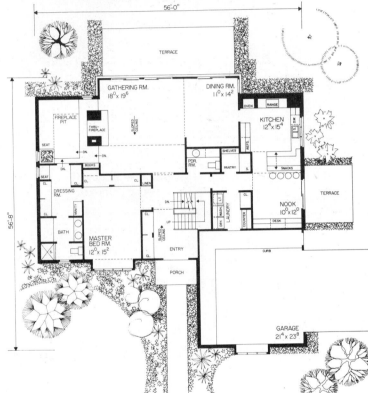

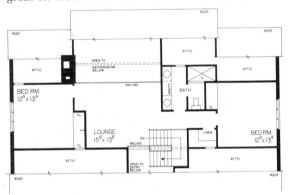

Design 11104
1,396 Sq. Ft. - First Floor
574 Sq. Ft. - Second Floor; 31,554 Cu. Ft.

● Here is a home whose front elevation makes one think of early New England. The frame exterior is highlighted by authentic double-hung windows with charming shutters; the attractive front entrance detail flanked by the traditional side lites and the projecting two-car garage with its appealing double doors.

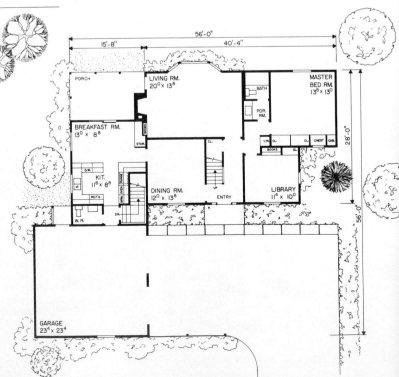

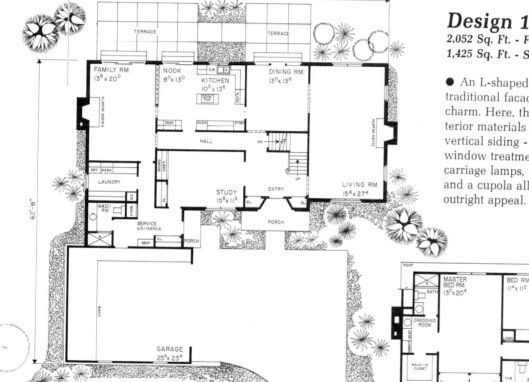

Design 12757

2,052 Sq. Ft. - First Floor
1,425 Sq. Ft. - Second Floor; 56,775 Cu. Ft.

● An L-shaped story-and-a-half with a traditional facade is hard to beat for pure charm. Here, the use of contrasting exterior materials - fieldstone, brick, vertical siding - along with delightful window treatment, recessed front door, carriage lamps, two massive chimneys and a cupola all make a contribution to outright appeal.

Design 12569

1,102 Sq. Ft. - First Floor
764 Sq. Ft. - Second Floor; 29,600 Cu. Ft.

● What an enchanting updated version of the popular Cape Cod cottage. There are facilities for both formal and informal living pursuits. Note first floor laundry.

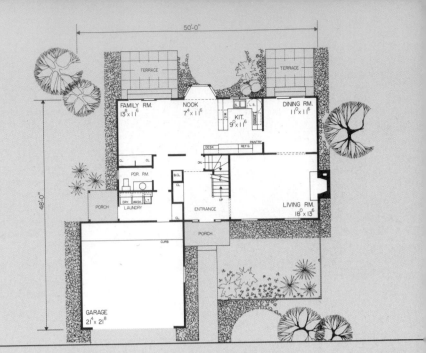

Design 12559

1,388 Sq. Ft. - First Floor
809 Sq. Ft. - Second Floor; 36,400 Cu. Ft.

● Imagine, a 26 foot living room with fireplace, a quiet study with built-in bookshelves and excellent dining facilities. Within such an appealing exterior, too.

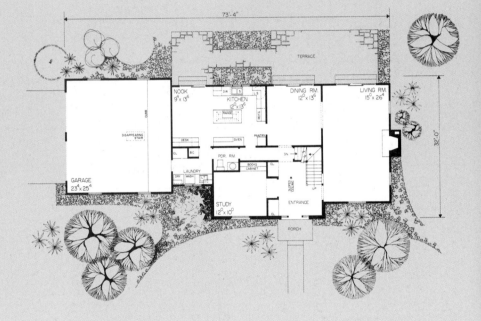

Design 12563

1,500 Sq. Ft. - First Floor
690 Sq. Ft. - Second Floor; 38,243 Cu. Ft.

● You'll have all kinds of fun deciding just how your family will function in this dramatically expanded half-house. There is lots of attic storage, too. Observe three-car garage.

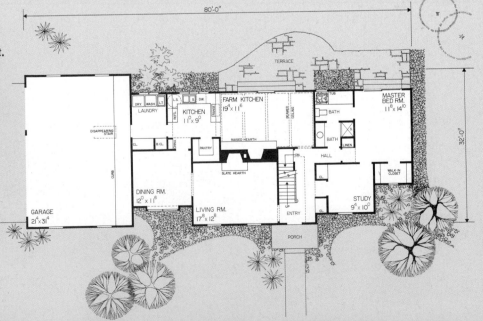

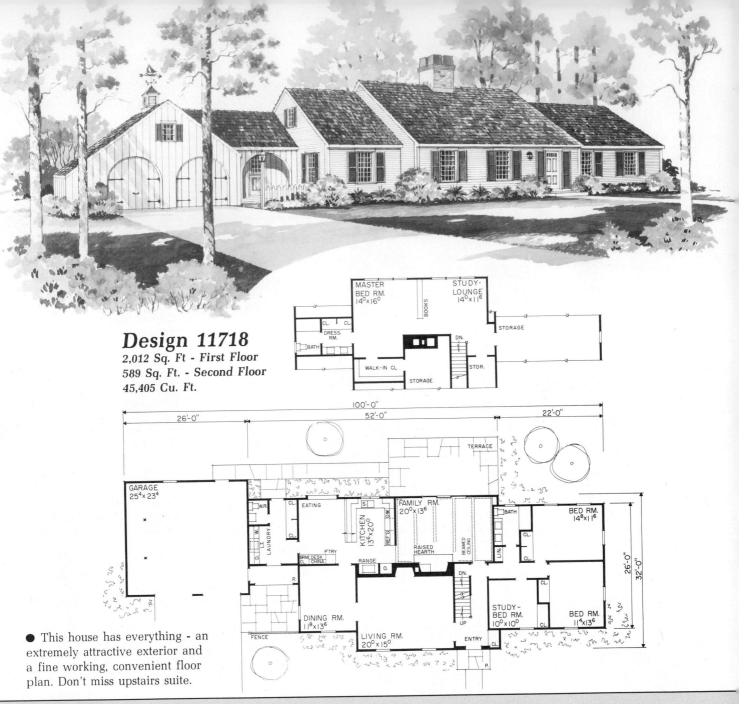

Design 11718

2,012 Sq. Ft - First Floor
589 Sq. Ft - Second Floor
45,405 Cu. Ft.

MASTER BED RM. 14⁰x16⁰
STUDY-LOUNGE 14⁰x11⁶
BOOKS
CL. CL.
DRESS. RM.
BATH
DN.
STORAGE
WALK-IN CL
STORAGE
STOR.

100'-0"
26'-0"   52'-0"   22'-0"

TERRACE

GARAGE 25⁴x 23⁴

W.R.
CL.
EATING
S.
FAMILY RM. 20⁰x13⁶
BATH
BED RM. 14⁸x11⁶

W.
LT.
D.
LAUNDRY
CL.
KITCHEN 13⁶x20⁰
REF'G
DW
RAISED HEARTH
BEAMED CEILING
CL.
LIN.
CL.

BRM
CL
DESK
CHINA
P'TRY
RANGE
O.
DN.
UP
STUDY-BED RM. 10⁰x10⁰
BED RM. 11⁴x13⁶

DINING RM. 11⁸x13⁶
LIVING RM. 20⁰x15⁰
ENTRY
CL.

FENCE
P.
P.

32'-0"
26'-0"

● This house has everything - an extremely attractive exterior and a fine working, convenient floor plan. Don't miss upstairs suite.

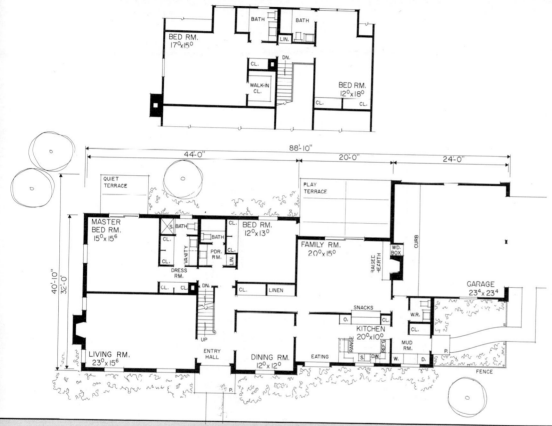

Design 11794

2,122 Sq. Ft. - First Floor
802 Sq. Ft. - Second Floor
37,931 Cu. Ft.

● The inviting warmth of this delightful story-and-a-half home catches the eye of even the most casual observer. Imagine, four big bedrooms! Formal and informal living can be enjoyed throughout this charming plan. Two fireplaces. One has a raised hearth and an adjacent wood box. A very private, formal dining room for those very special occasions. A U-shaped kitchen with pass-thru to family room. Note the two distinct rear terraces.

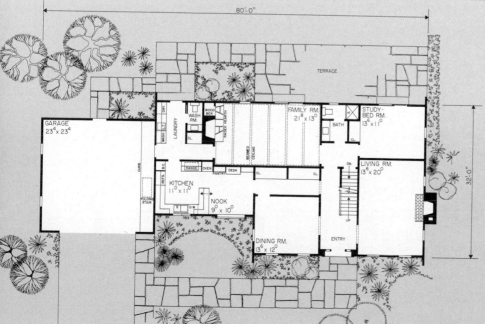

Design 11987

1,632 Sq. Ft. - First Floor
980 Sq. Ft. - Second Floor
35,712 Cu. Ft.

● The comforts of home will surely be endless and enduring when experienced and enjoyed in this Colonial adaptation. What's your favorite feature?

Design 11964

2,150 Sq. Ft. - First Floor
680 Sq. Ft. - Second Floor
39,927 Cu. Ft.

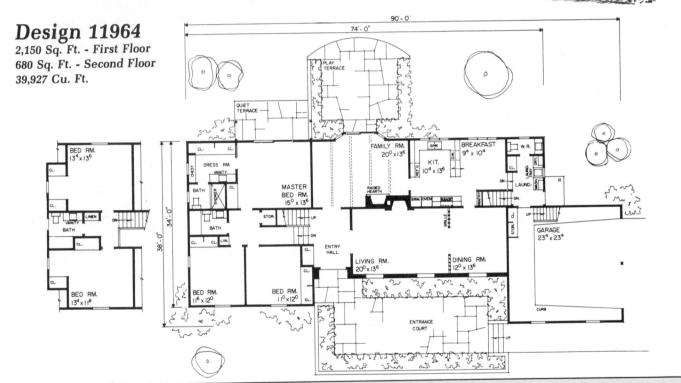

Design 11967

1,804 Sq. Ft. - First Floor
496 Sq. Ft. - Second Floor
40,173 Cu. Ft.

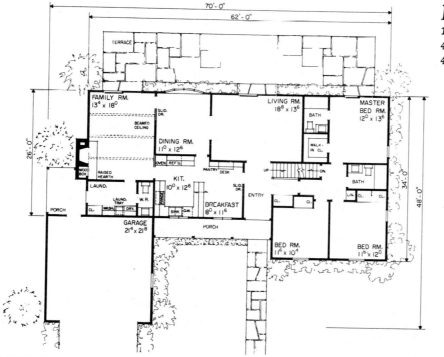

Design 11780

2,018 Sq. Ft. - First Floor
568 Sq. Ft. - Second Floor
37,586 Cu. Ft.

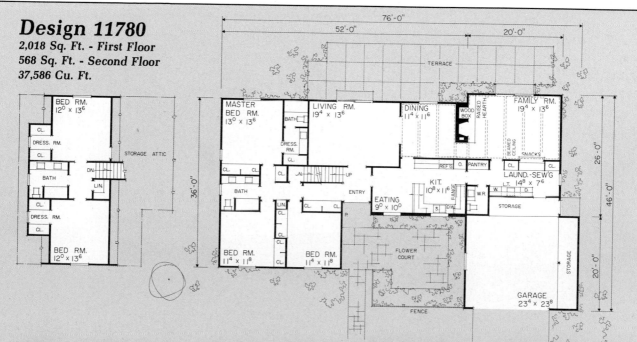

223

Design 12273

1,357 Sq. Ft. - First Floor
1,065 Sq. Ft. - Second Floor
38,303 Cu. Ft.

● Picture this as your new home. It will represent a most worthy lifetime investment. Its traditional charm will be ageless. Like 12279 on opposing page, note development of basement.

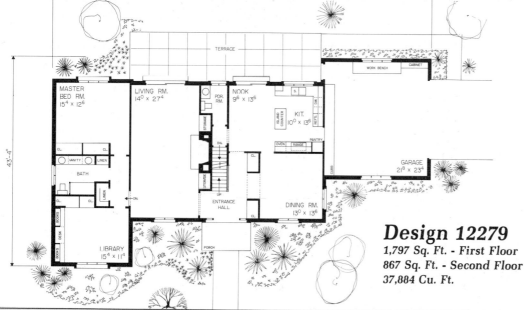

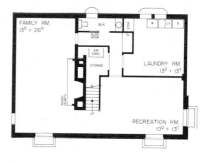

Design 12279

1,797 Sq. Ft. - First Floor
867 Sq. Ft. - Second Floor
37,884 Cu. Ft.

Design 12237

2,714 Sq. Ft. - First Floor
1,010 Sq. Ft. - Second Floor
55,719 Cu. Ft.

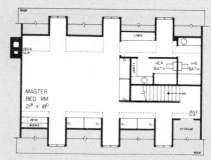

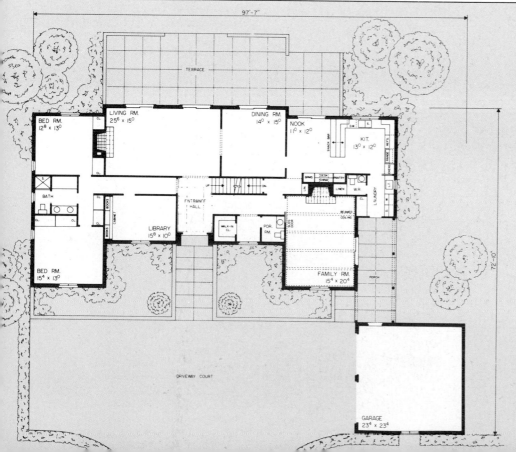

● Here is a gracious country-estate home with unsurpassed distinction outside, plus unexcelled convenience and livability inside.

Design 12286

1,496 Sq. Ft. - First Floor
751 Sq. Ft. - Second Floor
32,165 Cu. Ft.

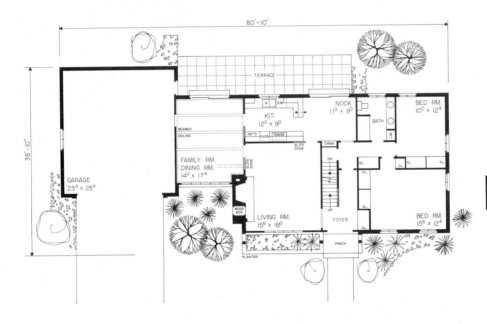

● A touch of Tudor styling houses four bedrooms, two baths and a sizeable family/dining room with a cozy beamed ceiling. Note access to rear terrace.

Design 12284

1,677 Sq. Ft. - First Floor
897 Sq. Ft. - Second Floor
40,413 Cu. Ft.

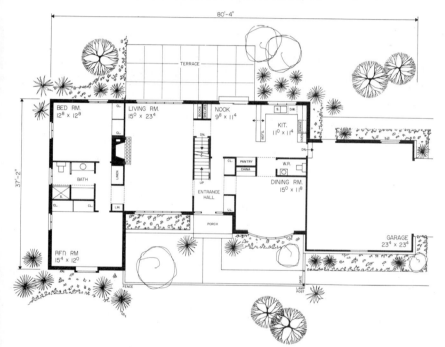

● This low-slung traditional design features four bedrooms plus three baths and a wash room. For family recreational and hobby space there is the basement.

Design 12285

1,118 Sq. Ft. - First Floor
821 Sq. Ft. - Second Floor
28,585 Cu. Ft.

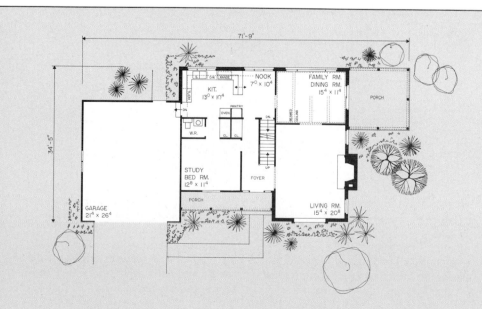

● An appealing home for the modest budget. There is exceptional livability for the average sized family. And there is plenty of flexibility. Note room use options on first floor.

Design 12342

2,824 Sq. Ft. - First Floor
1,013 Sq. Ft. - Second Floor
59,882 Cu. Ft.

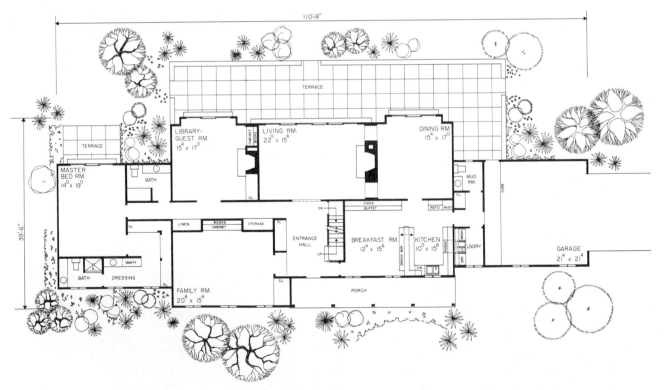

● A distinctive exterior characterized by varying roof planes, appealing window treatment, attractive chimneys and a covered front porch with prominent vertical columns. The main portion of the house is effectively balanced by the master bedroom wing on the one side and the garage wing on the other. As a buffer between house and garage is the mud room and the laundry. The kitchen is U-shaped, efficient, and strategically located to serve the breakfast and dining rooms. Notice how the rooms at the rear function through sliding glass doors with the outdoor terrace areas. Fireplaces highlight both the spacious living room and the large library. The big family room features built-in book shelve and cabinet. Upstairs, two bedrooms and a study alcove.

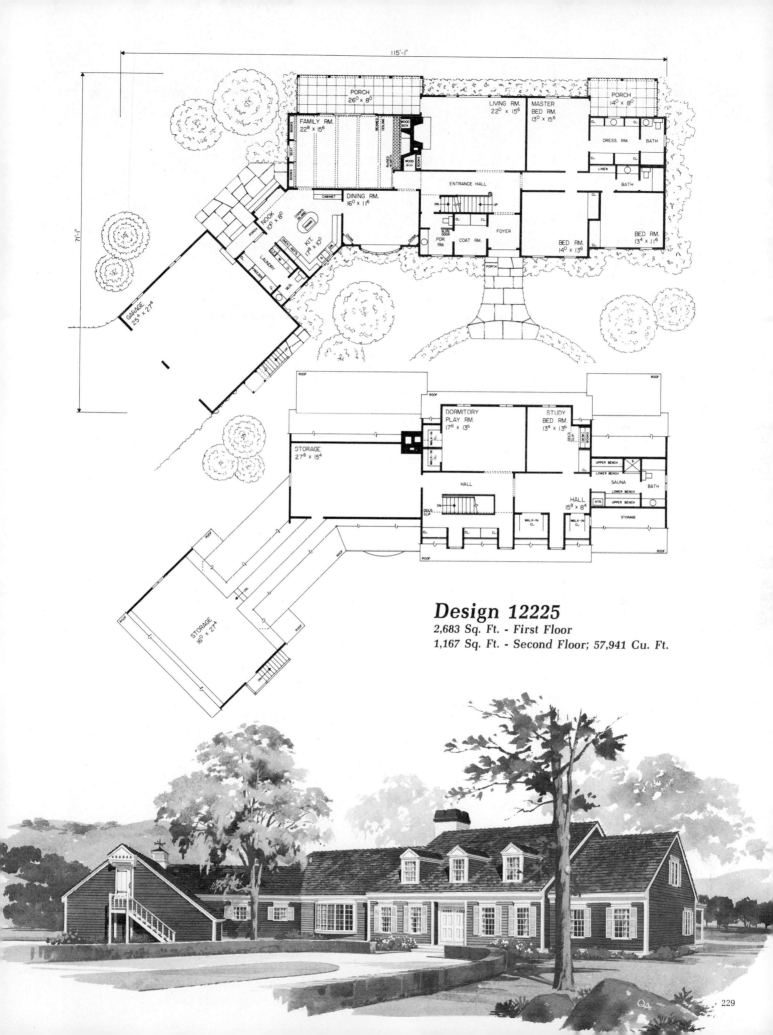

First Floor Plan Labels:

115'-1"

71'-1"

PORCH 26⁰ x 8⁰

FAMILY RM. 22⁸ x 15⁶

WOOD BOX

LIVING RM. 22⁰ x 15⁶

MASTER BED RM. 13⁰ x 15⁶

PORCH 14⁰ x 8⁰

DRESS. RM.

BATH

LINEN

BATH

DINING RM. 16⁰ x 11⁶

CABINET

ENTRANCE HALL

NOOK 10⁰ x 8⁰

COPPER ISLAND

KIT. 17⁸ x 10⁰

DN.

UP

FOYER

BED RM. 14⁰ x 13⁶

BED RM. 13⁴ x 11⁶

LAUNDRY

W.R.

PDR. RM.

COAT RM.

PORCH

GARAGE 25⁴ x 27⁴

Second Floor Plan Labels:

ROOF

ROOF

DORMITORY PLAY RM. 17⁸ x 13⁶

STUDY BED RM. 13⁴ x 13⁶

ROOF

STORAGE 27⁸ x 15⁴

WALK-IN

HALL

UPPER BENCH

LOWER BENCH

SAUNA

BATH

LOWER BENCH

HALL 15⁸ x 8⁴

HTR

UPPER BENCH

STORAGE

DN.

WALK-IN CL.

WALK-IN CL.

STORAGE

STORAGE 16⁰ x 27⁴

ROOF

ROOF

Design 12225
2,683 Sq. Ft. - First Floor
1,167 Sq. Ft. - Second Floor; 57,941 Cu. Ft.

Design 11766 1,638 Sq. Ft. - First Floor; 1,006 Sq. Ft. - Second Floor; 35,352 Cu. Ft.

● Here is a home that truly fits the description of traditional charm. The symmetry is, indeed, delightful. A certain magnetic aura seems to reach out with a whisper of welcome. Observe the spacious family-kitchen area, the study, the separate dining room and the extra bath.

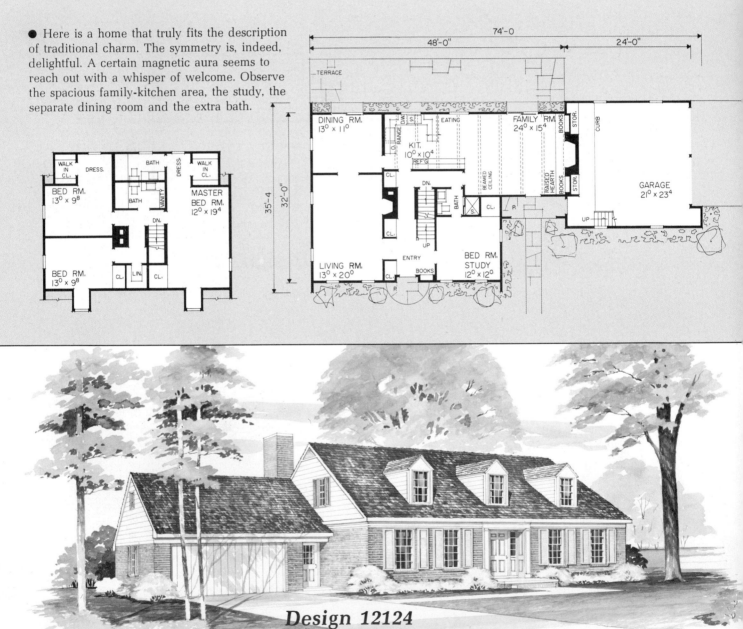

Design 12124
1,180 Sq. Ft. - First Floor
1,018 Sq. Ft. - Second Floor; 29,854 Cu. Ft.

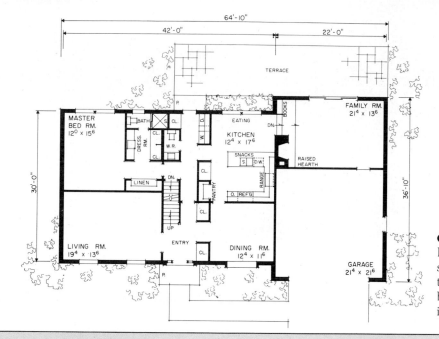

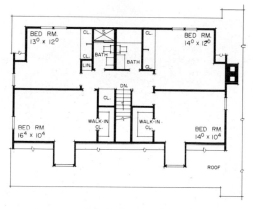

● This cozy home has over 2,600 square feet of livable floor area! And the manner in which this space to put to work to function conveniently for the large family is worth studying. Imagine five bedrooms, three full baths, living, dining and family rooms. Note large kitchen.

Design 11701 1,344 Sq. Ft. - First Floor; 948 Sq. Ft. - Second Floor; 33,952 Cu. Ft.

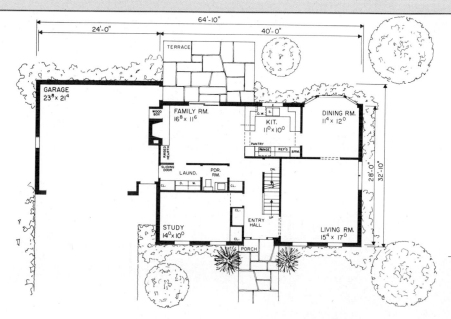

● Surely your list of favorite features will be fun to compile. It certainly will be a long one. The center entry hall helps establish excellent traffic patterns and good zoning. The formal living and dining rooms function well together, as do the kitchen and family room. Note laundry and study.

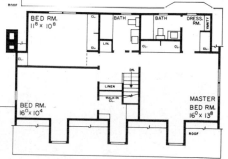

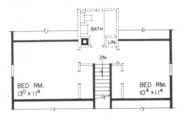

Design 11372

768 Sq. Ft. - First Floor
432 Sq. Ft. - Second Floor
17,280 Cu. Ft.

● Low cost livability could hardly ask for more. Here, is an enchanting exterior and a four bedroom floor plan. Note stairs to basement.

Design 12162

741 Sq. Ft. - First Floor
504 Sq. Ft. - Second Floor
17,895 Cu. Ft.

● This economical design delivers great exterior appeal and fine livability. In addition to kitchen eating space there is a separate dining room.

Design 11394

832 Sq. Ft. - First Floor
512 Sq. Ft. - Second Floor
18,453 Cu. Ft.

● The growing family with a restricted building budget will find this a great investment - a convenient living floor plan inside an attractive facade.

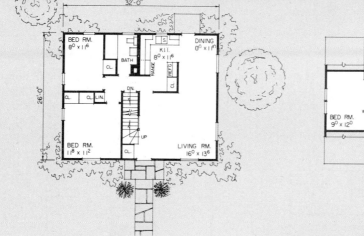

Design 12510

1,191 Sq. Ft. - First Floor
533 Sq. Ft. - Second Floor
27,500 Cu. Ft.

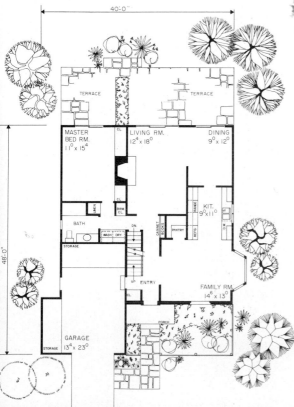

● The pleasant in-line kitchen is flanked by a separate dining room and a family room. The master bedroom is on the first floor with two more bedrooms upstairs.

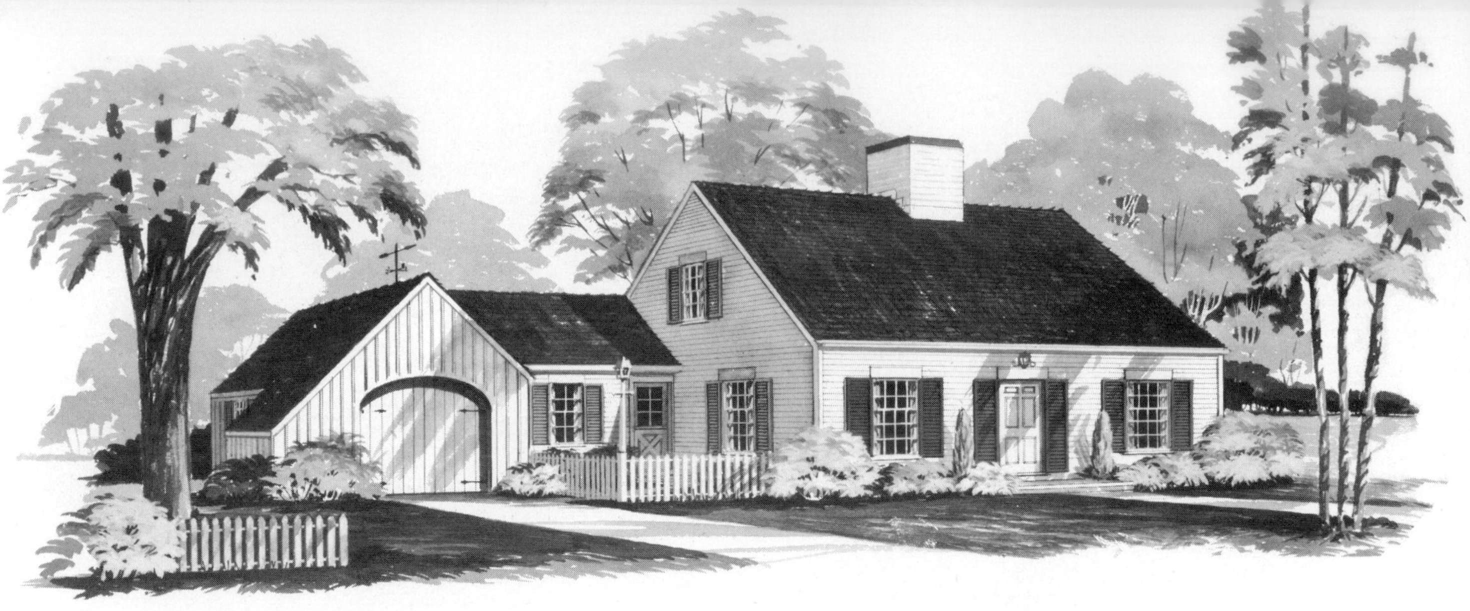

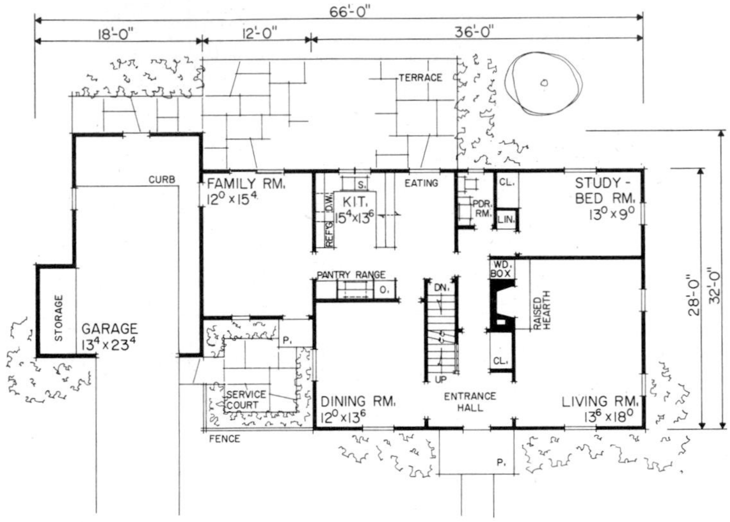

66'-0"
18'-0"
12'-0"
36'-0"
TERRACE
CURB
FAMILY RM.
12⁰x15⁴
S.
EATING
KIT.
15⁴x13⁶
D.W.
REF'G.
PDR. RM.
CL.
LIN.
STUDY-BED RM.
13⁰x9⁰
PANTRY RANGE
O.
DN.
WD. BOX
RAISED HEARTH
28'-0"
32'-0"
STORAGE
GARAGE
13⁴x23⁴
P.
SERVICE COURT
UP
CL.
DINING RM.
12⁰x13⁶
ENTRANCE HALL
LIVING RM.
13⁶x18⁰
FENCE
P.

● Colonial charm could hardly be more appealingly captured than it is by this winsome design. List the features and study the living patterns.

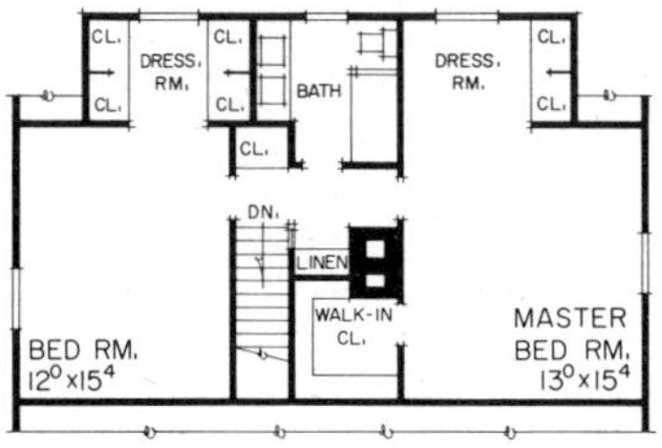

CL.
DRESS. RM.
CL.
BATH
DRESS. RM.
CL.
CL.
CL.
CL.
CL.
DN.
LINEN
WALK-IN CL.
BED RM.
12⁰x15⁴
MASTER BED RM.
13⁰x15⁴

Design 11901

1,200 Sq. Ft. - First Floor
744 Sq. Ft. - Second Floor; 27,822 Cu. Ft.

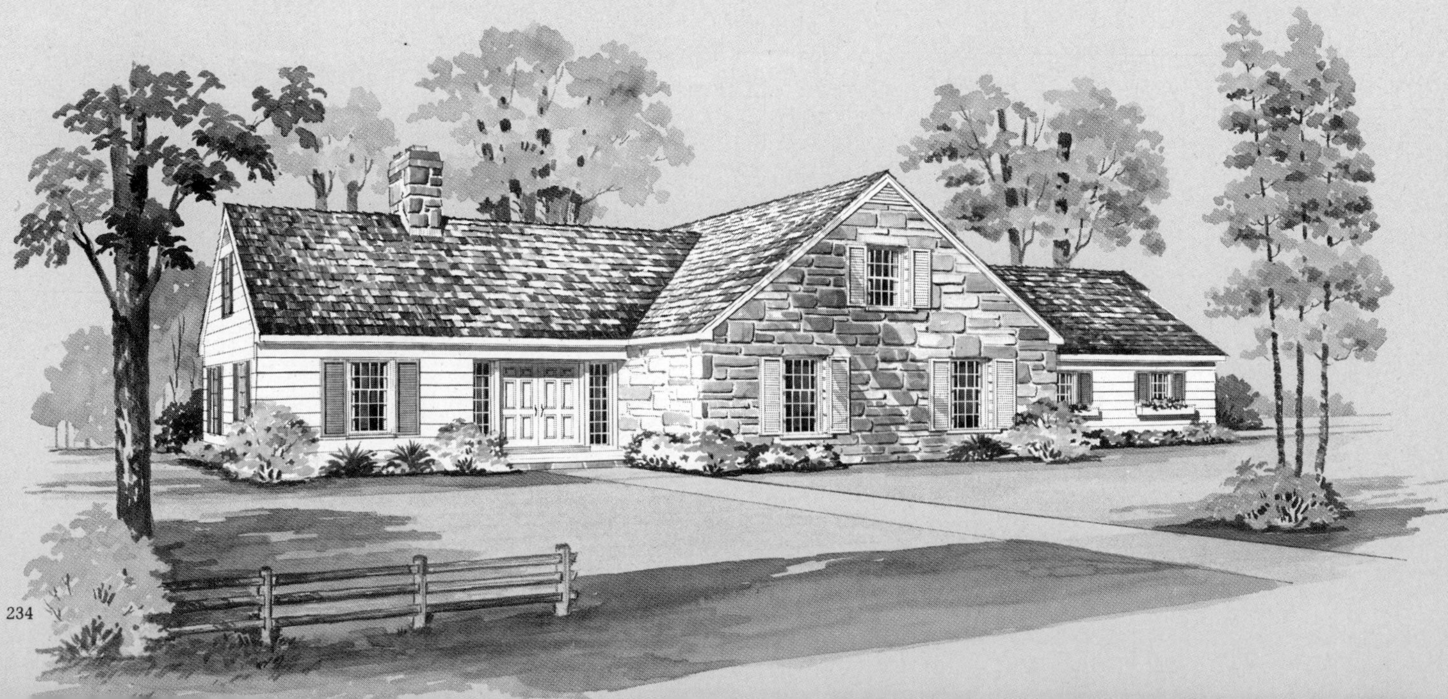

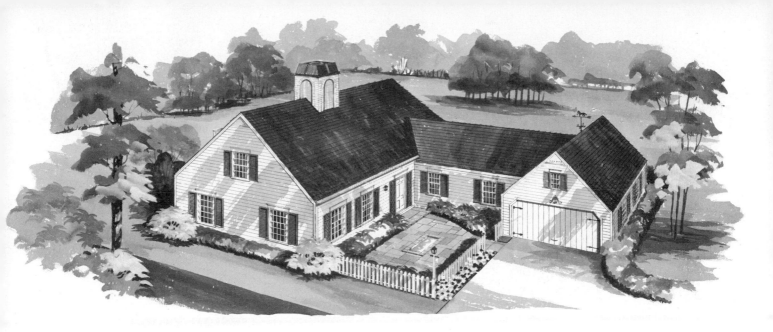

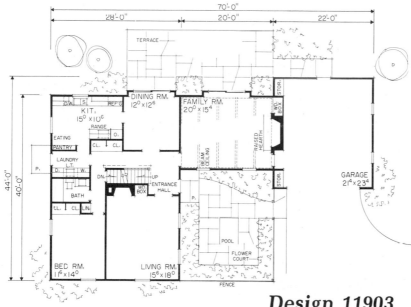

● Picturesque, indeed. This L-shaped one-and-a-half story home would attract its full share of attention even on Cape Cod. Study the excellent plan.

TERRACE

KIT.
15⁰ x 10⁶

DINING RM.
12⁰ x 12⁶

FAMILY RM.
20⁰ x 15⁴

STOR.

MASTER BED RM.
13⁸ x 14⁴

EATING

PANTRY

RANGE

O.

CL.

CL.

VANITY

CL.

LAUNDRY
L.T.

D.

W.

BEAM CEILING

RAISED HEARTH

DRESS. RM.

BATH

LIN.

BATH

DN.

UP

ENTRANCE HALL

WD. BOX

GARAGE
21⁴ x 23⁴

WALK-IN CL.

BATH

CL.

LIN.

BED RM.
11⁶ x 14⁰

LIVING RM.
15⁶ x 18⁰

POOL

FLOWER COURT

FENCE

BED RM.
10⁰ x 12⁰

BED RM.
11⁰ x 14⁴

Design 11903

1,460 Sq. Ft. - First Floor; 854 Sq. Ft. - Second Floor; 32,647 Cu. Ft.

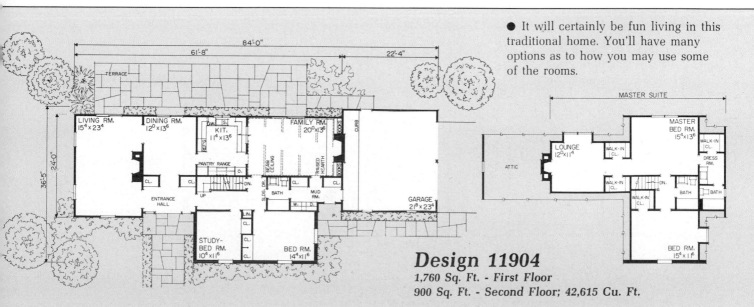

● It will certainly be fun living in this traditional home. You'll have many options as to how you may use some of the rooms.

TERRACE

LIVING RM.
15⁴ x 23⁴

DINING RM.
12⁰ x 13⁶

KIT.
11⁴ x 13⁶

FAMILY RM.
20⁰ x 13⁶

CURB

MASTER SUITE

PANTRY RANGE

O.

CL.

BEAM CEILING

RAISED HEARTH

ENTRANCE HALL

UP

DN.

SLDG. DR.

BATH

MUD RM.

W.

D.

GARAGE
21⁸ x 23⁴

ATTIC

LOUNGE
12⁰ x 11⁴

WALK-IN CL.

MASTER BED RM.
15⁴ x 13⁶

WALK-IN CL.

DRESS. RM.

STUDY-BED RM.
10⁴ x 11⁶

BED RM.
14⁴ x 11⁶

WALK-IN CL.

DN.

BATH

BATH

BED RM.
15⁴ x 11⁶

Design 11904

1,760 Sq. Ft. - First Floor
900 Sq. Ft. - Second Floor; 42,615 Cu. Ft.

Design 21365
975 Sq. Ft. - First Floor
583 Sq. Ft. - Second Floor
20,922 Cu. Ft.

● Here are three wonderfully livable houses. Each provides facilities to function as either three or four bedroom, two bath homes. Compare each of the three designs. Consider them in light of your building budget and your family's living requirements. Whichever design you choose it will be a credit to your family's design taste.

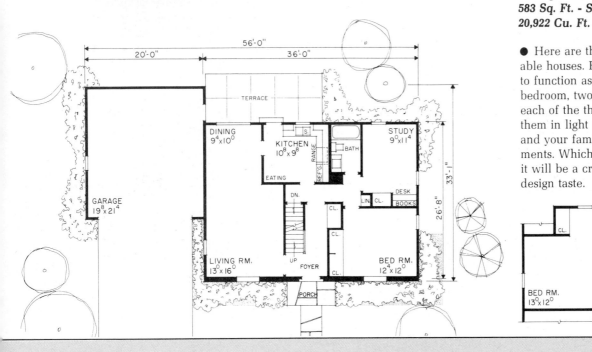

Design 12395
1,481 Sq. Ft. - First Floor
861 Sq. Ft. - Second Floor
34,487 Cu. Ft.

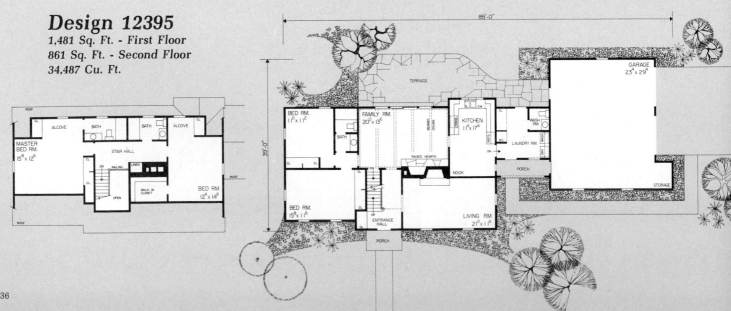

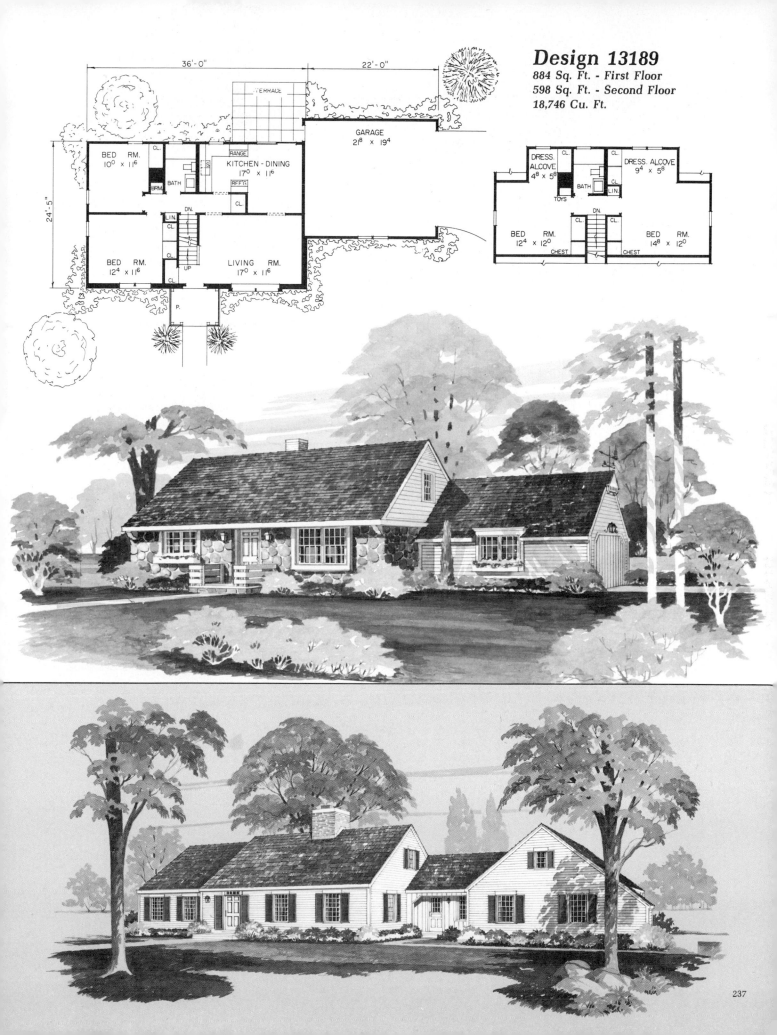

Design 13189

884 Sq. Ft. - First Floor
598 Sq. Ft. - Second Floor
18,746 Cu. Ft.

36'-0" 22'-0"

TERRACE

GARAGE
21⁸ x 19⁴

BED RM.
10⁰ x 11⁶

CL.

RANGE

KITCHEN - DINING
17⁰ x 11⁶

BATH

BRM

REF'G

24'-5"

DN.

LIN
CL.

CL.

BED RM.
12⁴ x 11⁶

CL.

LIVING RM.
17⁰ x 11⁶

UP

CL.

P.

DRESS.
ALCOVE
4⁸ x 5⁸

CL.

CL.

DRESS. ALCOVE
9⁴ x 5⁸

BATH

TOYS

LIN.

DN.

CL.

CL.

BED RM.
12⁴ x 12⁰

CHEST

BED RM.
14⁸ x 12⁰

CHEST

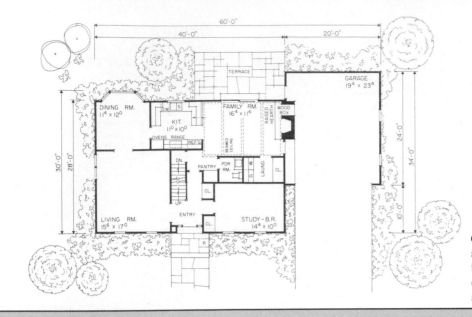

Design 11791

1,157 Sq. Ft. - First Floor
875 Sq. Ft. - Second Floor
27,790 Cu. Ft.

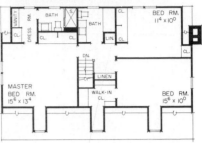

● Wherever you build this moderately sized house an aura of Cape Cod is sure to unfold. The symmetry is pleasing, indeed. The authenic center entrance seems to project a beckoning call.

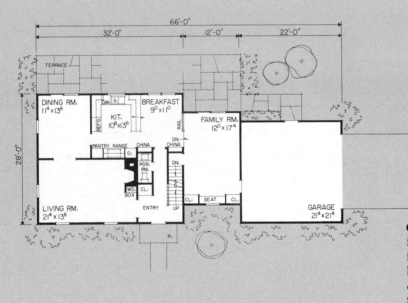

Design 11870

1,136 Sq. Ft. - First Floor
936 Sq. Ft. - Second Floor
26,312 Cu. Ft.

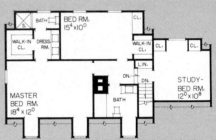

● Besides an enchanting exterior, this home has formal dining and living rooms, plus informal family and breakfast rooms. Built-ins are located in both of these informal rooms. U-shaped, the kitchen will efficiently service both of the dining areas. Study the sleeping facilities of the second floor.

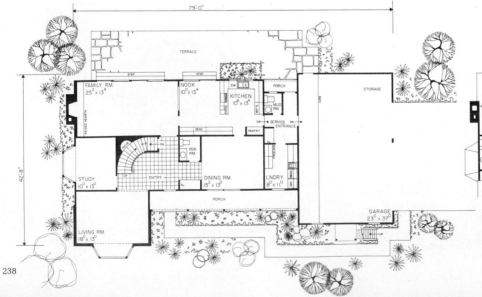

Design 12513

1,799 Sq. Ft. - First Floor
1,160 Sq. Ft. - Second Floor
47,461 Cu. Ft.

● What an appealing story-and-a-half design. Delightful, indeed, is the colonial detailing of the garage. The large entry hall with its open curving staircase is dramatic.

239

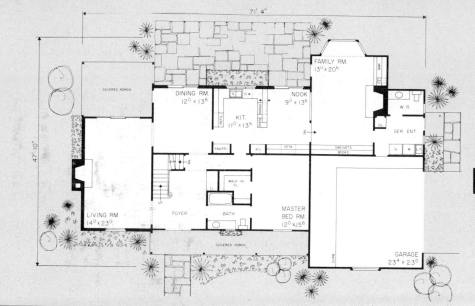

Design 12500

1,851 Sq. Ft. - First Floor
762 Sq. Ft. - Second Floor
43,052 Cu. Ft.

● The large family will enjoy the wonderful living patterns offered by this charming home. Don't miss the covered rear porch and the many features of the family room.

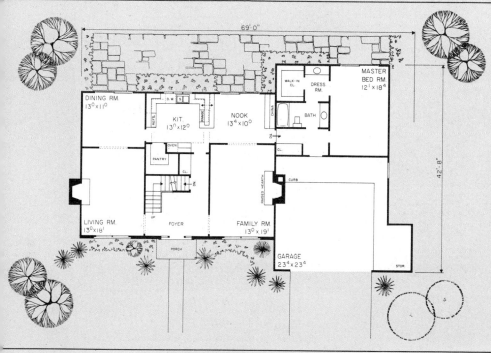

Design 12501

1,699 Sq. Ft. - First Floor
758 Sq. Ft. - Second Floor
37,693 Cu. Ft.

● Whether you build this inviting home with a fieldstone front, or substitute with a different material of your choice, you can be assured that you've selected a great home for your family.

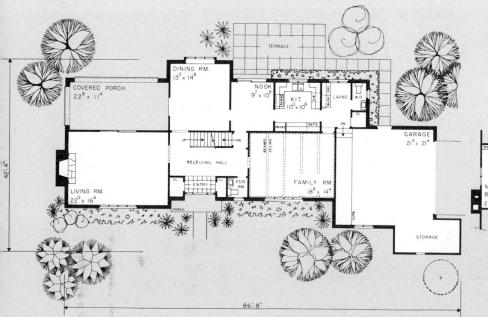

Design 12338

1,505 Sq. Ft. - First Floor
1,219 Sq. Ft. - Second Floor
38,878 Cu. Ft.

● A spacious receiving hall is a fine setting for the welcoming of guests. Here traffic flows effectively to all areas of the plan. Outstanding livability throughout the entire plan.

241

Design 12776

1,134 Sq. Ft. - First Floor
874 Sq. Ft. - Second Floor; 31,600 Cu. Ft.

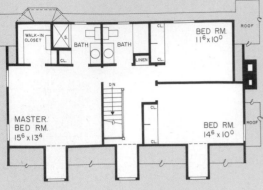

WALK-IN CLOSET
BATH
BATH
CL.
CL.
LINEN
CL.
BED RM.
11⁶ x 10⁰
ROOF
DN
MASTER BED RM.
15⁶ x 13⁴
CL.
CL.
BED RM.
14⁶ x 10⁰
ROOF

● The covered front porch of this one-and-a-half story will surely be a delight on those warm summer evenings. Basement included.

61'-4"
TERRACE
CURB
DINING RM. 11⁴ x 10⁰
KITCHEN 11⁰ x 10⁰
FAMILY RM. 16⁴ x 15⁶
OVEN RANGE REF'G
RAISED HEARTH
GARAGE 21⁰ x 21⁴
38'-0"
DN
UP
SERVICE ENTRANCE
LIVING RM. 15⁶ x 17⁰
ENTRANCE
BRM CL.
PDR. RM.
W.
D.
CL.
LAUNDRY
SEAT
CL.
PORCH

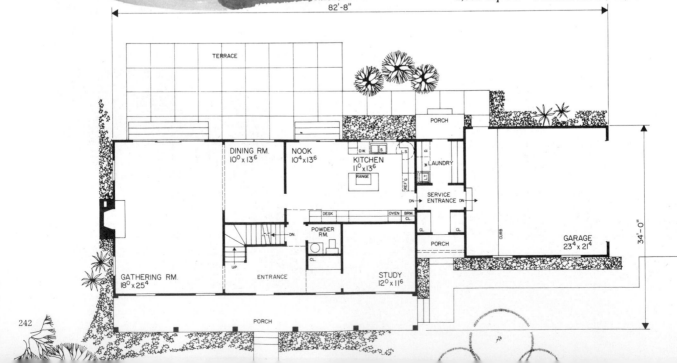

Design 12650

1,451 Sq. Ft. - First Floor
1,091 Sq. Ft. - Second Floor; 43,555 Cu. Ft.

82'-8"
TERRACE
PORCH
DINING RM. 10⁰ x 13⁶
NOOK 10⁴ x 13⁶
KITCHEN 11⁰ x 13⁶
RANGE
DW S
LS
LAUNDRY
D
REF'G
SERVICE ENTRANCE
DN
DN
CURB
GARAGE 23⁴ x 21⁴
34'-0"
DESK
OVEN
BRM CL.
CL.
CL.
POWDER RM.
UP
DN
CL.
PORCH
GATHERING RM. 18⁰ x 25⁴
ENTRANCE
STUDY 12⁰ x 11⁶
PORCH

BED RM.
11⁴ x 10⁰

WALK-IN CLOSET

DRESSING RM.

BATH

SHELVES

BATH

CL

CL

CL

MASTER BED RM.
18⁰ x 14¹⁰

DN

SHELVES

LINEN

SHELVES

BED RM.
17⁰ x 12⁶

● The rear view of this design is just as appealing as the front. The dormers and the covered porch with pillars is a charming way to introduce this house to the on-lookers. Inside, the appeal is also outstanding. Note the size (18 x 25 foot) of the gathering room which is open to the dining room. Kitchen-nook area is very spacious and features an island range, built-in desk and more. Great convenience having the laundry in service area close to the kitchen. Imagine, a fireplace in both the gathering room and the master bedroom! Make special note of the service entrance doors leading to both the front and back of the house.

Design 12629

1,555 Sq. Ft. - First Floor
1,080 Sq. Ft. - Second Floor
38,479 Cu. Ft.

● This home will really be fun in which to live. In addition to the sizeable living, dining and family rooms, many extras will be found. There are two fireplaces one to serve each of the formal and the informal areas. The back porch is a delightful extra. It will be great to relax in after a long hard day. Note two half baths on the first floor and two full baths on the second floor to serve the three bedrooms. Count the number of closets in the spacious upstairs. The door from the bedroom leads to storage over garage.

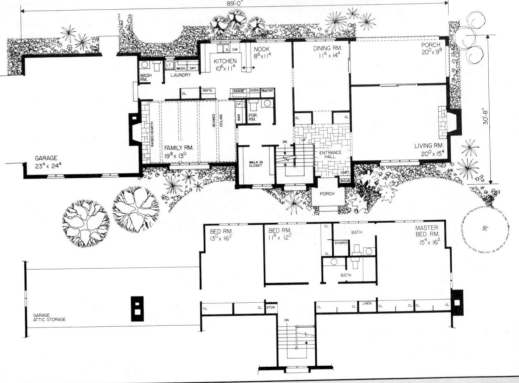

Design 12722

2,330 Sq. Ft. - First Floor
921 Sq. Ft. - Second Floor
60,075 Cu. Ft.

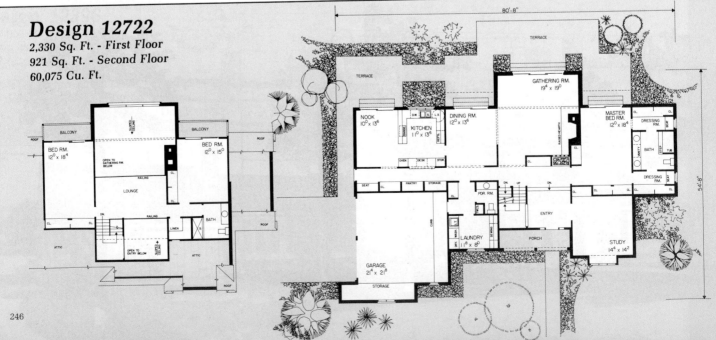

246

Design 12630

1,491 Sq. Ft. - First Floor
788 Sq. Ft. - Second Floor
35,575 Cu. Ft.

● This distinctive version of Tudor styling will foster many years of prideful ownership and unique, yet practical living patterns. The main portion of the facade is delightfully symmetrical. Inside, the family living will focus on the 29 foot great room with its dramatic fireplace and beamed ceiling. The kitchen is outstanding with snack bar and dining nook nearby. Note the three large bedrooms each having its own dressing room. Extra storage space is available above the garage or may be developed into another room. Oversized garage includes a built-in work bench. Study plan carefully. It has much to offer.

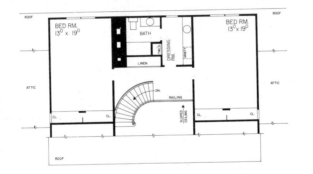

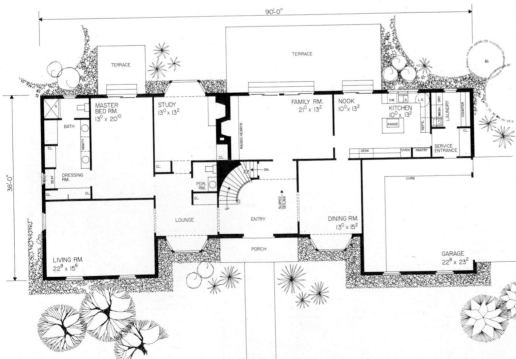

Design 12724

2,543 Sq. Ft. - First Floor
884 Sq. Ft. - Second Floor
53,640 Cu. Ft.

● Impressive at first glance! The double front doors of this one-and-a-half story home lead to the foyer which includes a sloped ceiling and curved staircase. The formal dining room and the lounge each offer a bay window. In the living room there are full-length paned windows. Also an abundance of livability. In the spacious family room, a raised-hearth fireplace runs the full length of one wall and has double doors to the terrace. Also a study with a fireplace and a rear bay window. In the kitchen, an island range and lots of built-ins make life easy. Two eating areas, the informal nook and the formal dining room, will be delightfully served by the L-shaped kitchen. The master bedroom suite is on the first floor and has a private terrace. The second floor houses two more bedrooms and a bath. A design sure to provide enjoyment.

Design 12614

1,701 Sq. Ft. - First Floor
1,340 Sq. Ft. - Second Floor
31,380 Cu. Ft.

● Pleasing appearance! With
an excellent floor plan. Notice how all the rooms are
accessible from a hall. That's
a plus for easy housekeeping.
Some other extras. An exceptionally large room, more
than 20' by 15' . . . with a
beamed ceiling and traditional fireplace. Plus a sliding
glass door onto the terrace. A
gracious living room, too,
complemented by paned-glass
windows and a fireplace with
a built-in woodbox. A formal
dining room adjacent to the
kitchen/nook area as well.
Four large bedrooms. Including a master suite with private dressing room and bath.
Something more! A secluded
guest suite, accessible only by
the back stairs. You could use
it as a spacious library, playroom or a hobby area. On the
same floor, a huge storage
area . . . or perhaps another
room since there are win-
dows at both ends. Note storage area in garage.

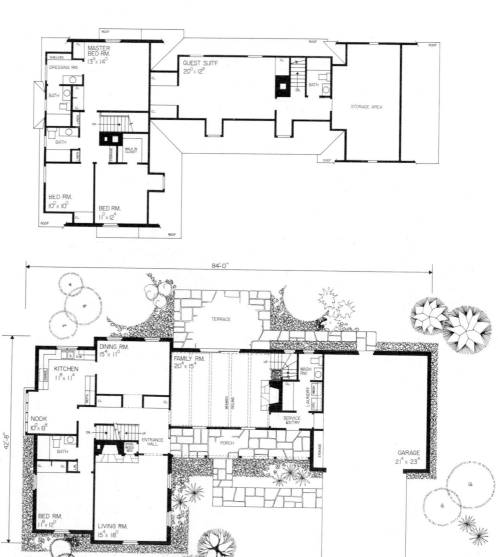

● You don't need a mansion to live graciously. What you do need is a practical floor plan which takes into consideration the varied activities of the busy family. This story-and-a-half design will not require a large piece of property. Its living potential is tremendous.

Design 11241
1,064 Sq. Ft. - First Floor
898 Sq. Ft. - Second Floor; 24,723 Cu. Ft.

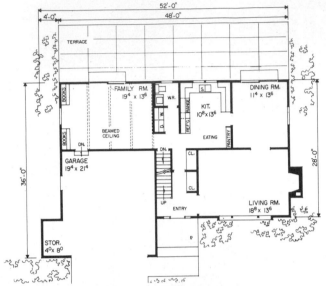

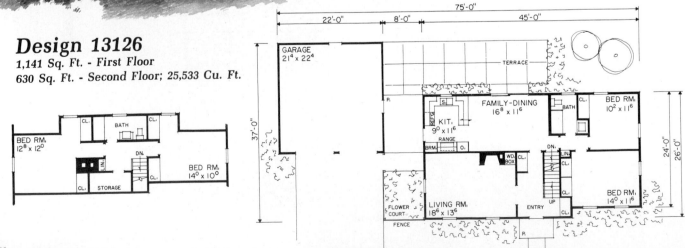

● Positively outstanding. From the delightful flower court to the upstairs storage room, this New England adaptation has much about which to talk. There is the U-shaped kitchen, the family-dining room, the four bedrooms, the two full baths, the fireplace, the numerous closets, the covered porch and two-car garage.

Design 13126
1,141 Sq. Ft. - First Floor
630 Sq. Ft. - Second Floor; 25,533 Cu. Ft.

Contemporary Designs
For A Refreshing New Look

Design 11783 2,412 Sq. Ft. - First Floor; 640 Sq. Ft. - Second Floor; 36,026 Cu. Ft.

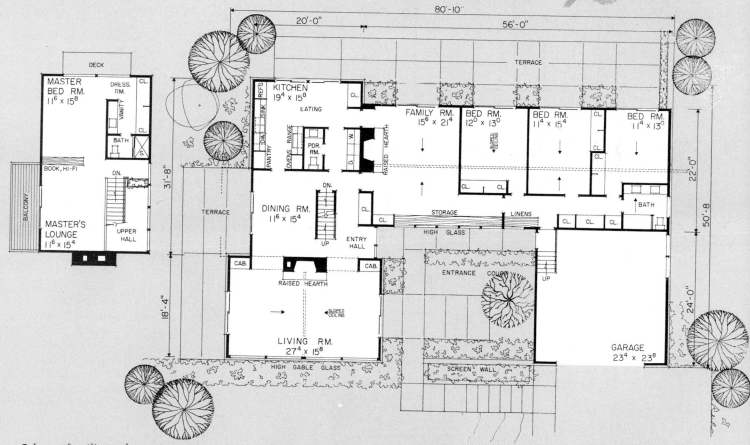

● Large families, take notice! Here is an impressive contemporary that is not only going to be fun to live in, but to look at, as well. Contributing to the appeal of this design are the interesting roof levels, their exposed rafters and wide overhangs. A big entrance court, screened from the street by a masonry wall, heightens the drama of the front exterior. The 27 foot living room is captivating, indeed. It can function through sliding glass doors, with either the front court or the side terrace. Eating patterns can be quite flexible with the extra space in the kitchen, a formal dining room and also a dining terrace. Don't miss sloping ceilings.

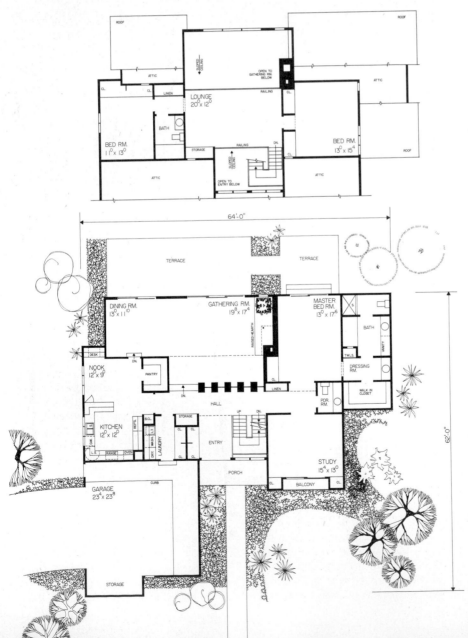

Design 12708
2,108 Sq. Ft. - First Floor
824 Sq. Ft. - Second Floor
52,170 Cu. Ft.

● Here is a one-and-a-half story home whose exterior is distinctive. It has a contemporary feeling, yet it retains some of the fine design features and proportions of traditional exteriors. Inside the appealing double front doors there is livability galore. The sunken rear living-dining area is delightfully spacious and is looked down into from the second floor lounge. The open end fireplace, with its raised hearth and planter, is another focal point. The master bedroom features a fine compartmented bath with both shower and tub. The study is just a couple steps away. The U-shaped kitchen is outstanding. Notice the pantry and laundry. Upstairs provides children with their own sleeping, studying and TV quarters. Absolutely a great design! Study all the fine details closely with your family.

Design 12782

2,060 Sq. Ft. - First Floor
897 Sq. Ft. - Second Floor
47,750 Cu. Ft.

● What makes this such a distinctive four bedroom design? Let's list some of the features. This plan includes great formal and informal living for the family at home or when entertaining guests. The formal gathering room and informal family room share a dramatic raised-hearth fireplace. Other features of the sunken gathering room include: high, sloped ceilings, built-in planter and sliding glass doors to the front entrance court. The kitchen has a snack bar, many built-ins, a pass-thru to dining room and easy access to the large laundry/wash room. The master bedroom suite is located on the main level for added privacy and convenience. There's even a study with a built-in bar. The upper level has three more bedrooms, a bath and a lounge looking down into the gathering room.

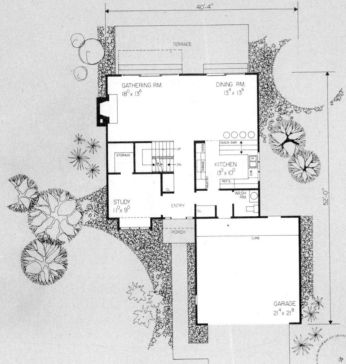

Design 12711 975 Sq. Ft. - First Floor
1,024 Sq. Ft. - Second Floor; 31,380 Cu. Ft.

● Special features! A complete master suite with a private balcony plus two more bedrooms and a bath upstairs. The first floor has a study with a storage closet. A convenient snack bar between kitchen and dining room. The kitchen offers many built-in appliances. Plus a gathering room and dining room that measures 31 feet wide. Note the curb area in the garage and fireplace in gathering room.

Design 12748
1,232 Sq. Ft. - First Floor
720 Sq. Ft. - Second Floor
27,550 Cu. Ft.

● This four bedroom contemporary will definitely have appeal for the entire family. The U-shaped kitchen-nook area with its built-in desk, adjacent laundry/wash room and service entrance will be very efficient for the busy kitchen activities. The living and family rooms are both sunken one step.

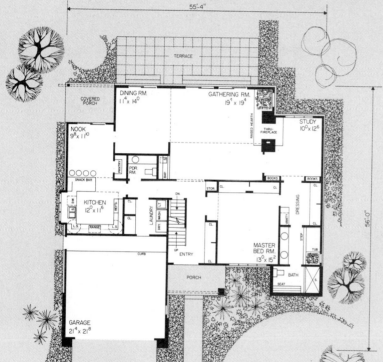

Design 12701 1,909 Sq. Ft. - First Floor
891 Sq. Ft. - Second Floor; 50,830 Cu. Ft.

● A snack bar in the kitchen! Plus a breakfast nook and formal dining room. Whether it's an elegant dinner party or a quick lunch, this home provides the right spot. There's a wet bar in the gathering room. Built-in bookcases in the study. And between these two rooms, a gracious fireplace. Three large bedrooms. Including a luxury master suite. Plus a balcony lounge overlooking gathering room below.

Design 12834

1,775 Sq. Ft. - Main Level; 1,041 Sq. Ft. - Upper Level
1,128 Sq. Ft. - Lower Level; 55,690 Cu. Ft.

● This passive solar design offers 4,200 square feet of livability situated on three levels. The primary passive element will be the lower level sun room which admits sunlight for direct-gain heating. The solar warmth collected in the sun room will radiate into the rest of the house after it passes the sliding glass doors. During the warm summer months, shades are put over the skylight to protect it from direct sunlight. This design has the option of incorporating active solar heating panels to the roof. The collectors would be installed on the south-facing portion of the roof. They would absorb the sun's warmth for both domestic water and supplementary space heating. An attic fan exhausts any hot air out of the house in the summer and circulates air in the winter. With or without the active solar panels, this is a marvelous two-story contemporary.

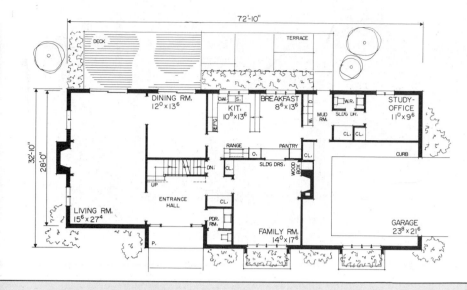

Design 11898

1,726 Sq. Ft. - First Floor
1,364 Sq. Ft. - Second Floor
41,975 Cu. Ft.

● A house with "everything" is often a matter of interpretation. Yet, here is a sparkling design that does have a full measure of outstanding features to assure complete livability.

First floor labels: DECK, TERRACE, DINING RM. 12⁰×13⁶, KIT. 10⁸×13⁶, BREAKFAST 8⁶×13⁶, MUD RM., STUDY-OFFICE 11⁰×9⁶, W.R., SLD'G DR., CL., CL., REFG., RANGE, O., PANTRY, CL., SLDG DRS., WOOD BOX, CURB, DN., UP, ENTRANCE HALL, PDR. RM., LIVING RM. 15⁶×27⁴, P., FAMILY RM. 14⁰×17⁶, GARAGE 23⁸×21⁶. Dimensions: 72'-10", 32'-10", 28'-0".

Second floor labels: BALCONY, BED RM. 15⁰×13⁶, WALK-IN CL., DRESS. RM., CL., CL., CL., CL., BATH, S., MASTER BED RM. 19⁰×13⁶, GLASS GABLE, LINEN, DN., BED RM. 11⁸×13⁶, WALK-IN CL., BATH, GRILLE, WALK-IN CL., BED RM. 13⁶×13⁶.

Design 11855

1,536 Sq. Ft. - First Floor
1,440 Sq. Ft. - Second Floor
37,056 Cu. Ft.

● Like its two-story contemporary companions above, this home has wonderful livability to offer. Start your study of this plan by observing the five bedrooms and the baths.

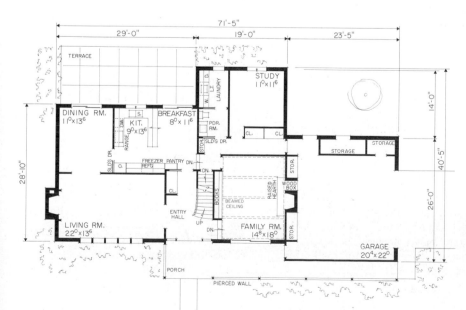

First floor labels: TERRACE, DINING RM. 11⁰×13⁶, KIT. 9⁰×13⁶, DW., S., RANGE, BREAKFAST 8⁰×11⁶, LT., LAUNDRY, W., D., STUDY 11⁰×11⁶, PDR. RM., SLD'G DR., CL., CL., SLD'G DR., FREEZER, PANTRY, REFG., DN., CL., STORAGE, STORAGE, STOR., WOOD BOX, BOOKS, BEAMED CEILING, RAISED HEARTH, STOR., ENTRY HALL, UP, DN., FAMILY RM. 14⁸×18⁰, LIVING RM. 22⁰×13⁶, PORCH, GARAGE 20⁴×22⁰, PIERCED WALL. Dimensions: 71'-5", 29'-0", 19'-0", 23'-5", 28'-10", 40'-5", 26'-0", 14'-0".

Second floor labels: BED RM. 11⁰×13⁸, CL., BATH, CL., BED RM. 12⁰×10⁰, BATH, VANITY, VANITY, WALK-IN CL., DRESS. RM., SLD'G DR., LINEN, S., BOOKS, STOR., STOR., DN., CL., CL., WALK-IN CL., BED RM. 14⁴×15⁴, BED RM. 11⁰×13⁰, MASTER BED RM. 14⁸×19⁰.

265

Design 12130 1,608 Sq. Ft. - First Floor; 924 Sq. Ft. - Second Floor; 34,949 Cu. Ft.

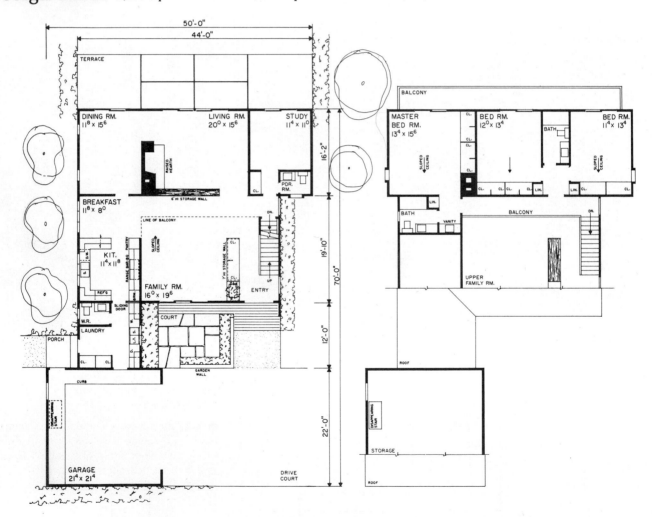

● Ring in the new. Here is a fresh forward-looking design which exemplifies some of the up-to-date imagery of today's architecture. This contemporary is a good study in the interest developed by the introduction of angles. These angles, plus the varying roof planes, blank wall masses, simple glass areas and the overall shape resulting from the orientation of the living components, make this an outstanding design. Inside, the floor planning will offer a lifetime of enjoyable living patterns. Study the various room relationships. Notice the practical zoning which results in a separation of functions to guarantee convenient living. Observe the homemaker's kitchen/laundry area. Also, formal dining, living rooms.

266

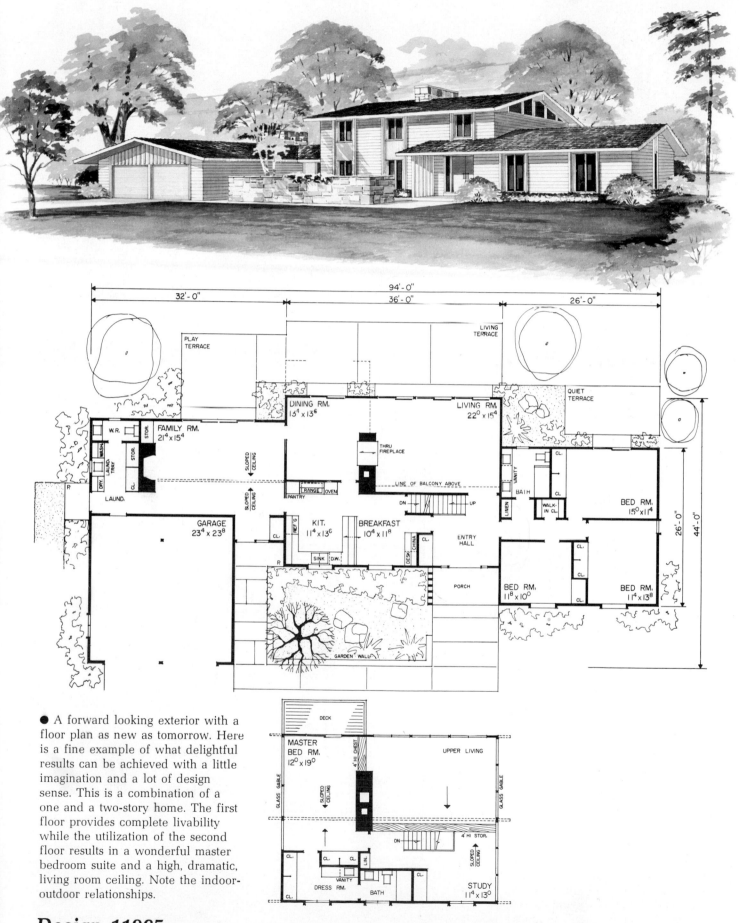

● A forward looking exterior with a floor plan as new as tomorrow. Here is a fine example of what delightful results can be achieved with a little imagination and a lot of design sense. This is a combination of a one and a two-story home. The first floor provides complete livability while the utilization of the second floor results in a wonderful master bedroom suite and a high, dramatic, living room ceiling. Note the indoor-outdoor relationships.

Design 11965 2,228 Sq. Ft. - First Floor; 682 Sq. Ft. - Second Floor; 42,556 Cu. Ft.

New Dimension in Exterior Appeal; Interior

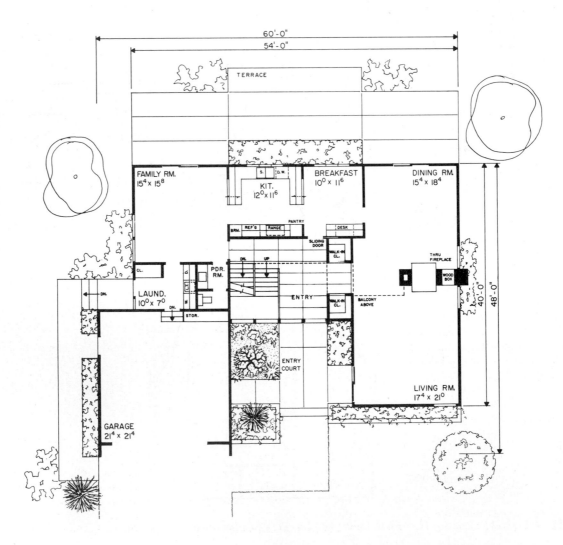

Design 12123 1,624 Sq. Ft. - First Floor; 1,335 Sq. Ft. - Second Floor; 42,728 Cu. Ft.

Livability

● If yours is a preference for contemporary styling with a real flair for the dramatic then this two-story should suit your fancy. There is nothing here that is reminiscent of the past - only prophetic of the future. The formal entry court has as its

backdrop, spectacular glass panels which rise to a height of 15 feet. Also facing the entry court are glass sliding doors of the living room. Above the doors is a glass panel which follows the line of the living room's sloping ceiling. The rear ele-

vation is hardly less dramatic than the front. It has large glass areas and an outdoor balcony accessible from the second floor bedrooms. The window detail at the side of the house is appealing. A great house for those with unique tastes.

You will never tire of its distinction. Inside there is close to 3,000 square feet of uniquely planned floor area. The spacious, well-lighted entry has, of course, a high sloping ceiling. A second floor balcony looks down from above. This area features

two walk-in closets. Between the dining and living rooms is a thru fireplace which may be enjoyed from either room. Between the garage and the family room is the laundry and the compartmented powder room. The second floor ceilings

slope and, consequently, add to the feeling of spaciousness. Count the closets. Note the master bedroom's private bath and dressing room, plus its generous lounge area which looks down on the living room. Also three family bedrooms.

Design 12780

2,006 Sq. Ft. - First Floor
718 Sq. Ft. - Second Floor; 42,110 Cu. Ft.

● This 1½-story contemporary has more fine features than one can imagine. The livability is outstanding and can be appreciated by the whole family. Note the fine indoor-outdoor living relationships.

Design 12772

1,579 Sq. Ft. - First Floor
1,240 Sq. Ft. - Second Floor; 39,460 Cu. Ft.

● This four-bedroom two-story contemporary design is sure to suit your growing family needs. The rear U-shaped kitchen, flanked by the family and dining rooms, will be very efficient to the busy homemaker. Parents will enjoy all the convenience of the master bedroom suite.

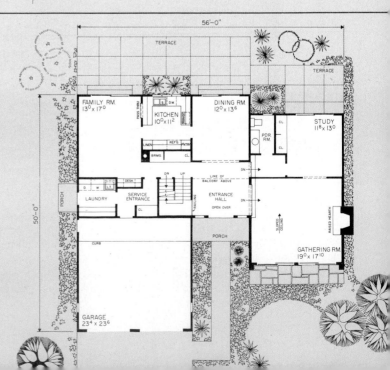

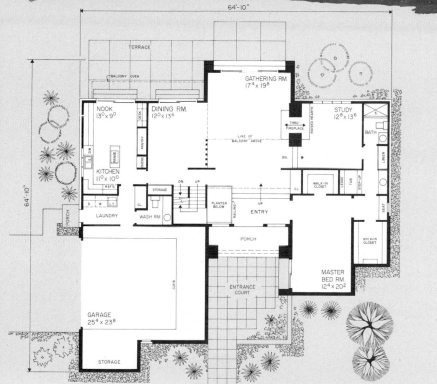

TERRACE

BALCONY OVEN

GATHERING RM.
17⁴ x 19⁸

NOOK
13⁰ x 9⁰

DINING RM.
12⁰ x 13⁶

DESK

PANTRY

THRU-FIREPLACE

RAISED HEARTH

STUDY
12⁸ x 13⁶

BATH

LINE OF BALCONY ABOVE

LINEN

KITCHEN
11⁰ x 10⁰

RANGE

OVENS

REF'G

DN

UP

CL

WALK-IN CLOSET

LEDGE

TUB

STEP-UP

D W LT

CL

STORAGE

DN UP

PLANTER BELOW

RAILING

UP

ENTRY

SEAT

LAUNDRY

WASH RM

PORCH

WALK-IN CLOSET

GARAGE
25⁴ x 23⁸

CURB

ENTRANCE COURT

MASTER BED RM.
12⁴ x 20²

STORAGE

Design 12771

2,087 Sq. Ft. - First Floor

816 Sq. Ft. - Second Floor; 53,285 Cu. Ft.

● This design will provide an abundance of livability for your family. The second floor is highlighted by an open lounge which overlooks both the entry and the gathering room below.

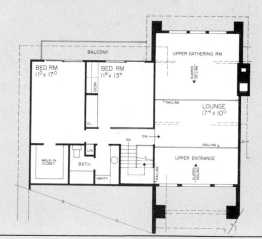

BALCONY

UPPER GATHERING RM.

BED RM.
11⁰ x 17⁰

BED RM.
11⁸ x 13⁶

DESK

SLOPED CEILING

RAILING

LOUNGE
17⁴ x 10⁰

CL

WALK-IN CLOSET

LIN

BATH

DN DN

RAILING

UPPER ENTRANCE

VANITY

RAILING

SLOPED CEILING

● Here is another contemporary two-story which offers fine contemporary living patterns. Four bedrooms, 2½ baths, family room. Blueprints include optional non-basement details.

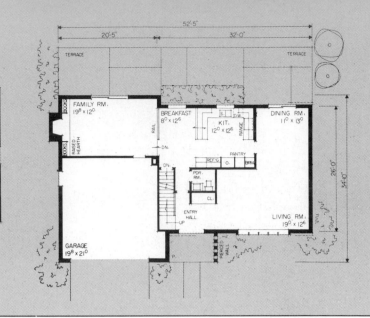

Design 11908
1,122 Sq. Ft. - First Floor
896 Sq. Ft. - Second Floor; 27,064 Cu. Ft.

Design 11879
1,008 Sq. Ft. - First Floor
1,008 Sq. Ft. - Second Floor
27,518 Cu. Ft.

● An engaging contemporary two-story which will be most economical to build. Thus, the return on your construction dollar in the way of liva-bility will be weighted in your favor. Consider; four bedrooms - three for the kids and one for the parents; one main bath with vanity for the younger set, one private bath and dressing room for Mr. and Mrs., and an extra powder room downstairs for the convenience of everyone; two distinct eating areas - the informal breakfast room and the formal dining room; a family room only a step removed from the rear terrace and a quiet living room off by itself.

THE PLAN BOOKS

. . . are a most valuable tool for anyone planning to build a new home. A study of the hundreds of delightfully designed exteriors and the practical, efficient floor plans will be a great learning and fun-oriented family experience. You will be able to select your preferred styling from among Early American, Tudor, French, Spanish and Contemporary adaptations. Your ideas about floor planning and interior livability will expand. And, of course, after you have selected an appealing home design that satisfies your long list of living requirements, you can order the blueprints for further study of your favorite design in greater detail. Surely the hours spent studying the portfolio of Home Planners' designs will be both enjoyable and rewarding ones.

Kindly note: For detailed information about the complete home planning package, see pages 303 through 308.

HOME PLANNERS, INC.
Dept. BK, 23761 Research Drive
Farmington Hills, Michigan 48024

Phone Toll Free:
1-800-521-6797

PLAN BOOK ORDER FORM

Please mail me the following:

THE DESIGN CATEGORY SERIES - A great series of books specially edited by design type and size. Each book features interesting sections to further enhance the study of design styles, sizes and house types. A fine addition to the home or office library. Complete collection - over 1275 designs.

1. _____ 400 1½ & Two-Story Home Plans @ $5.95 ea . . . . $_____
2. _____ 210 One-Story - Over 2,000 sq. ft. @ $3.95 ea. . . . . $_____
3. _____ 350 One-Story - Under 2,000 sq. ft. @ $4.95 ea. . . . . $_____
4. _____ 205 Multi-Level Home Plans @ $3.95 ea. . . . . $_____
5. _____ 223 Vacation Homes @ $4.25 ea. . . . . $_____

OTHER CURRENT TITLES - The interesting series of plan books listed below have been edited to appeal to various style preferences and budget considerations. The majority of the designs highlighted in these books also may be found in the Design Category Series.

The Exterior Style Series-

6. _____ 120 Early American Home Plans @ $2.25 ea. $_____
7. _____ 125 Contemporary Home Plans @ $2.25 ea. $_____
8. _____ 135 English Tudor Homes @ $2.50 ea. . . . . $_____
9. _____ 112 Traditional & Contemporary Family Homes @ $2.75 ea. . . . . $_____
10. _____ 102 Home Plans @ $1.75 ea. . . . . $_____
11. _____ 130 Distinctive Home Designs @ $2.75 ea. (March '84) . . . .$_____

The Budget Series-

12. _____ 175 Low Budget Homes @ $2.75 ea. . . . . $_____
13. _____ 165 Affordable Home Plans @ $2.50 ea. . . . . $_____
14. _____ 142 Home Designs for Expanded Bldg. Budgets @ $2.75 ea. (May '84) $_____
15. _____ 110 Home Plans @ $2.75 ea. . . . . $_____

Books in Full Color-

16. _____ 116 Traditional & Contemporary Plans @ $4.95 ea. . . . . $_____
17. _____ 122 Home Designs @ $4.95 ea. . . . . $_____

Other Titles-

18. _____ 166 Most Popular Homes @ $2.75 ea. . . . . $_____
19. _____ Encyclopedia of Home Designs @ $8.95 ea. $_____

MAIL TODAY	**SATISFACTION GUARANTEED!** *Your order will be processed and shipped within 48 hours*	Sub Total $_____
		Michigan Residents kindly add 4% sales tax $_____
		TOTAL-Check enclosed $_____

Please Print

Name _____

Address _____

City _____ State _____ Zip _____

CV1

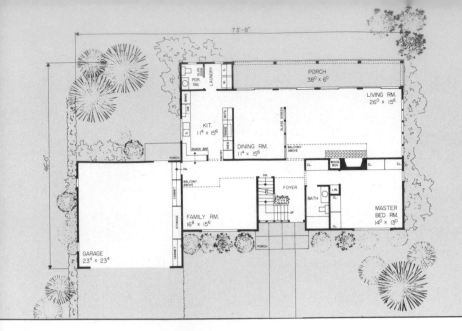

Design 12246

1,651 Sq. Ft. - First Floor
1,161 Sq. Ft. - Second Floor
52,382 Cu. Ft.

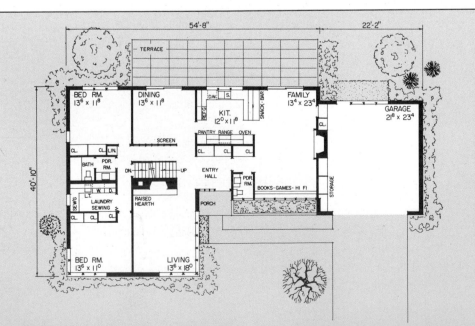

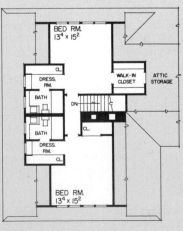

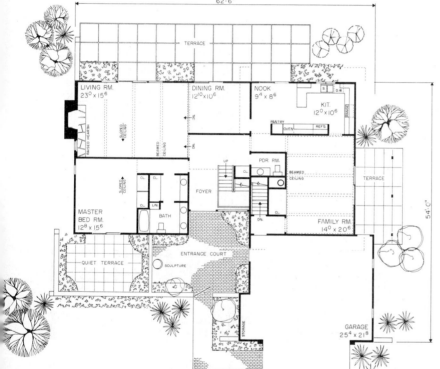

TERRACE

62'-6"

LIVING RM.
23⁰ x 15⁶

DINING RM.
12¹⁰ x 10⁶

NOOK
9⁴ x 8⁶

KIT.
12⁰ x 10⁶

PANTRY
OVEN   REFS.

RAISED HEARTH

BEAMED CEILING

SLOPED CEILING

SLOPED CEILING

PDR. RM.

FOYER

UP

CL

CL

LIN.

BATH

CL

MASTER
BED RM.
12⁸ x 15⁶

BEAMED CEILING

FAMILY RM.
14⁰ x 20⁶

TERRACE

QUIET TERRACE

SCULPTURE

ENTRANCE COURT

STORAGE

GARAGE
25⁴ x 21⁶

54'-0"

Design 12252

1,810 Sq. Ft. - First Floor
1,033 Sq. Ft. - Second Floor
33,629 Cu. Ft.

ROOF

STUDY
12⁰ x 13⁶

BOOKS

BED RM.
13⁰ x 13⁶

BEAMED CEILING

SLOPED CEILING

UPPER DINING RM.

RAILING

UPPER FOYER

BATH

CL

LINEN

BATH

CL

CL

DN

SLOPED CEILING

ROOF

OPEN TRELLIS

BED RM.
11⁶ x 12⁰

BED RM.
11⁶ x 11⁶

UP

PDR. RM.

AIR COND.

LNDRY.

OPTIONAL NON-BASEMENT

Design 11084

1,804 Sq. Ft. - First Floor
732 Sq. Ft. - Second Floor
33,842 Cu. Ft.

Design 12828 First Floor: 817 Sq. Ft. - Living Area; 261 Sq. Ft. - Foyer & Laundry
Second Floor: 852 Sq. Ft. - Living Area; 214 Sq. Ft. - Foyer & Storage; 34,690 Cu. Ft.

TWO COUPLES/SINGLES RESIDENCE

CONVERTIBLE ONE-FAMILY RESIDENCE

● This contemporary home has been designed as a two-couples/singles residence. A home of this type could be bought jointly by two couples or one couple could buy the entire home and rent out one of the units. Complete livability is offered on each floor of this two-story. Each floor has a living room, dining room, interior kitchen, bedroom and bath. At a later date this home could be converted into a one-family residence. The second floor unit would now be a bedroom area.

BASEMENT PLAN

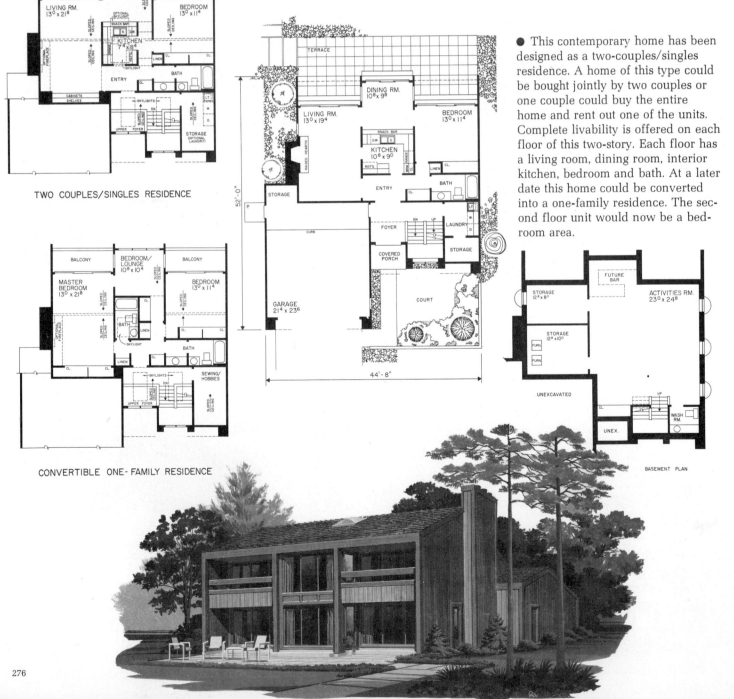

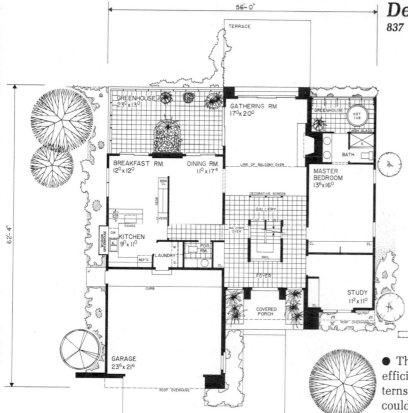

Design 12884 1,814 Sq. Ft. - First Floor
837 Sq. Ft. - Second Floor; 51,305 Cu. Ft.

First Floor labels:

TERRACE

GREENHOUSE 23⁰ x 13⁰

GATHERING RM 17⁰ x 20⁰

GREENHOUSE

HOT TUB

HIGH GLASS

BATH

BREAKFAST RM. 12⁰ x 12⁰

DINING RM. 11⁰ x 17⁴

LINE OF BALCONY OVER

MASTER BEDROOM 13⁶ x 16⁰

BRM. CL.

DESK

RANGE

OVENS

DECORATIVE SCREEN

GALLERY

BALCONY OVER

RAIL

CL.

CL.

DW.

KITCHEN 9⁰ x 11⁰

WINDOW

REF'G.

LAUNDRY

PDR. RM.

CL.

FOYER

CURB

STUDY 11² x 11⁰

COVERED PORCH

CL.

ROOF OVERHANG

ROOF OVERHANG

GARAGE 23⁶ x 21⁶

56'-0"

62'-4"

Second Floor labels:

UPPER GREENHOUSE

UPPER GATHERING RM.

SLOPED CEILING

ROOF

BALCONY RAIL

BEDROOM 15⁴ x 11⁴

DRESSING AREA

LINE OF WALL ABOVE

LOUNGE / T.V. LOFT 17⁰ x 11⁴

VANITY

CL.

ATTIC STORAGE

BALCONY RAIL

DN

BALCONY RAIL

CL.

BATH

BEDROOM 13⁰ x 11⁴

LINEN

UPPER FOYER

BALCONY RAIL

UP

ACCESS

ATTIC STORAGE

ROOF

● The greenhouse in this design enhances its energy-efficiency and allows for spacious and interesting living patterns. Being a one-and-a-half story design, the second floor could be developed at a later date when the space is needed.

● A refreshing two-story contemporary with dramatic brick masses, simple window treatment, a low-pitched, wide overhanging roof, delightful exterior planter and an exciting outdoor sun deck over the attached two-car garage.

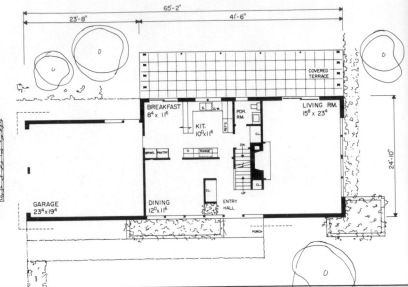

● Here are three distinctive contemporary two-story homes. Each with a refreshing flair of its own. This home features a fine bedroom suite over the garage. Note large L-shaped living-dining area.

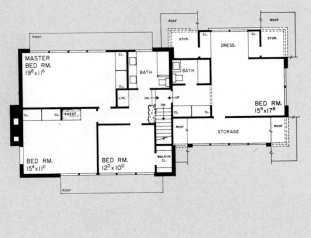

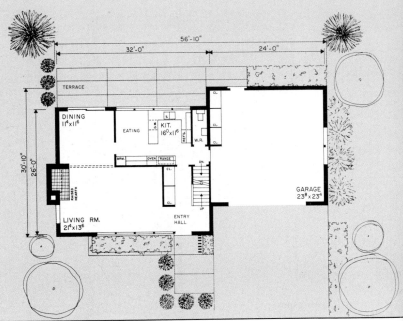

● Contemporary two-story living is dramatically illustrated here. The numerous roof planes with their wide overhangs result in a distinctive home.

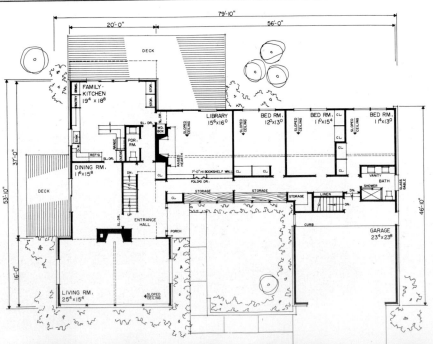

Design 13147
996 Sq. Ft. - First Floor; 996 Sq. Ft. - Second Floor
26,722 Cu. Ft.

Design 13194
853 Sq. Ft. - First Floor; 1,208 Sq. Ft. - Second Floor
25,324 Cu. Ft.

Design 11895
2,448 Sq. Ft. - First Floor; 746 Sq. Ft. - Second Floor
53,100 Cu. Ft.

Design 12309 1,719 Sq. Ft. - First Floor; 456 Sq. Ft. - Second Floor; 22,200 Cu. Ft.

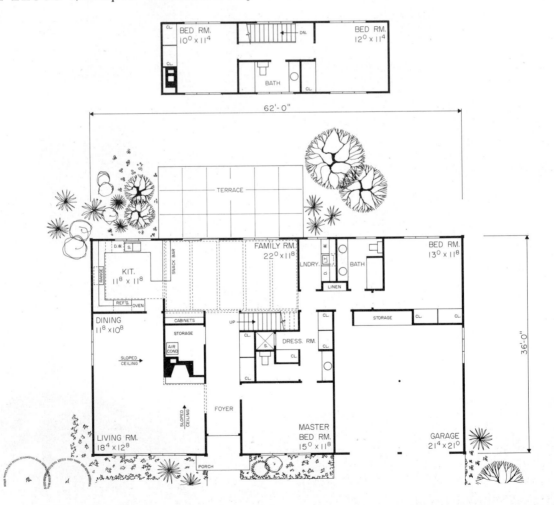

● Here's proof that the simple rectangle (which is relatively economical to build, naturally) can, when properly planned, result in unique living patterns. The exterior can be exceedingly appealing, too. Study the floor plan carefully. The efficiency of the kitchen could hardly be improved upon. It is strategically located to serve the formal dining room, the family room and even the rear terrace. The sleeping facilities are arranged in a most interesting manner. The master bedroom with its attached bath and dressing room will enjoy a full measure of privacy on the first floor. A second bedroom is also on this floor and has a full bath nearby. Upstairs there are two more bedrooms and a bath. Don't miss the laundry, the snack bar, the beamed ceiling or the sliding glass doors.

● Here is a contemporary Mansard roof adaptation that is dramatic, indeed. Because of its simplicity it will not fail to elicit its full measure of acclaim. The vertical 1 x 3 inch battens and the glass panels add a distinctive note. The unique appeal of this design continues to be apparent on the inside as well. The center entrance hall effectively routes traffic. To the right is the kitchen-laundry area. To the left, the well-lighted open stairwell to the second floor. At the top of the stairs you can look over the balcony railing down into a portion of the living room. In addition to the formal living and dining rooms (which function together), there is the large beamed ceilinged family room. Note the bar, game storage and sliding glass doors to terrace. Outstanding livability!

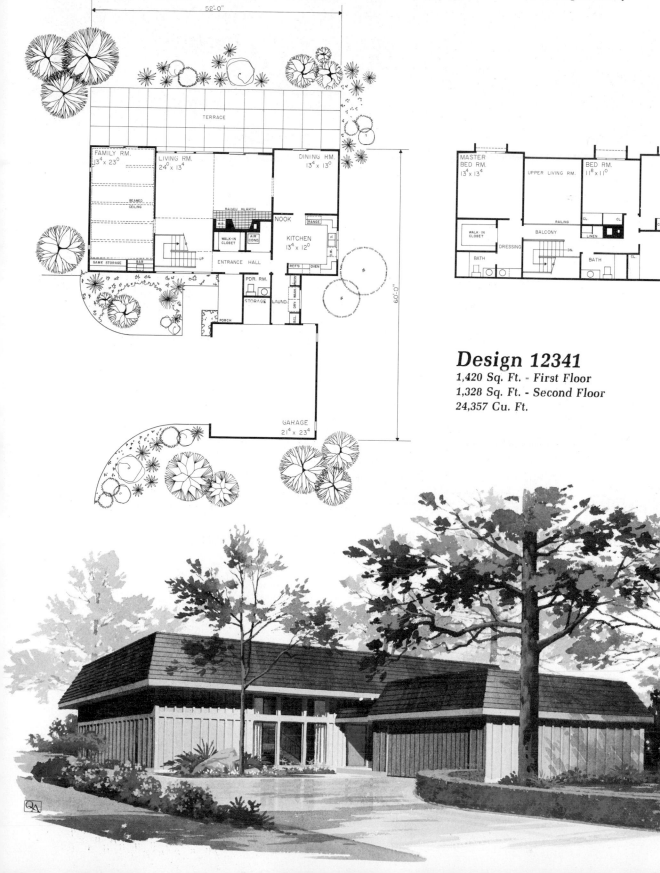

Design 12341

1,420 Sq. Ft. - First Floor
1,328 Sq. Ft. - Second Floor
24,357 Cu. Ft.

Design 12339 2,068 Sq. Ft. - First Floor; 589 Sq. Ft. - Second Floor; 27,950 Cu. Ft.

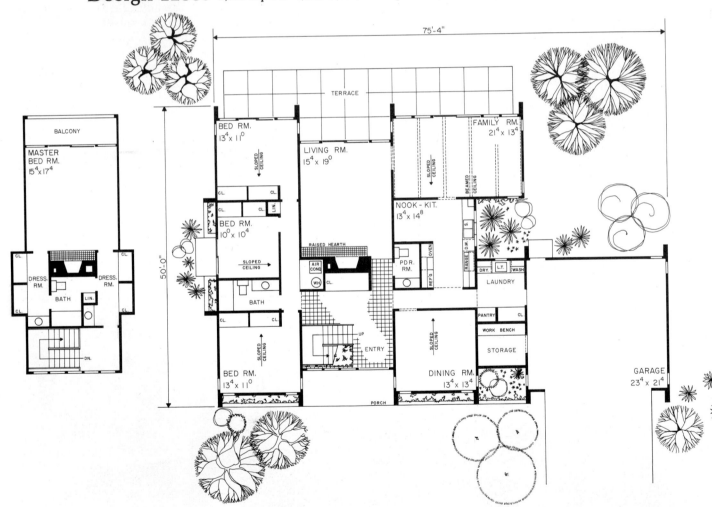

● These two pages show the influence that the Spanish Southwest has on today's design. Essentially a one-story home, the design above locates a big master bedroom on a second floor. However, the design on the opposing page is a full two-story

with all the sleeping facilities located upstairs. While each design has a similar amount of square footage, its use to deliver family livability could hardly be more diverse. Contrast the living patterns. They are interestingly different. Which seems to fit the

interests and activities of your family best? Note the sloped ceilings, the two fireplaces and the balcony of 12339 above. Observe the second floor terrace and balcony, the formal living area and the huge family room of 12315 at right.

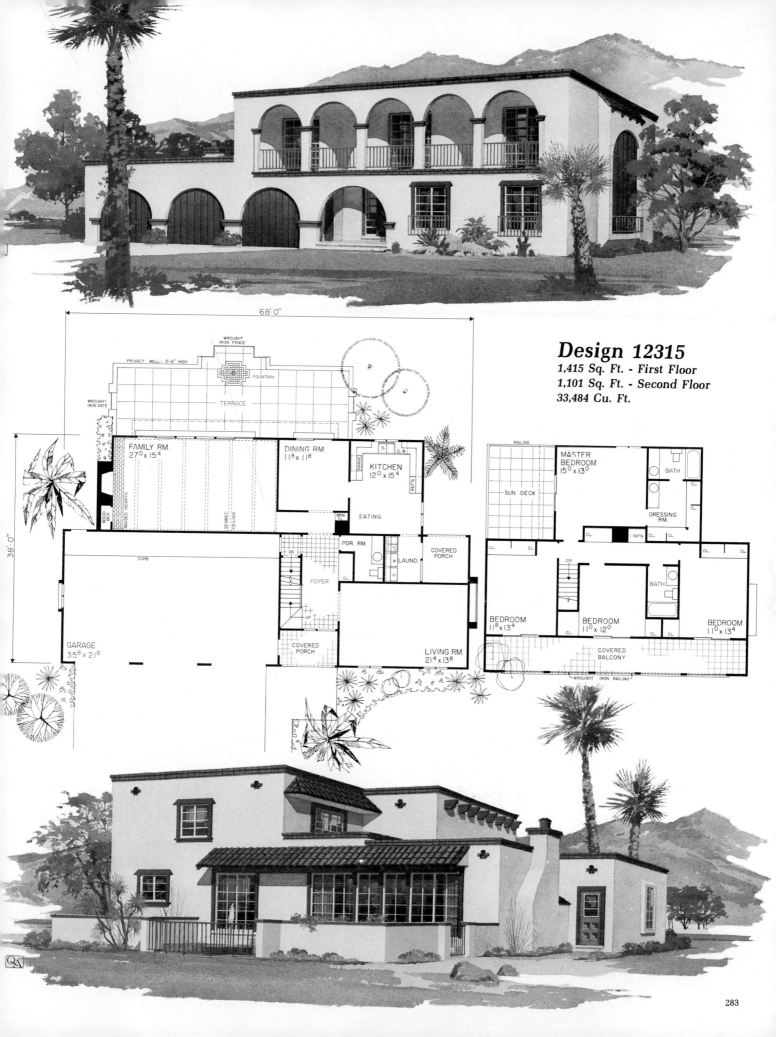

Design 12315

1,415 Sq. Ft. - First Floor
1,101 Sq. Ft. - Second Floor
33,484 Cu. Ft.

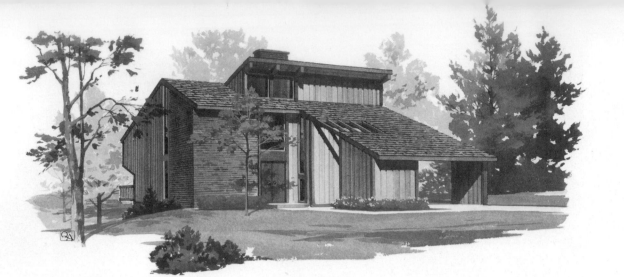

Design 12511

1,043 Sq. Ft. - Main Level
703 Sq. Ft. - Upper Level
794 Sq. Ft. - Lower Level
30,528 Cu. Ft.

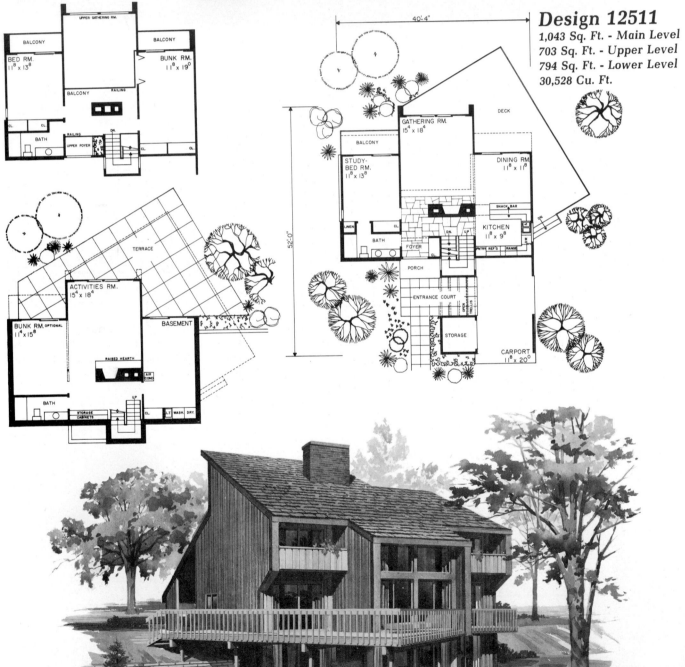

Upper Level

UPPER GATHERING RM.

BALCONY

BALCONY

BED RM.
11⁸ x 13⁸

BUNK RM.
11⁸ x 19⁰

BALCONY

RAILING

CL. CL.

BATH

UPPER FOYER

RAILING

DN.

CL.

CL.

Lower Level

TERRACE

ACTIVITIES RM.
15⁴ x 18⁴

BUNK RM. OPTIONAL
11⁴ x 15⁸

BASEMENT

RAISED HEARTH

AIR COND.

BATH

STORAGE CABINETS

UP

CL. H.T. WASH. DRY.

Main Level

40'-4"

52'-0"

GATHERING RM.
15⁴ x 18⁴

DECK

BALCONY

STUDY-
BED RM.
11⁸ x 13⁸

DINING RM.
11⁸ x 11⁸

SNACK BAR

LINEN

CL.

KITCHEN
11⁸ x 9⁸

BATH

FOYER

DN. UP

PANTRY REF'G RANGE

PORCH

ENTRANCE COURT

OPEN TRELLIS

STORAGE

CARPORT
11⁸ x 20⁰

Design 12823

1,370 Sq. Ft. - First Floor
927 Sq. Ft. - Second Floor
34,860 Cu. Ft.

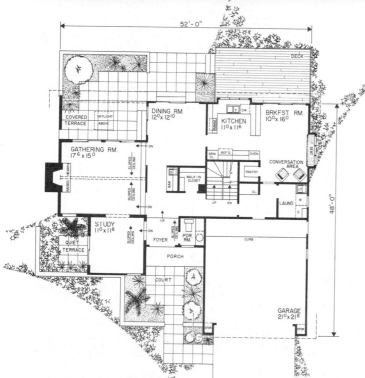

● The street view of this contemporary design features a small courtyard entrance as well as a private terrace off the study. Inside the livability will be outstanding. This design features spacious first floor activity areas that flow smoothly into each other. In the gathering room a raised hearth fireplace creates a dramatic focal point. An adjacent covered terrace, featuring a skylight, is ideal for outdoor dining and could be screened in later for an additional room.

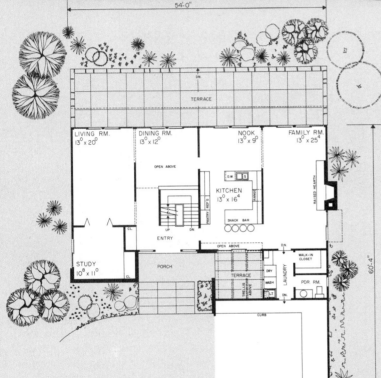

Design 12509

1,634 Sq. Ft. - First Floor
1,304 Sq. Ft. - Second Floor
44,732 Cu. Ft.

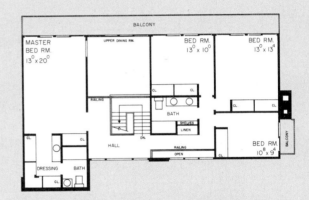

● A two-story with more livability will be hard to find. Notice how the various rooms are oriented with the terrace and balcony. The dining room has a high ceiling so its activities can be viewed from the upstairs hall.

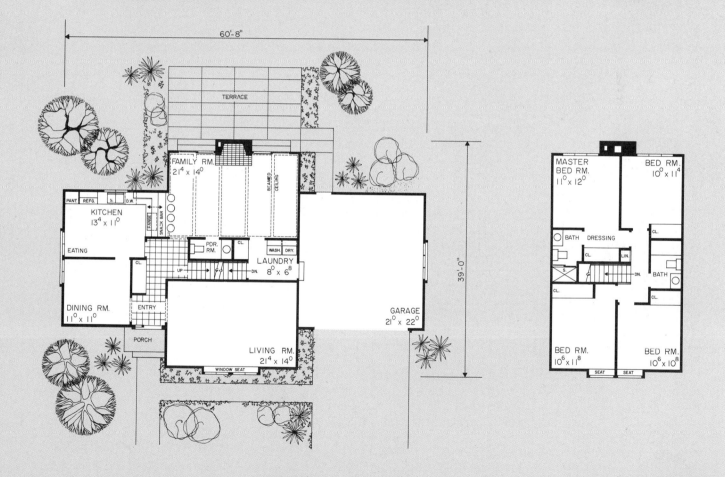

TERRACE

FAMILY RM.
21⁴ x 14⁰

BEAMED CEILING

PANT. REFG. S. D.W.

KITCHEN
13⁴ x 11⁰

RANGE SNACK BAR

EATING

CL.

DINING RM.
11⁰ x 11⁰

ENTRY

PORCH

PDR. RM.

CL.

WASH DRY.

LAUNDRY
8⁰ x 6⁸

UP

DN.

GARAGE
21⁰ x 22⁰

LIVING RM.
21⁴ x 14⁰

WINDOW SEAT

60'-8"

39'-0"

MASTER BED RM.
11⁰ x 12⁰

BED RM.
10⁰ x 11⁴

BATH DRESSING

CL.

LIN.

CL.

S

DN.

BATH

CL.

CL.

BED RM.
10⁶ x 11⁸

BED RM.
10⁶ x 10⁸

SEAT

SEAT

Design 12365 *1,194 Sq. Ft. - First Floor; 802 Sq. Ft. - Second Floor; 24,693 Cu. Ft.*

● This unadorned contemporary has an appeal all its own. The wide overhanging roof, the box bay window and the horizontal siding are features which set the character. A welcomed change of pace to any neighborhood will be the two-story middle section flanked by the projecting one-story wings. Inside, there is livability galore. The formal living room and the informal family room are of identical size. Both large, they are well-located to serve their family functions ideally. The kitchen offers eating space and around the corner is the formal dining room. On the second floor there are four fine bedrooms and two full baths. Notice the window seats of the projecting bay, in both the upstairs bedrooms and the living room.

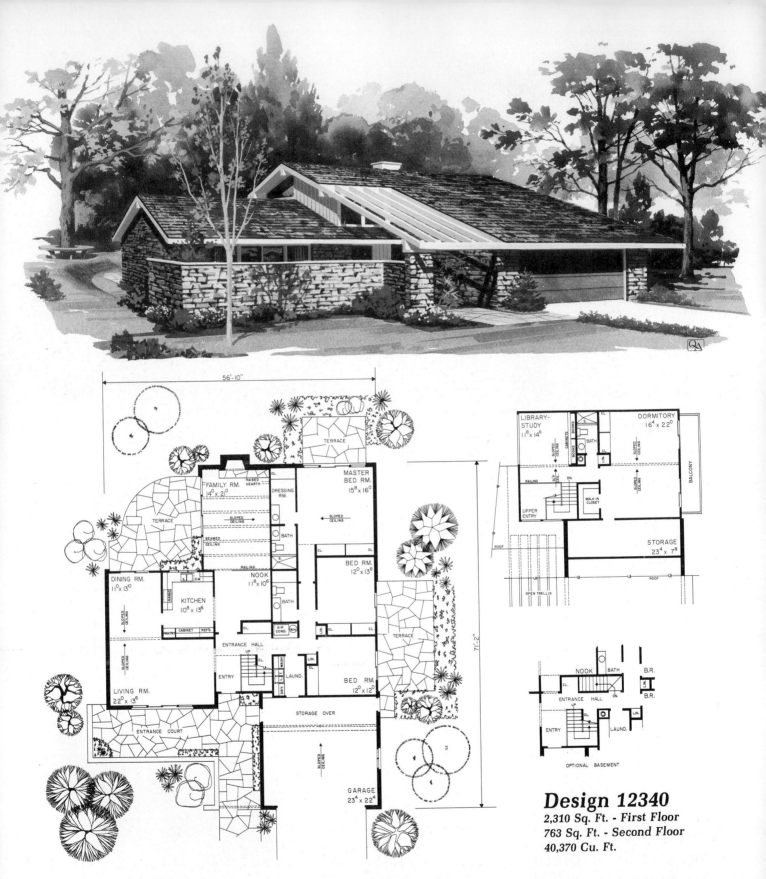

Design 12340
2,310 Sq. Ft. - First Floor
763 Sq. Ft. - Second Floor
40,370 Cu. Ft.

● If you have a flair for the extra-ordinary and wish to introduce your family to living patterns that will be delightfully different, then this design should fill the bill. Whether you build with quarried stone, brick veneer or some other exterior material of your choice, you'll surely experience pride of ownership here. However, inside is where your family's fun really begins. This is a highly integrated plan which allows for the full expression of a family's diverse activities. Study the effective zoning of the first floor.

There are the formal, the informal and the sleeping areas. Then, upstairs there is a library which can look down on the entrance hall. Also, the dormitory with its own bath, balcony and fine closet facilities. Note optional basement. Laundry remains upstairs.

Design 12582

1,195 Sq. Ft. - First Floor
731 Sq. Ft. - Second Floor
32,500 Cu. Ft.

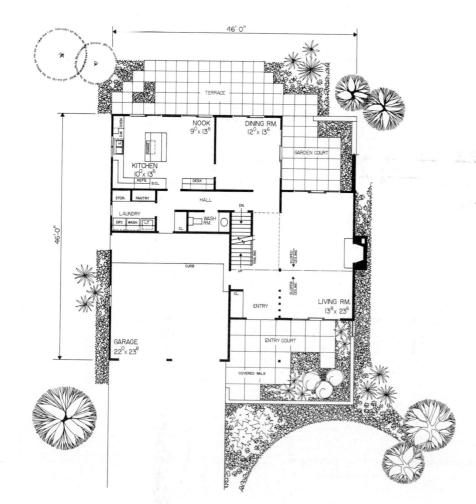

● This distinctive two-story will command attention wherever built. One of its significant features is that it doesn't require a huge piece of property. In slightly less than 2,000 square feet it offers tremendous livability. As a bonus, the basement can function as the family recreation and hobby areas. Of particular interest is the first floor laundry room. Don't miss the fine kitchen layout, the formal and informal dining facilities and the sloping ceiling of the living room. Notice the outstanding outdoor living facilities. Upstairs, three bedrooms and two baths will be found.

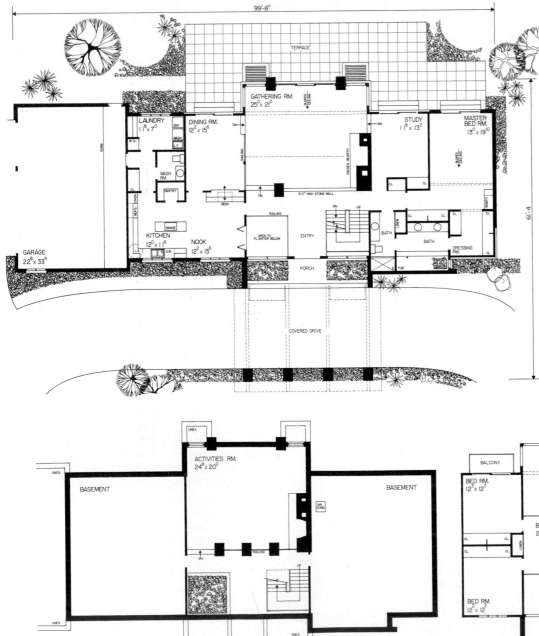

Design 12562
2,884 Sq. Ft. - First Floor
864 Sq. Ft. - Second Floor
73,625 Cu. Ft.

● Here is an exciting contemporary design for the large, active family. It can be called upon to function as either a four or five bedroom home. As a four bedroom home the parents will enjoy a wonderful suite with study and exceptional bath facilities. Note stall shower, plus sunken tub. The upstairs features the children's bedrooms and a spacious balcony lounge which looks down to the floor below. The sunken gathering room will be just that with its sloped beamed ceiling, dramatic raised hearth fireplace and direct access to the rear terrace.

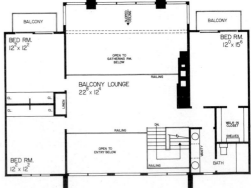

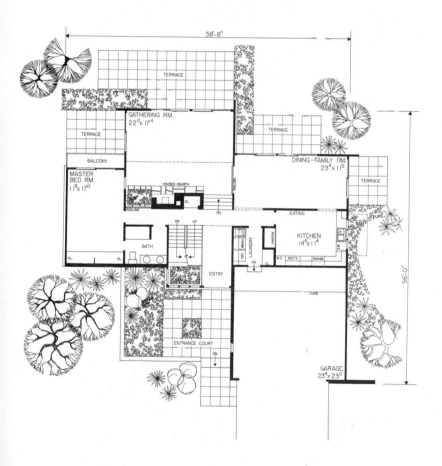

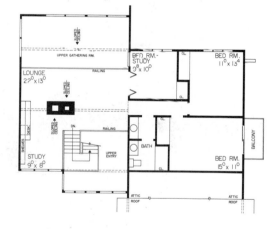

Design 12530

1,616 Sq. Ft. - First Floor
997 Sq. Ft. - Second Floor
41,925 Cu. Ft.

● This exciting contemporary with its dramatic roof lines and appealing glass areas could also be classified as a modified two-story home. Only the sunken living area qualifies it as a multi-level home. The interior planning is, indeed, unique. Study this plan carefully and consider how your family would function in it. The gathering room is a delightful area with its dramatic raised hearth fireplace and planter, and access to two terraces. The spaciousness of the dining/family room will surely make entertaining a memorable occasion. Note the privacy of the master bedroom. The second floor is devoted to the activities of the younger generation. The lounge looks down into the gathering room. Other features are the outdoor balconies, the first floor laundry and the basement.

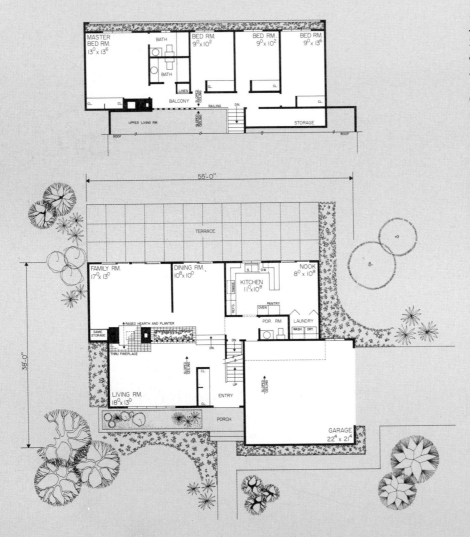

Design 12377

1,170 Sq. Ft. - First Floor
815 Sq. Ft. - Second Floor
22,477 Cu. Ft.

● What an impressive up-to-date home this is. Its refreshing configuration will command a full measure of attention. Note that all of the back rooms on the first floor are a couple steps lower than the entry and living room area. Separating the living room and the slightly lower level is a thru-fireplace which has a raised hearth in the family room. An adjacent planter with vertical members provides additional interest and beauty. The rear terrace is accessible from nook, family and dining rooms. Four bedrooms serviced by two full baths comprise the second floor which looks down into the living room. A large walk-in storage closet will be ideal for those seasonal items. An attractive outdoor planter extends across the rear just outside the bedroom windows. This will surely be a house that will be fun in which to live.

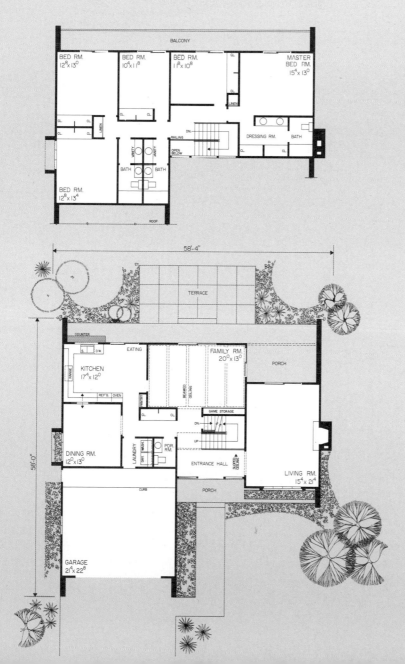

Design 12390

1,368 Sq. Ft. - First Floor
1,428 Sq. Ft. - Second Floor
37,734 Cu. Ft.

● If yours is a large family and you like the architecture of the Far West don't look further. Particularly if you envision building on a modest sized lot. Projecting the garage to the front contributes to the drama of this contemporary two-story. Its stucco exterior is beautifully enhanced by the clay tiles of the varying roof surfaces. Inside the double front doors is just about everything a large, active family would require for pleasurable, convenient living. The focal point, of course, is the five bedroom (count'em), three bath second floor. Four bedrooms have access to the outdoor balcony. The first floor offers two large living areas - the formal living and the informal family rooms - plus, two eating areas. Although there is the basement, the laundry is on the first floor. Don't overlook the covered porch accessible by family and living rooms.

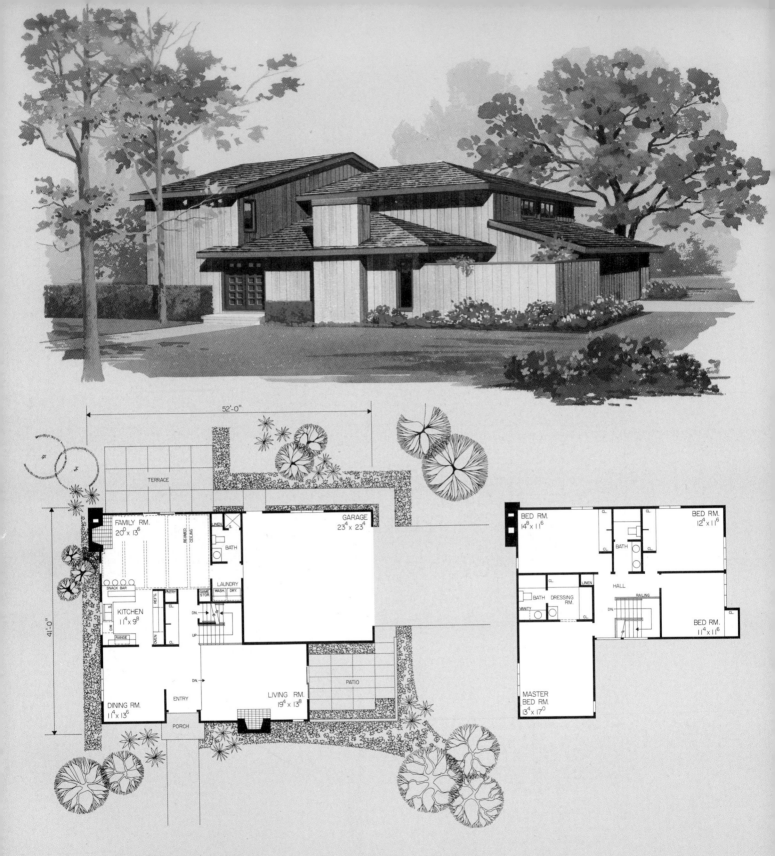

Design 12602 *1,154 Sq. Ft. - First Floor; 1,120 Sq. Ft. - Second Floor; 30,370 Cu. Ft.*

● Varying roof planes, wide overhangs, interestingly shaped blank wall areas and patterned double front doors provide the distinguishing characteristics of this refreshing, contemporary two-story design. The extension of the front wall results in an enclosed, private outdoor patio area accesssible from the living room. Inside the compact plan there is a fine feeling of spaciousness. The living area features open planning. The U-shaped kitchen is but a step or two from the dining room and the family room. There is a snack bar, laundry area, full bath with stall shower, pantry and game storage, and two fireplaces located on the first floor. Upstairs, four good-sized bedrooms, two baths, a dressing room and plenty of closets.

Design 12552 1,437 Sq. Ft. - First Floor; 1,158 Sq. Ft. - Second Floor; 43,000 Cu. Ft.

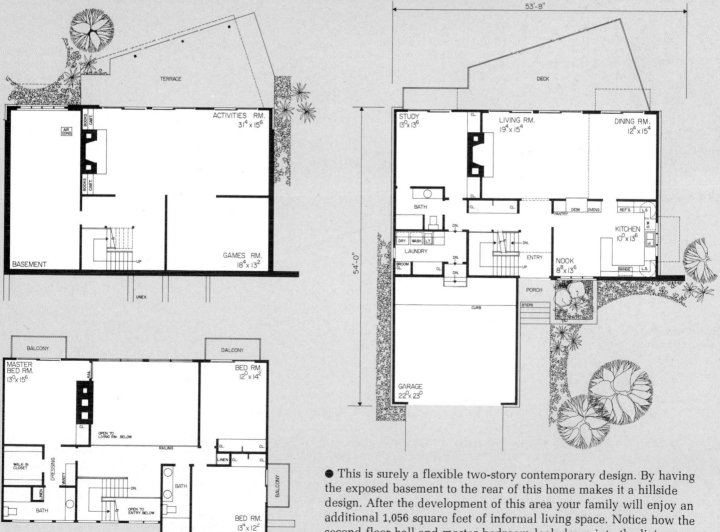

● This is surely a flexible two-story contemporary design. By having the exposed basement to the rear of this home makes it a hillside design. After the development of this area your family will enjoy an additional 1,056 square feet of informal living space. Notice how the second floor hall and master bedroom look down into the living room.

295

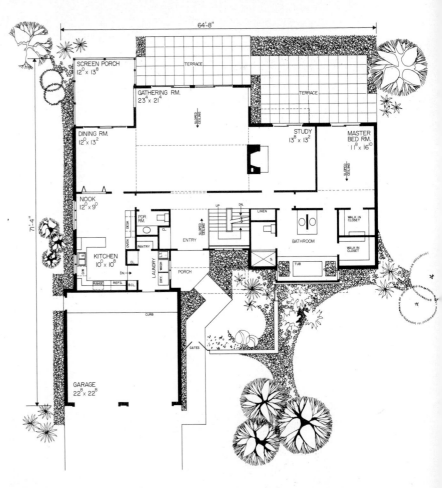

Design 12581

2,125 Sq. Ft. - First Floor
903 Sq. Ft. - Second Floor
54,476 Cu. Ft.

● Here is something of a smaller version of Design 12562 on page 290. There are many differences, not the least of which is the exterior with its projecting, front entrance garage. This feature in itself is significant since it results in the need of a much smaller building site; perhaps an important consideration in this day of high land costs. You will have fun contrasting the differences in these two designs in spite of their similarities. Don't miss the sizeable screened-in porch above. Notice the location of the fireplace in the study. The partially enclosed front flower court adds a dramatic touch to the entrance area. This design also has a basement which may be developed for additional living and hobby pursuits. Notice the pass-thru between the nook and the dining room.

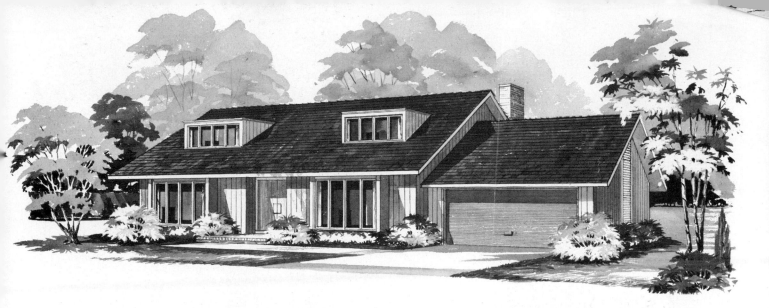

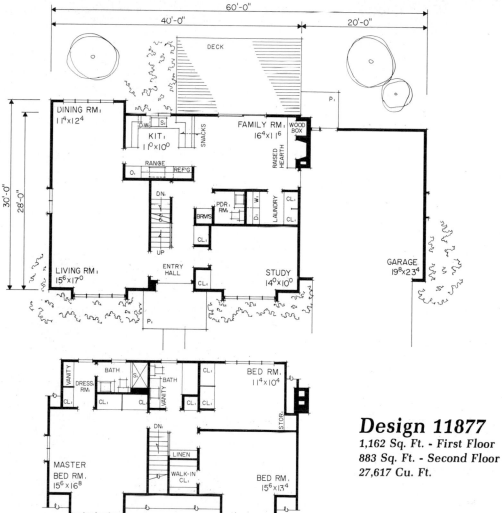

DINING RM.
11⁴x12⁴

KIT.
11⁰x10⁰

DECK

FAMILY RM.
16⁴x11⁶

WOOD BOX

RANGE

REF'G

RAISED HEARTH

DN.

UP

PDR.
RM.

LAUNDRY

BRMS

CL.

LIVING RM.
15⁶x17⁰

ENTRY HALL

CL.

STUDY
14⁰x10⁰

GARAGE
19⁸x23⁴

60'-0"
40'-0"
20'-0"
30'-0"
28'-0"

VANITY

BATH

BATH

CL.

BED RM.
11⁴x10⁴

DRESS. RM.

CL.

VANITY

CL.

STOR.

DN.

LINEN

WALK-IN CL.

MASTER BED RM.
15⁶x16⁸

BED RM.
15⁶x13⁴

Design 11877
1,162 Sq. Ft. - First Floor
883 Sq. Ft. - Second Floor
27,617 Cu. Ft.

● This simple, straightforward plan has much to offer in the way of livability and economical construction costs. Worthy of particular note are the excellent traffic patterns and the outstanding use of space. There is no wasted space here. Notice the cozy family room with its raised hearth fireplace, wood box and sliding glass doors to the sweeping outdoor deck. The efficient kitchen is flanked by the informal snack bar and the formal dining area. Open planning between the living and dining areas promotes a fine feeling of spaciousness. The study is a great feature. It may function as just that or become, the sewing or TV room, the guest room or even the fourth bedroom. Note the powder room and laundry. Study the second floor facilities.

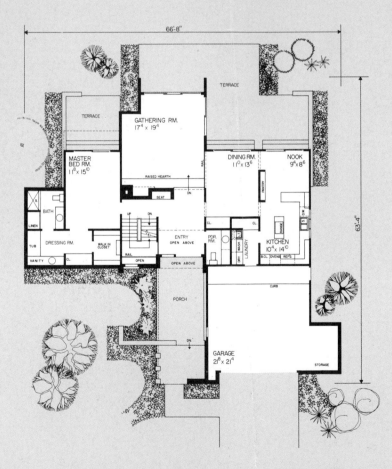

Design 12729
1,590 Sq. Ft. - First Floor
756 Sq. Ft. - Second Floor
39,310 Cu. Ft.

● Entering this home will surely be a pleasure through the sheltered walk-way to the double front doors. And the pleasure and beauty does not stop there. The entry hall and sunken gathering room are open to the upstairs for added dimension.

There's even a built-in seat in the entry area. The kitchen-nook area is very efficient with its many built-ins and the adjacent laundry room. There is fine indoor-outdoor living relationship in this design. Note the private terrace off the luxurious

master bedroom suite, a living terrace accessible from the gathering room, dining room and nook plus the balcony off the upstairs bedroom. Upstairs there is a total of two bedrooms, each having its own private bath and plenty of closets.

Design 12379 1,525 Sq. Ft. - First Floor; 748 Sq. Ft. - Second Floor; 26,000 Cu. Ft.

● A house that has "everything" may very well look just like this design. Its exterior is well-proportioned and impressive. Inside the inviting double front doors there are features galore. The living room and family room level are sunken. Separating these two rooms is a dramatic thru fireplace. A built-in bar, planter and beamed ceiling highlight the family room. Nearby is a full bath and a study which could be utilized as a fourth bedroom. The fine functioning kitchen has a pass-thru to the snack bar in the breakfast nook. The adjacent dining room overlooks the living room and has sliding doors to the covered porch. Upstairs three bedrooms, two baths and an outdoor balcony. Blueprints for this design include optional basement details.

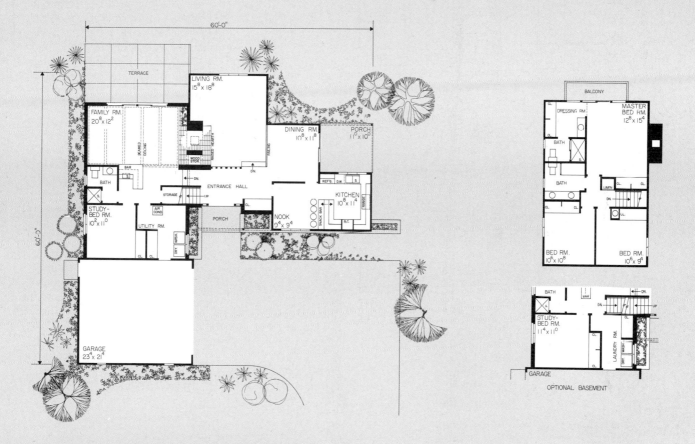

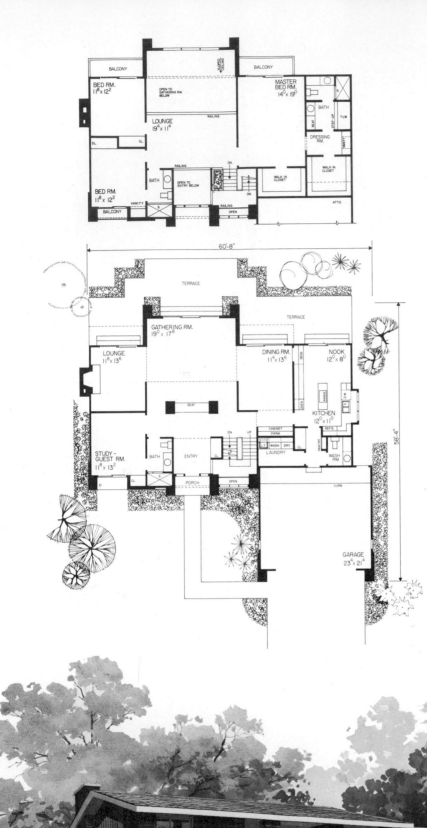

Design 12749
1,716 Sq. Ft. - First Floor
1,377 Sq. Ft. - Second Floor
72,885 Cu. Ft.

● This is positively a refreshingly dramatic two-story contemporary. The use of the vertical pane windows highlight the exterior along with the projecting garage. Upon entrance to this home, one will enjoy the open entry and the bench seat. The indoor-outdoor living relationship is present in all the back rooms of this design both on the first and second floor. The first floor can utilize the large back terrace through sliding glass doors in the quiet lounge (which also has a fireplace), the large gathering room which will have great family living flexibility, the formal dining room and the informal breakfast nook. On the second floor the two rear bedrooms plus the front bedroom each has its own private balcony. The optional fourth bedroom is on the first floor and has sliding doors to the patio. Note the lounge on the second floor which is open on two sides so you can look down into the gathering room and entry hall below.

Design 12709

2,471 Sq. Ft. - First Floor
2,038 Sq. Ft. - Second Floor
73,125 Cu. Ft.

● A lower-level conversation pit! Above, a skylight. And on the first and second floors, open balconies. . . .offering a view of both the conversation pit and skylight. That's just the beginning. Develop the basement area around the conversation pit and add 1,435 square feet to your informal living area. The gathering room features a balcony overlooking an indoor garden . . . part of the scenery in the family room. Fireplace in both those rooms. An enormous kitchen with a walk-in pantry, island range, built-in desk. Four large bedrooms, including a luxury master suite. Observe the storage potential.

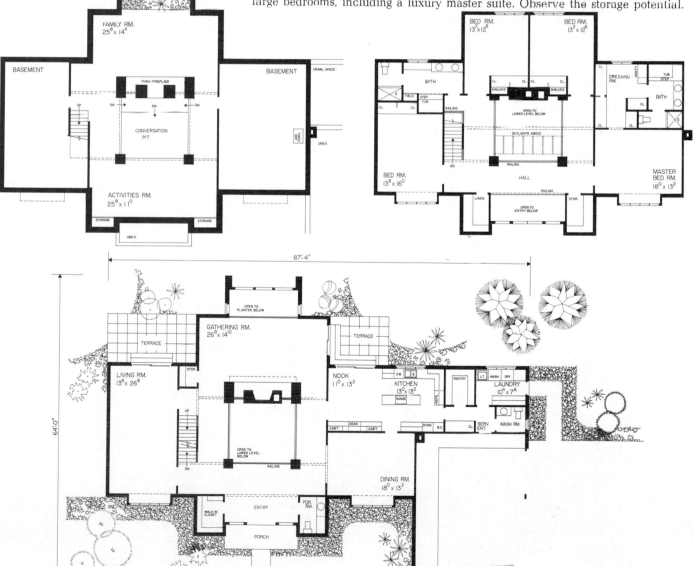

Design 12781

2,132 Sq. Ft. - First Floor
1,156 Sq. Ft. - Second Floor
47,365 Cu. Ft.

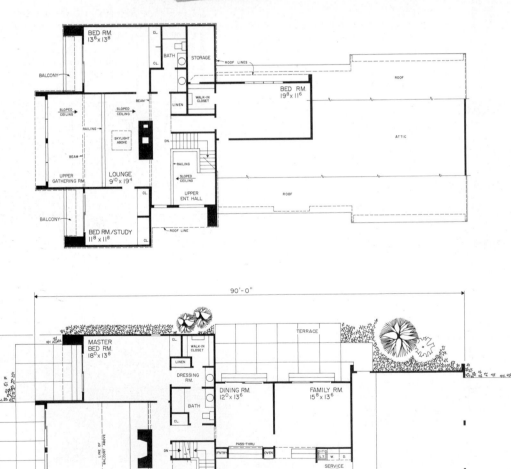

● This beautifully designed two-story could be considered a dream house of a lifetime. The exterior is sure to catch the eye of anyone who takes sight of its unique construction. The front kitchen features an island range, adjacent breakfast nook and pass-thru to formal dining room. The master bedroom suite with its privacy and convenience on the first floor has a spacious walk-in closet and dressing room. The side terrace is accessible thru sliding glass doors from the master bedroom, gathering room and study. The second floor has three bedrooms and storage space galore. Also notice the lounge which has sloped ceilings and a skylight above. This delightful area looks down into the gathering room. The outdoor balconies overlook the wrap-around terrace. Surely an outstanding trend house for the '80's and for decades to come.

ALL the "TOOLS" you and your builder need...

... to, first select an exterior and a floor plan for your new house that satisfy your tastes and your family's living patterns ...

... then, to review the blueprints in great detail and obtain a construction cost figure ... also, to price out the structural materials required to build ... and, finally, to review and decide upon the specifications to which your home is to be built. Truly, an invaluable set of "tools" to launch your home planning and building programs.

1. THE PLAN BOOKS
Home Planners' unique Design Category Series makes it easy to look at and study only the types of designs for which you and your family have an interest. Each of five plan books features a specific type of home, namely: 1½ and 2-Story, One-Story Over 2000 Sq. Ft., One-Story Under 2000 Sq. Ft., Multi-Levels and Vacation Homes. In addition to the convenient Design Category Series, there is an impressive selection of other current titles. While the home plans featured in these books are also to be found in the Design Category Series, they, too, are edited for those with special tastes and requirements. Your family will spend many enjoyable hours reviewing the delightfully designed exteriors and the practical floor plans. Surely your home or office library should include a selection of these popular plan books. Your complete satisfaction is guaranteed.

2. THE CONSTRUCTION BLUEPRINTS
There are blueprints available for each of the designs published in Home Planners' current plan books. Depending upon the size, the style and the type of home, each set of blueprints consists of from five to ten large sheets. Only by studying the blueprints is it possible to give complete and final consideration to the proper selection of a design for your next home. The blueprints provide the opportunity for all family members to familiarize themselves with the features of all exterior elevations, interior elevations and details, all dimensions, special built-in features and effects. They also provide a full understanding of the materials to be used and/or selected. The low-cost of our blueprints makes it possible and indeed, practical, to study in detail a number of different sets of blueprints before deciding upon which design to build.

3. THE MATERIAL LIST
A list of materials is an integral part of the plan package. It comprises the last sheet of each set of blueprints and serves as a handy reference during the period of construction. Of course, at the pricing and the material ordering stages, it is indispensable.

4. THE SPECIFICATION OUTLINE
Each order for blueprints is accompanied by one Specification Outline. You and your builder will find this a time-saving tool when deciding upon your own individual specifications. An important reference document should you wish to write your own specifications.

THE PLAN BOOKS

The Design Category Series . . .

. . . A great selection of five plan books specially edited for ease in studying specific design types. Features most of the house plans shown in other current titles. The five book Complete Collection guarantees many enjoyable hours of happy house hunting. A fine set of books for the home or office reference library.

1. 400 1½ and TWO-STORY HOME PLANS - Those interested in studying a wide variety of 1½ and two-story exteriors and floor plans need look no further. New England Gambrels, Salt Boxes, Tudor, French Mansards, Georgians, Southern Colonials, Cape Cods, Virginia Tidewater, Farmhouses and Contemporary exteriors are featured. Family living floor plans with two to six bedrooms.

2. 210 ONE-STORY HOME PLANS - Over 2,000 Square Feet - Designs for those who prefer one-story living and all the convenience that goes with it. A selection of homes with varying exterior styles housing practical and efficient family living floor plans. Gathering rooms, family rooms, formal and informal dining areas.

3. 350 ONE-STORY HOME PLANS - Under 2,000 Square Feet - A wide selection of one-story homes for the modest building budgets. Delightful Traditional exteriors as well as exciting Contemporaries. Fine functioning floor plans for both the small and large family. Plans with optional elevations.

4. 205 MULTI-LEVEL HOME PLANS - For those who wish to experience new dimensions in total livability. This fine collection includes split foyer bi-levels and tri-levels for flat and sloping sites. Also, homes with exposed lower levels.

5. 223 VACATION HOMES - A popularly acclaimed vacation and leisure-living book of exteriors and floor plans. A-Frames, Chalets, Hexagons and other interesting shapes with decks, balconies and terraces. 96 exciting full color pages.

1 320 Pages, $5.95
0-918894-26-3

2 192 Pages, $3.95
0-918894-27-1

3 256 Pages, $4.95
0-918894-28-X

4 192 Pages, $3.95
0-918894-29-8

5 176 Pages, $4.25
0-918894-30-1

The Exterior Style Series . . .

. . . Delightfully edited for those who wish to review home plans of their favorite exterior styling. Ideal for those who want to compare the unique appeal of various pleasing facades.

6. 120 EARLY AMERICAN PLANS - and other Colonial Adaptations is a unique plan book. Devoted exclusively to Early American architectural interpretations adapted for today's living patterns. Exquisitely detailed exteriors retain all of the charm of a proud heritage.

7. 125 CONTEMPORARY HOME PLANS - Here is an exciting book featuring a wide variety of home designs for the 1980's and far beyond. The exteriors of these homes are refreshing with their practical and progressive "new look".

8. 135 ENGLISH TUDOR HOMES - and other Popular Family Plans is a favorite of many. The current popularity of the English Tudor home design is phenomenal and here is a book which is loaded with Tudors for all budgets.

9. 112 TRADITIONAL and CONTEMPORARY FAMILY HOMES - A delightful collection of designs for traditional and contemporary tastes. All sizes and types of designs for family living. Over 300 exterior and floor plan illustrations.

10. 102 HOME PLANS - An excellent selection of home designs featuring a wide variety of exterior styles. There are Early American, Tudor, Spanish, French and Contemporary facades. A special 16 page feature section in full color.

11. 130 DISTINCTIVE HOME DESIGNS - Commencing with the Early American Homes and continuing through the Tudor, French, Spanish and Contemporary designs, this delightful book will be enjoyed by all. The pleasingly proportioned exteriors and the exciting floor plans assure hours of rewarding home planning.

6 112 Pages, $2.25
0-918894-23-9

7 112 Pages, $2.25
0-918894-24-7

8 104 Pages, $2.50
0-918894-32-8

9 96 Pages, $2.75
0-918894-35-2

10 96 Pages, $1.75
0-918894-22-0

11 112 Pages, $2.75
0-918894-39-5

The Budget Series . . .

. . . Construction costs are influenced to a significant extent by the size of the house. The houses and plans in this series have been edited according to square footage ranges. Each book highlights a wide variety of design styles and types.

12 96 Pages, $2.75
0-918894-36-0

175 LOW BUDGET HOMES - The house designs in this book average 1505 square feet. From 1165 square foot average for the one-story houses to an 1812 average for two-stories. 1½-Story and tri-level averages fall within this range, too. Many designs have expansive potential where sleeping areas may be finished off later. Wide selection of styles. Two to five bedrooms Family rooms, extra baths, formal and informal dining rooms. This book is a must for those with a restricted building budget.

13 112 Pages, $2.50
0-918894-31-X

165 AFFORDABLE HOME PLANS - Designs averaging 2052 square feet are featured in this collection of houses. They range from a 1581 square foot average for the one-stories, to 2261 for the two-story homes, to 2381 for the tri-levels. Tudor, French, Early American, Spanish and Contemporary exteriors are featured throughout the book. Efficient, family living floor plans. This wide selection of houses and plans will fit the medium budget. Basement and non-basement designs.

14 112 Pages, $2.75
0-918894-40-5

142 HOME DESIGNS FOR EXPANDED BUILDING BUDGETS - This selection of designs highlight houses with an average square footage of 2551. One-story plans average 2069; two-stories, 2735; multi-levels, 2825. As the family's size and income grows so does its need for, and ability to finance, a larger home grow. A fine group of designs for all exterior style tastes and livability requirements. Spacious homes featuring raised hearth fireplaces, beamed ceilings, open planning and efficient kitchens.
COMING MAY 1984

15 112 Pages, $2.75
0-918894-33-6

110 HOME PLANS FOR VARYING BUILDING BUDGETS - Edited in appealing two-color featuring designs for all budgets. One, 1½, two-story and multi-levels. Colonial, Tudor, Spanish, French and Contemporary exteriors, among the most popular, are featured. Special section of energy-oriented designs with solariums, atriums, skylights, collectors, etc. Trend houses and history house designs. Houses designed for flat and hillside sites. Exposed lower levels are also available.

Two Great Books in Full Color . . .

For Plan Book Order Form
Kindly turn to page 273.

116 TRADITIONAL and CONTEMPORARY PLANS - A beautifully illustrated home plan book in complete, full color. One, 1½, two-story and split-level designs featured in all of the most popular exterior styles. Varied building budgets will be satisfied by the numerous plans for all budget sizes. Designs for flat and hillside sites, including those with exposed lower levels. Also, homes for that sought after leisure-living. A truly beautiful plan book. An ideal gift item that will help the family in their house hunting.

16 96 Pages, $4.95
0-918894-15-8

122 HOME DESIGNS - A new book in delightfully dramatic full color throughout. More than 120 eye-pleasing, colored illustrations. Tudor, French, Spanish, Early American and Contemporary exteriors featuring one, 1½ and two-story and multi-level designs. The interiors house efficient, step-saving family living floor plans. Formal and informal living areas along with convenient work centers. Two to six bedroom sleeping areas. Interesting traffic patterns. Surely a book for your permanent library.

17 96 Pages, $4.95
0-918894-34-4

A collection of Most Popular Designs

166 MOST POPULAR HOMES - A book of best-selling house plans containing over 400 illustrations. Houses range in size from 1,050 to 5,308 square feet. Tudor, Early American, Spanish and French exteriors. Plus Contemporary elevations and floor plans. Homes featuring atriums, balconies, decks, sloping beamed ceilings, exposed lower levels and much more. Truly an outstanding plan book of popular homes.

18 112 Pages, $2.75
0-918894-37-9

An Encyclopedia of Home Designs

450 HOUSE PLANS - For those who wish to review and study perhaps the largest selection of designs available in a single volume. This edition will provide countless hours of enjoyable family home planning. Varying exterior styles, plus interesting and practical floor plans for all building budgets. Formal, informal living patterns; indoor-outdoor living; small, growing, large family facilities. A book for your permanent library.

19 320 Pages, $8.95
0-918894-38-7

1 Frontal Sheet

2 Foundation Plan

3 Detailed Floor Plan

FIRST FLOOR PLAN

SECOND FLOOR PLAN

4 House Cross-Sections

CROSS SECTION C-C

SECTION DD

5 Interior Elevations

FULL SIZE TYPICAL TRIM

6 Exterior Elevations

LEFT SIDE

ELEVATION

7 Material List

MATERIAL LIST

The Blueprints...

1. FRONTAL SHEET.

Artist's landscaped sketch of the exterior and ink-line floor plans are on the frontal sheet of each set of blueprints.

2. FOUNDATION PLAN.

¼" Scale basement and foundation plan. All necessary notations and dimensions. Plot plan diagram for locating house on building site.

3. DETAILED FLOOR PLAN.

¼" Scale first and second floor plans with complete dimensions. Cross-section detail keys. Diagrammatic layout of electrical outlets and switches.

4. HOUSE CROSS-SECTIONS.

Large scale sections of foundation, interior and exterior walls, floors and roof details for design and construction control.

5. INTERIOR ELEVATIONS.

Large scale interior details of the complete kitchen cabinet design, bathrooms, powder room, laundry, fireplaces, paneling, beam ceilings, built-in cabinets, etc.

6. EXTERIOR ELEVATIONS.

¼" Scale exterior elevation drawings of front, rear, and both sides of the house. All exterior materials and details are shown to indicate the complete design and proportions of the house.

7. MATERIAL LIST.

Complete lists of all materials required for the construction of the house as designed are included in each set of blueprints.

THIS BLUEPRINT PACKAGE

will help you and your family take a major step forward in the final appraisal and planning of your new home. Only by spending many enjoyable and informative hours studying the numerous details included in the complete package, will you feel sure of, and comfortable with, your commitment to build your new home. To assure successful and productive consultation with your builder and/or architect, reference to the various elements of the blueprint package is a must. The blueprints, material list and specification outline will save much consultation time and expense. Don't be without them.

The Material List...

With each set of blueprints you order you will receive a material list. Each list shows you the quantity, type and size of the non-mechanical materials required to build your home. It also tells you where these materials are used. This makes the blueprints easy to understand.

Influencing the mechanical requirements are geographical differences in availability of materials, local codes, methods of installation and individual preferences. Because of these factors, your local heating, plumbing and electrical contractors can supply you with necessary material take-offs for their particular trades.

Material lists simplify your material ordering and enable you to get quicker price quotations from your builder and material dealer. Because the material list is an integral part of each set of blueprints, it is not available separately.

Among the materials listed:

• Masonry, Veneer & Fireplace • Framing Lumber • Roofing & Sheet Metal • Windows & Door Frames • Exterior Trim & Insulation • Tile Work, Finish Floors • Interior Trim, Kitchen Cabinets • Rough & Finish Hardware

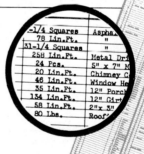

The Specification Outline...

This fill-in type specification lists over 150 phases of home construction from excavating to painting and includes wiring, plumbing, heating and air-conditioning. It consists of 16 pages and will prove invaluable for specifying to your builder the exact materials, equipment and methods of construction you want in your new home. One Specification Outline is included free with each order for blueprints. Additional Specification Outlines are available at $3.00 each.

CONTENTS
• General Instructions, Suggestions and Information • Excavating and Grading • Masonry and Concrete Work • Sheet Metal Work • Carpentry, Millwork, Roofing, and Miscellaneous Items • Lath and Plaster or Drywall Wallboard • Schedule for Room Finishes • Painting and Finishing • Tile Work • Electrical Work • Plumbing • Heating and Air-Conditioning

Before you order

1. STUDY THE DESIGNS . . . found in Home Planners current publications. As you review these delightful custom homes, you should keep in mind the total living requirements of your family — both indoors and outdoors. Although we do not make changes in plans, many minor changes can be made prior to the period of construction. If major changes are involved to satisfy your personal requirements, you should consider ordering one set of blueprints and having them redrawn locally. Consultation with your architect is strongly advised when contemplating major changes.

2. HOW TO ORDER BLUEPRINTS . . . After you have chosen the design that satisfies your requirements, or if you have selected one that you wish to study in more detail, simply clip the accompanying order blank and mail with your remittance. However, if it is not convenient for you to send a check or money order, you can use your credit card, or merely indicate C.O.D. shipment. Postman will collect all charges, including postage and C.O.D. fee. C.O.D. shipments are not permitted to Canada or foreign countries. Should time be of essence, as it sometimes is with many of our customers, your telephone order usually can be processed and shipped in the next day's mail. Simply call toll free 1-800-521-6797, (Michigan residents call collect 0-313-477-1854).

3. OUR SERVICE . . . Home Planners makes every effort to process and ship each order for blueprints and books within 48 hours. Because of this, we have deemed it unnecessary to acknowledge receipt of our customers orders. See order coupon for the postage and handling charges for surface mail, air mail or foreign mail.

4. A NOTE REGARDING REVERSE BLUEPRINTS . . . As a special service to those wishing to build in reverse of the plan as shown, we do include an extra set of reversed blueprints for only $20.00 additional with each order. Even though the lettering and dimensions appear backward on reversed blueprints, they make a handy reference because they show the house just as it's being built in reverse from the standard blueprints — thereby helping you visualize the home better.

5. OUR EXCHANGE POLICY . . . Since blueprints are printed up in specific response to your individual order, we cannot honor requests for refunds. However, the first set of blueprints in any order (or the one set in a single set order) for a given design may be exchanged for a set of another design at a fee of $10.00 plus $2.00 for postage and handling via surface mail; $3.00 via air mail.

How many sets of blueprints should be ordered?

This question is often asked. The answer can range anywhere from 1 to 7 sets, depending upon circumstances. For instance, a single set of blueprints of your favorite design is sufficient to study the house in greater detail. On the other hand, if you are planning to get cost estimates, or if you are planning to build, you may need as many as seven sets of blueprints. Because the first set of blueprints in each order is $85.00, and because additional sets of the same design in each order are only $20.00 each (and with package sets even more economical), you save considerably by ordering your total requirements now. To help you determine the exact number of sets, please refer to the handy check list.

How Many Blueprints Do You Need?

___ OWNER'S SET

___ BUILDER (Usually requires at least 3 sets: 1 as legal document; 1 for inspection; and at least 1 for tradesmen — usually more.)

___ BUILDING PERMIT (Sometimes 2 sets are required.)

___ MORTGAGE SOURCE (Usually 1 set for a conventional mortgage; 3 sets for F.H.A. or V.A. type mortgages.)

___ SUBDIVISION COMMITTEE (If any.)

___ TOTAL NO. SETS REQUIRED

Blueprint Ordering Hotline

Phone toll free: 1-800-521-6797. Orders received by 11 a.m. (Detroit time) can usually be processed and shipped to you the same day. Use of this line restricted to blueprint ordering only. Michigan residents simply call collect 0-313-477-1854.

In Canada Mail To: Home Planners, Inc., 772 King St. W. Kitchener, Ontario N2G 1E8

TO: **HOME PLANNERS, INC., 23761 RESEARCH DRIVE FARMINGTON HILLS, MICHIGAN 48024**

Please rush me the following:

____ SET(S) BLUEPRINTS FOR DESIGN NO(S). _____ $_____
Single Set, $85.00; Additional Identical Sets in Same Order $20.00 ea.
4 Set Package of Same Design, $125.00 (Save $20.00)
7 Set Package of Same Design, $160.00 (Save $45.00)
(Material Lists and 1 Specification Outline included)

____ SPECIFICATION OUTLINES @ $3.00 EACH . . . . $_____

Michigan Residents add 4% sales tax $_____

FOR POSTAGE AND HANDLING PLEASE CHECK ✔ & REMIT
☐ $2.00 Added to Order for Surface Mail – Any Mdse.
☐ $3.00 Added for Air Mail of One Set of Blueprints only.
☐ $4.00 Added for Air Mail of Two or more Sets of Blueprints only. ⎱
☐ For Foreign Mail add $2.00 to above applicable rates. ⎰ $_____

☐ C.O.D. PAY POSTMAN
(C.O.D. Within U.S.A. Only)

TOTAL in U.S.A. funds $_____

PLEASE PRINT

Name _____

Street _____

City _____ State _____ Zip _____

CREDIT CARD ORDERS ONLY: Fill in the boxes below   Prices subject to change without notice

Credit Card No. ☐☐☐☐☐☐☐☐☐☐☐☐☐☐☐☐   Expiration Date Month/Year ☐☐☐☐

CHECK ONE: ☐ VISA   ☐ MasterCard

CV1   Your Signature _____

BLUEPRINTS SHIPPED WITHIN 48 HOURS!

TO: **HOME PLANNERS, INC., 23761 RESEARCH DRIVE FARMINGTON HILLS, MICHIGAN 48024**

Please rush me the following:

____ SET(S) BLUEPRINTS FOR DESIGN NO(S). _____ $_____
Single Set, $85.00; Additional Identical Sets in Same Order $20.00 ea.
4 Set Package of Same Design, $125.00 (Save $20.00)
7 Set Package of Same Design, $160.00 (Save $45.00)
(Material Lists and 1 Specification Outline included)

____ SPECIFICATION OUTLINES @ $3.00 EACH . . . . $_____

Michigan Residents add 4% sales tax $_____

FOR POSTAGE AND HANDLING PLEASE CHECK ✔ & REMIT
☐ $2.00 Added to Order for Surface Mail – Any Mdse.
☐ $3.00 Added for Air Mail of One Set of Blueprints only.
☐ $4.00 Added for Air Mail of Two or more Sets of Blueprints only. ⎱
☐ For Foreign Mail add $2.00 to above applicable rates. ⎰ $_____

☐ C.O.D. PAY POSTMAN
(C.O.D. Within U.S.A. Only)

TOTAL in U.S.A. funds $_____

PLEASE PRINT

Name _____

Street _____

City _____ State _____ Zip _____

CREDIT CARD ORDERS ONLY: Fill in the boxes below   Prices subject to change without notice

Credit Card No. ☐☐☐☐☐☐☐☐☐☐☐☐☐☐☐☐   Expiration Date Month/Year ☐☐☐☐

CHECK ONE: ☐ VISA   ☐ MasterCard

CV1   Your Signature _____

Two-Story Homes
A Potpourri of Family Living Plans

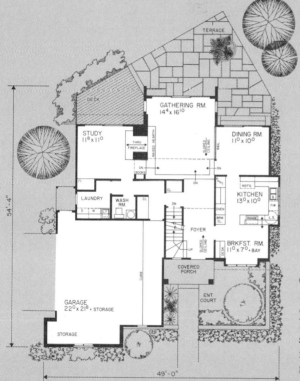

ALTERNATE KITCHEN / DINING RM. / BREAKFAST RM. FLOOR PLAN

Design 12826
1,112 Sq. Ft. - First Floor
881 Sq. Ft. - Second Floor; 32,770 Cu. Ft.

● This is an outstanding example of the type of informal, traditional-style architecture that has captured the modern imagination. The interior plan houses all the features that people want most - a spacious gathering room, formal and informal dining areas, efficient, U-shaped kitchen, master bedroom, two children's bedrooms, second-floor lounge, entrance court and rear terrace and deck. Study all areas of this plan carefully.

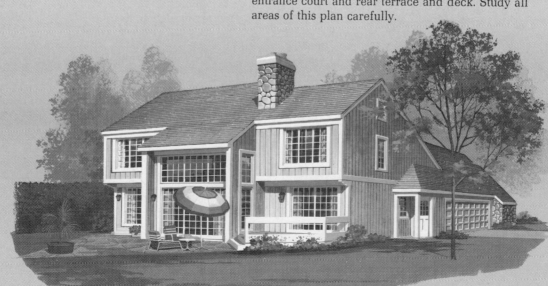

Design 12655

893 Sq. Ft. - First Floor
652 Sq. Ft. - Second Floor; 22,555 Cu. Ft.

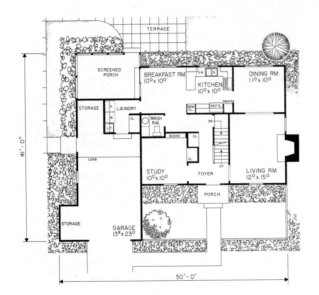

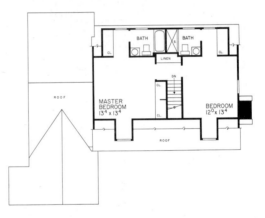

● Wonderful things can be enclosed in small packages. This is the case for this one-and-a-half story design. The total square footage is a mere 1,545 square feet yet its features are many, indeed. Its exterior appeal is very eye-pleasing with horizontal lines and two second story dormers. Livability will be enjoyed in this plan. The front study is ideal for a quiet escape. Nearby is a powder room also convenient to the kitchen and breakfast room. Two bedrooms and two full baths are located on the second floor.

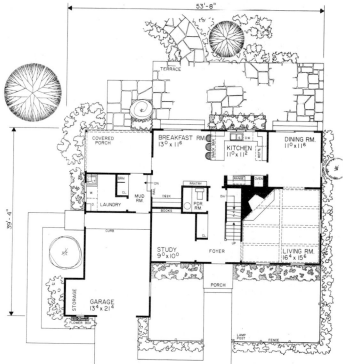

Design 53'-8"

COVERED PORCH

TERRACE

BREAKFAST RM. 13⁰ x 11⁶

KITCHEN 11⁰ x 11²

SNACK BAR

DINING RM. 11⁰ x 11⁶

W. LAUNDRY

MUD RM.

CL

BRM

PANTRY

BOOKS

PDR. RM.

CL

RANGE OVEN

REF.

STUDY 9⁰ x 10⁰

FOYER

UP

LIVING RM. 16⁴ x 15⁶

PORCH

39'-4"

CURB

STORAGE

GARAGE 13⁴ x 21⁴

FLOWER BOX

LAMP POST

FENCE

BEDROOM 12⁰ x 13⁰

BATH

MASTER BEDROOM 12⁸ x 16⁰

LIN.

LINEN

CL

DN

ROOF

BEDROOM 12⁰ x 11⁰

DRESSING RM.

BATH

ROOF

Design 12656 1,122 Sq. Ft. - First Floor
884 Sq. Ft. - Second Floor; 31,845 Cu. Ft.

● This charming Cape cottage possesses a great sense of shelter through its gambrel roof. Dormers at front and rear pierce the gambrel roof to provide generous, well-lit living space on the second floor which houses three bedrooms. This design's first floor layout is not far different from that of the Cape cottages of the 18th century. The large kitchen and adjoining dining room recall cottage keeping rooms both in function and in location at the rear of the house.

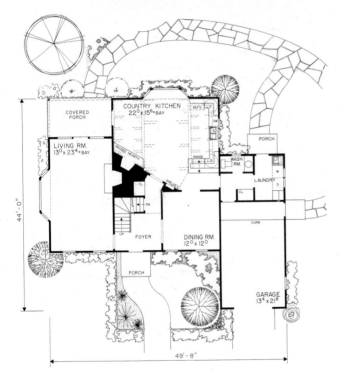

Design 12657 1,217 Sq. Ft. - First Floor
868 Sq. Ft. - Second Floor; 33,260 Cu. Ft.

● Deriving its design from the traditional Cape Cod style, this facade features clap board siding, small-paned windows and a transom-lit entrance flanked by carriage lamps. A central chimney services two fireplaces, one in the country-kitchen and the other in the formal living room which is removed from the disturbing flow of traffic. The master suite is located to the left of the upstairs landing. A full bathroom services two additional bedrooms.

Design 12658

1,218 Sq. Ft. - First Floor
764 Sq. Ft. - Second Floor; 29,690 Cu. Ft.

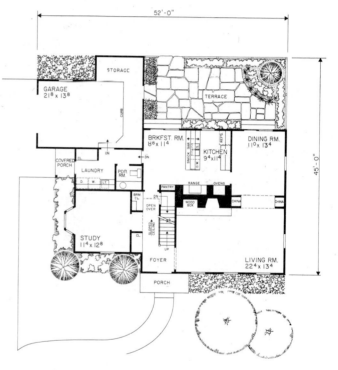

● Traditional charm of yesteryear is exemplified delightfully in this one-and-a-half story home. The garage has been conveniently tucked away in the rear of the house which makes this design ideal for a corner lot. Interior livability has been planned for efficient living. The front living room is large and features a fireplace with wood box. The laundry area is accessible by way of both the garage and a side covered porch. Enter the rear terrace from both eating areas, the formal dining room and the informal breakfast room.

Design 12644
1,349 Sq. Ft. - First Floor
836 Sq. Ft. - Second Floor
36,510 Cu. Ft.

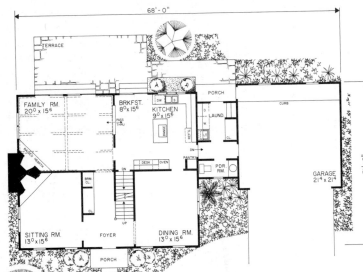

● What a delightful, compact two-story this is! This design has many fine features tucked within its framework. The bowed roofline of this house stems from late 17th-Century architecture.

Design 12661

1,020 Sq. Ft. - First Floor
777 Sq. Ft. - Second Floor; 30,745 Cu. Ft.

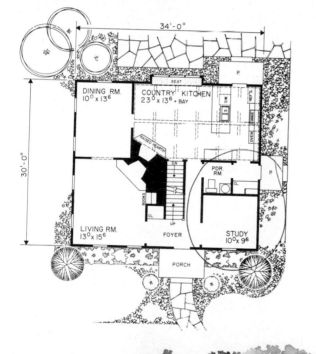

● Any other starter house or retirement home couldn't have more charm than this design. Its compact frame houses a very livable plan. An outstanding feature of the first floor is the large country kitchen. Its fine attractions include a beamed ceiling, raised hearth fireplace, built-in window seat and a door leading to the outdoors. A living room is in the front of the plan and has another fireplace which shares the single chimney. The rear dormered second floor houses the sleeping and bath facilities.

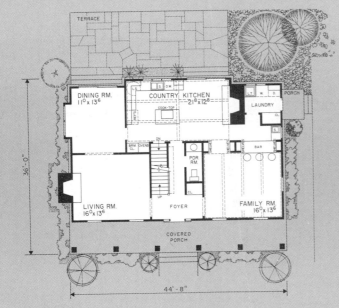

● The exterior of this full two-story is highlighted by the covered porch and balcony. Many enjoyable hours will be spent at these outdoor areas. The interior is highlighted by a spacious country kitchen. Be sure to notice its island cook-top, fireplace and the beamed ceiling. A built-in bar is in the family room.

Design 12664
1,308 Sq. Ft. - First Floor
1,262 Sq. Ft. - Second Floor; 49,215 Cu. Ft.

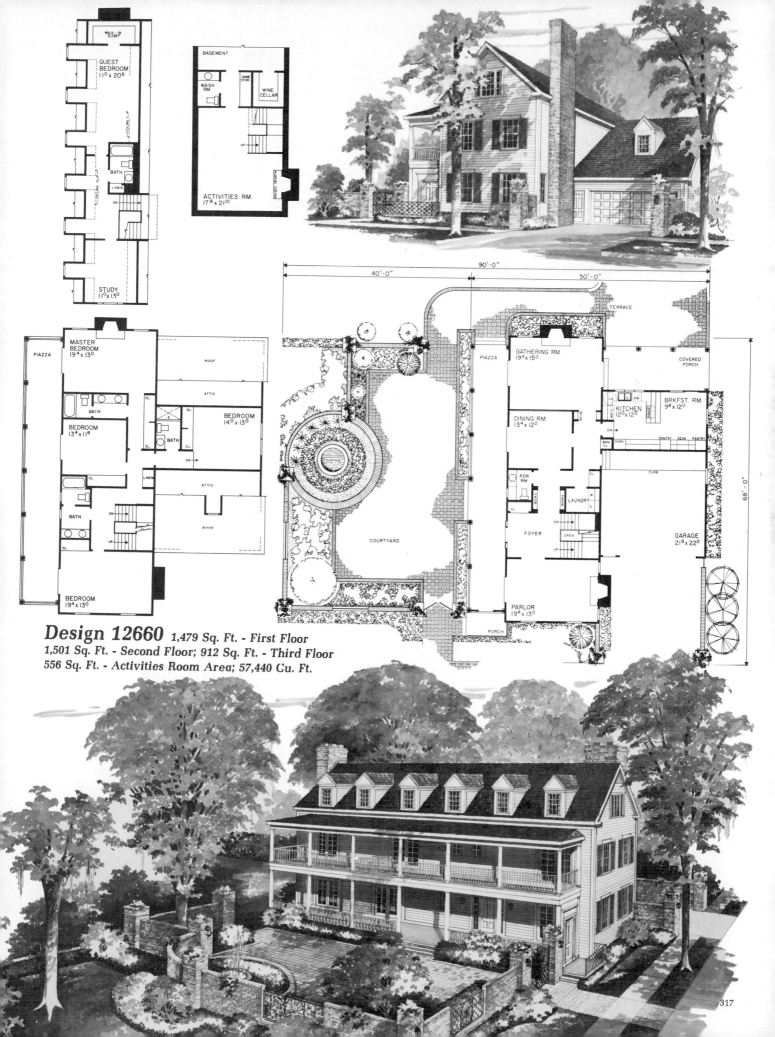

WALK-IN CLOSET

GUEST BEDROOM
11⁰ x 20⁶

BATH

LINEN

DN

STUDY
11⁰ x 13⁰

BASEMENT

WASH RM.

GAME STOR.

WINE CELLAR

UP

ACTIVITIES RM.
17⁸ x 21¹⁰

RAISED HEARTH

MASTER BEDROOM
19⁴ x 13⁰

PIAZZA

ROOF

ATTIC

BATH

BEDROOM
13⁴ x 11⁸

BEDROOM
14⁰ x 13⁰

BATH

LINEN

ATTIC

BATH

DN

UP

ROOF

BEDROOM
19⁴ x 13⁰

40'-0"   90'-0"   50'-0"

TERRACE

COURTYARD

FOUNTAIN

PIAZZA

GATHERING RM.
19⁴ x 15⁰

COVERED PORCH

DINING RM.
13⁴ x 12⁰

NICHE

KITCHEN
12⁰ x 12⁰

BRKFST. RM.
9⁸ x 12⁰

PANTRY   DESK   PANTRY

OVEN

BRM CL

CURB

PDR RM

BOOKS

LAUNDRY

CL

FOYER

OPEN

UP

GARAGE
21⁸ x 22⁰

68'-0"

PARLOR
19⁴ x 13⁰

PORCH

Design 12660 1,479 Sq. Ft. - First Floor
1,501 Sq. Ft. - Second Floor; 912 Sq. Ft. - Third Floor
556 Sq. Ft. - Activities Room Area; 57,440 Cu. Ft.

Design 12794

1,680 Sq. Ft. - First Floor
1,165 Sq. Ft. - Second Floor
867 Sq. Ft. - Apartment
55,900 Cu. Ft.

● This exceptionally pleasing Tudor design has a great deal of interior livability to offer its occupants. Use the main entrance, enter into the foyer and begin your journey throughout this design. To the left of the foyer is the study, to the right, the formal living room. The living room leads to the rear, formal dining room. This room has access to the outdoors and is conveniently located adjacent to the kitchen. A snack bar divides the kitchen from the family room which also has access to outdoors plus it has a fireplace as does the living room. The second floor houses the family's four bedrooms. Down six steps from the mud room is the laundry and entrance to the garage, up six steps from this area is a complete apartment. This is an excellent room for a live-in relative. It is completely private by gaining access from the outdoor balcony.

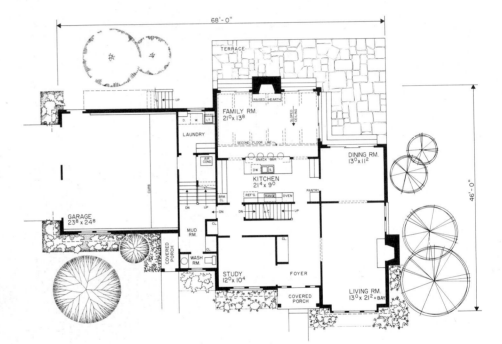

● This Tudor design has many fine features. The exterior is enhanced by front and side bay windows in the family and dining rooms. Along with an outstanding exterior, it also contains a modern and efficient floor plan within its modest proportions. Flanking the entrance foyer is a comfortable living room. The U-shaped kitchen is conveniently located between the dining and breakfast rooms.

Design 12800 999 Sq. Ft. - First Floor
997 Sq. Ft. - Second Floor; 31,390 Cu. Ft.

● The charm of old England has been captured in this outstanding one-and-a-half story design. Interior livability will efficiently serve the various needs of all family members. The first floor offers both formal and informal areas along with the work centers. Features include: a wet-bar in the dining room, the kitchen's snack bar, first floor laundry and rear covered porch.

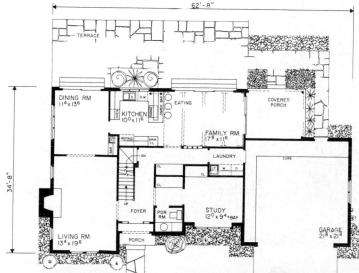

Design 12854 1,261 Sq. Ft. - First Floor
950 Sq. Ft. - Second Floor; 36,820 Cu. Ft.

319

● Natural stone, board-and-batten, multi-paned windows, overhanging eaves and the covered front porch highlight the exterior of this two-story home. Not only is the exterior well designed, but so is the interior. The sunken gathering room's ceiling is open to the second floor and is sloped for an even more dramatic appeal. Note the efficiency of the kitchen and dining area. A skylight will illuminate this area.

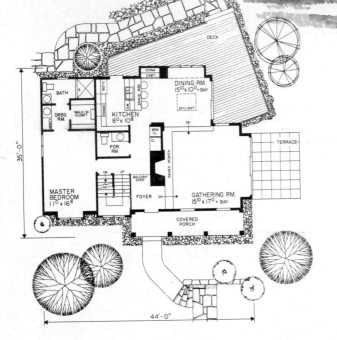

Design 12853

1,161 Sq. Ft. - First Floor
475 Sq. Ft. - Second Floor
28,715 Cu. Ft.

Design 12801 1,172 Sq. Ft. - First Floor
884 Sq. Ft. - Second Floor; 32,510 Cu. Ft.

● Built-ins in the breakfast room for china and pantry goods are certainly features to be mentioned up-front. A second china cabinet is located adjacent to the formal dining room. The great room will be just that. It is sunken two steps, has a beamed ceiling, the beauty of a fireplace and two sets of sliding glass doors to a front and rear courtyard.